D1189714

CHILDREN OF LOS ALAMOS

An Oral History of the Town Where the Atomic Age Began

Katrina R. Mason has interviewed a wide range of people who spent all or parts of their childhoods in Los Alamos, New Mexico—the place where scientists built the atomic bomb that ushered in the nuclear age. To create this engaging and provocative portrait of a place that has come to epitomize the scientific advances and moral ambiguities of this century, Mason has synthesized the recollections of those who lived in Los Alamos from its muddy beginnings in 1943—when the town was an army secret and residents officially lived at P.O. Box 1663—to the late 1950s, after the Laboratory had come under the auspices of the Atomic Energy Commission. Exploring how the children have dealt with their often conflicting feelings about their parents' involvement in the creation of nuclear weaponry, Mason illuminates the personal and often very emotional dimensions of a fascinating historical era.

Katrina R. Mason is a journalist who lives in Bethesda, Maryland. She is a graduate of Smith College and received her M.A. in English literature from the University of Pennsylvania.

"*Children of Los Alamos* is a grand achievement. It captures the unreal reality of the secret city where the atom bomb was born, depicts America in the 1940s, and presents a portrait of childhood—all at the same time."
—Rose DeWolf, Staff Writer, *Philadelphia Daily News*

"Katrina Mason has the skill to conceal the immense toil involved in projects like this. From a mountain of difficult material, she has made a powerful story that seems to tell itself."
—Henry Taylor, former Poet Laureate of Virginia

"Katrina Mason has produced a compelling and comprehensive collection of reminiscences of Los Alamos as seen by its wartime children. Her detailed narrative comes alive through these accounts, which include not only those of the children of the scientists and administrators, but also of lesser-known participants in the project such as security guards, carpenters, and cooks. With open-mindedness and insight, Ms. Mason has put a human face on a subject that is so much in the news yet so poorly understood."

—Hedy Mannheimer Dunn
Director, Los Alamos Historical Museum

KATRINA R. MASON

CHILDREN OF LOS ALAMOS

An Oral History of the Town
Where the Atomic Age Began

TWAYNE PUBLISHERS
An Imprint of Simon & Schuster Macmillan
New York

PRENTICE HALL INTERNATIONAL
London   Mexico City   New Delhi   Singapore   Sydney   Toronto

Twayne's Oral History Series No. 19

Children of Los Alamos: An Oral History of the Town Where the Atomic Age Began
Katrina R. Mason

Twayne Publishers
An Imprint of Simon & Schuster Macmillan
866 Third Avenue
New York, New York 10022

Library of Congress Cataloging-in-Publication Data

Mason, Katrina R.
   Children of Los Alamos : an oral history of the town where the atomic age
began / Katrina R. Mason.
      p.   cm.—(Twayne's oral history series)
   Includes bibliographical references and index.
   ISBN 0-8057-9138-8 (hc)—ISBN 0-8057-9139-6 (pb)
   1. Atomic bomb—New Mexico—Los Alamos—History.   2. Children—
New Mexico—Los Alamos—Biography.   3. Los Alamos (N.M.)—Description
and travel.   I. Title.   II. Series.
QC773.3.U5M29   1995
623.4'5119—dc20   95–13825
                                                                             CIP

The paper used in this publication meets the minimum requirements of American
National Standard for Information Sciences—Permanence of Paper for Printed
Library Materials. ANSI Z3948–1984.∞™

10 9 8 7 6 5 4 3 2 1 (hc)
10 9 8 7 6 5 4 3 2 1 (pb)

Printed in the United States of America.

Contents

Foreword

A half century after atomic bombs fell on Hiroshima and Nagasaki, it is appropriate to examine the birthplace of the atomic age. Katrina Mason has recreated the atmosphere of Los Alamos, New Mexico, during the 1940s—through the eyes of the children of those who worked on the Manhattan Project. A polyglot of Europeans, Anglo Americans, African Americans and Hispanic Americans, these children grew up behind barbed wire. They were as innocent of what was happening within their isolated desert locality as were any Americans, and would later feel just as guilty over its consequences. The memories that persist within the scientists' families measure the contribution that community spirit made to the scientific achievements of its citizens, and the disruption of friendships and destruction of reputations that followed in the Red Scare after the war. Telling personal stories at times humorous and poignant, the children of Los Alamos offer glimpses into the "secret city" from the inside out.

Oral history may well be the twentieth century's substitute for the written memoir. In exchange for the immediacy of diaries or correspondence, the retrospective interview offers a dialogue between the participant and the informed interviewer. Having prepared sufficient preliminary research, interviewers can direct the discussion into areas long since "forgotten" or no longer considered of consequence. "I haven't thought about that in years" is a common response, uttered just before an interviewee commences with a surprisingly detailed description of some past incident. The quality of the interview, its candidness and depth, generally will depend as much on the interviewer as the interviewee, and the confidence and rapport between the two adds a special dimension to the spoken memoir.

Interviewers represent a variety of disciplines and work either as part of a collective effort or individually. Regardless of their different interests or the variety of their subjects, all interviewers share a common imperative: to collect memories while they are still available. Most oral historians feel an additional responsibility to make their interviews accessible for use beyond their own research needs. Still, important collections of vital, vibrant interviews lie scattered in archives throughout every state, undiscovered or simply not used.

Twayne's Oral History Series seeks to identify those resources and to publish selections of the best materials. The series lets people speak for themselves, from their own unique perspectives on people, places, and events. But to be more than a babble of voices, each volume organizes its interviews around particular situations and events and ties them together with interpretative essays that place individuals into the larger historical context. The styles and format of individual volumes vary with the material from which they are drawn, demonstrating again the diversity of oral history and its methodology.

Whenever oral historians gather in conference, they enjoy retelling experiences about inspiring individuals they met, unexpected information they elicited, and unforgettable reminiscences that would otherwise have never been recorded. The result invariably reminds listeners of others who deserve to be interviewed, provides them with models of interviewing techniques, and inspires them to make their own contribution to the field. I trust that the oral historians in this series, as interviewers, editors, and interpreters, will have a similar effect on their readers.

DONALD A. RITCHIE
Series Editor, Senate Historical Office

Introduction

In the 1940s the town of Los Alamos did not appear on any map. Its very name was classified, not to pass the lips of those who lived there, even within the fences that circumscribed the isolated wooded mesa in northern New Mexico. Surrounded by mountains, barbed wire, and armed guards, scientists were working on a new kind of weapon, more powerful than anything yet imagined. They believed they were in a race against Hitler to create a weapon that could well determine the outcome of the war. The bomb they built has been used twice, both times against Japan. On 6 August 1945 it was dropped on Hiroshima, and three days later it was dropped on Nagasaki. Although it has not been used again in war, the atomic bomb has hovered over all military and political planning ever since.

The scientists at the Los Alamos Scientific Laboratory were striving to transform a theoretical possibility into an explosive reality. They were attempting to develop two kinds of bomb at once: one to be fueled by enriched uranium and the other by plutonium. Because neither fuel was yet available in significant quantities, calculations and experiments had to be done with something similar or with small, impure quantities of the real thing. The scientists were told to have the bombs ready by the time the fuels would be ready in sufficient quantities—probably the summer of 1945.

As the wife of one scientist recalls, there was "the feeling that you've *got* to make that bomb, you've *got* to get it done; others are working on it; Germans are working on it; hurry! hurry! hurry! This is going to save our boys! . . . Get that damn bomb done!"[1]

To attract top scientists from such institutions as Harvard and Stanford, along with other civilian workers needed for the project, the government allowed employees of the project to bring their families. The children who came to Los Alamos entered a town unlike any other—one that would have a profound effect on their lives. The town of Los Alamos had been hastily constructed on the site of a small preparatory boarding school for boys, the Los Alamos Ranch School. The name *Los Alamos* was derived from the cottonwood trees that thrive on the hillsides and in the canyons. At 7,200 feet above sea level, Los Alamos is just a bit higher than Santa Fe, 35 miles south and east, but the two locales are separated by a wide valley. The road connecting them descends into the valley then rises steeply, especially on the final approach to Los Alamos. Here the narrow winding road hugs the jagged, rocky cliffs as it climbs by switchbacks. The road from Santa Fe led up a steep incline; much of it was unpaved—dust in the dry season, almost impenetrable mud when it rained. Climbing that hill to the place where it levels off as the Pajarito Plateau on one-lane rutted roads is an experience the children never forgot. The first view of Los Alamos is still strong in the recollections of children old enough to remember their arrival; many of them arrived with a churning stomach and a cringing fear that the car would go over the cliff.

Part way up the hill are Los Alamos's nearest neighbors, the Native Americans of the San Ildefonso pueblo, whose ancestors had carved out homes in the cliffs of what had become the Bandelier National Monument and who now were sharing their land and traditions with this strange band of newcomers.

Some years before the Pilgrims arrived at Plymouth Rock, Spanish explorers already had established a provincial capital in northern New Mexico, just north of present-day Española. Their Spanish-American descendents homesteaded the Pajarito Plateau (*Pajarito* means "little bird") and became farmers around the area of Los Alamos Lab sites. The first Anglo homesteader to brave the region's snows with a year-round ranch was an intrepid lumberjack named Harold Hemingway Brook. He filed on 160 acres of land in 1911— a year before New Mexico became the forty-seventh state. Constructing a series of log buildings, he called his place Alamos Ranch. Seven years later, at the tail end of World War I, Ashley Pond bought the ranch from Brook, renaming it the Los Alamos Ranch School. In December 1942 the headmaster called the boys together to tell them that the school would close in February. Its land and buildings were being taken over for a special project to help the war effort. The army soon moved in with a clamor of heavy machines. Amid the chaos and commotion, contractors threw up homes as fast as they could for the military, the scientists, the machinists, and the technicians.

During the war the average age among Los Alamos residents was 24. There were no unemployed, elderly, or disabled individuals; there were no garages or sidewalks and very few street names. There were few paved roads and plenty of mud. The residents officially lived at P.O. Box 1663, Santa Fe. Many called their home simply "The Hill." The Los Alamos of the war years can be considered a plateau of privileges unknown in the surrounding valleys or anywhere else in the state. Because of the importance of its mission, it had the best of everything. Its commissaries stocked items not found in those at other military bases or even in civilian stores—like chocolate bars. And the brand-new school was exceptionally well equipped with books and art supplies.

To encourage wives to work, the army arranged to hire women from the San Ildefonso pueblo as housekeepers. Each morning an army bus arrived at the pueblo to bring the women to the new town. Some were soon looked upon as nannies or even extended family members. The children of Los Alamos have fond memories of their Indian caregivers and cherish the pueblo culture they assimilated. Some trace their sense of spirituality to association with the Indians. Others were fascinated by the nonverbal communication they developed with the Indians. Still others recall with awe the experience of watching the dances on feast days. Almost all took away some treasured Indian craft—a black pottery bowl, or pottery animal. To the children born at Los Alamos, the Indian housekeepers often gave a name in the Tewa language, which these children recall with affection.

While the children of Los Alamos did not think of themselves as unique when they were children, as adults they realize that many circumstances they accepted were peculiar, that, as one of them puts it, "this was not the way in which most people grew up." They lived in a community that was not only secret but intense (and often tense), carefully selected, and diverse in geographic and cultural background. These children were a microcosm of the United States—children of scientists, many of whom had grown up in Europe; of machinists and technicians from around the country; of construction workers from Texas and Oklahoma; and of Spanish Americans.

Uniting this group of children from such diverse backgrounds was their physical isolation from the rest of the country. Still another dimension was added by the urgency of the town's mission, combined with the sense of impermanence of the town itself. With the exception of many of the Spanish Americans, everyone else in the town came from somewhere else. The children quickly accepted the town's unusual aspects—its fences, guard gate, soldiers, PX—all of which were less interesting than the wonders of the cliffs and canyons, the woods fragrant with the scent of piñon, and the nearby valleys of tall grass and wildflowers.

Still, that early secrecy has left a mark. One daughter of a physicist, now in her fifties and an administrator at the Los Alamos Scientific Laboratory, has trouble shaking the idea that "you don't ask." The son of a metallurgist says the years of silence created a communication chasm that he and his father were never able to bridge. And in the decades that passed after the secret was made public in August 1945, many parents never did talk about those years. Their children know generally what their parents did but are left to guess how they felt about it.

The recollections of those who were children in Los Alamos from 1943 to 1952 reveal three common threads. One is a magnetic attraction to and sense of connection with the land. The second is a sense of security—that

Los Alamos was a place where children felt safe. With a fence around it and constantly patrolling military police, what little danger there was involved getting lost in the woods or canyons, and there were plenty of soldiers to help find a lost child. Since everyone had a job and had been investigated, there was no fear of crime. The third common thread is multiculturalism. Almost all the children list interest in other cultures and ability to get along with all kinds of people as very important to them, and they attribute this interest directly to their experience at Los Alamos.

"There was a tremendous sort of melting-pot thing that occurred," observes Jim Bradbury, son of Norris Bradbury, director of the Laboratory from 1945 to 1970. "The Ulams [from Poland and France], the Fermis [from Italy], the Kistiakowskys [from Poland]. Their children mixing with . . . the [Native-American] Atencios and the [Spanish-American] Sandovals. . . . Here you had this tremendous diversity in people . . . in nationalities and ethnic groups, in roles, yet somehow . . . you had this bond of something happening that kept you all together." Some of the children go so far as to say, "The children felt no prejudice—none." Others disagree, noting that in some important ways Los Alamos was an unusually stratified community, but by education and occupation, not ethnic origin.

On one point all agree: academic success was the leveler. Scholastic achievement, not family background, determined one's place in the children's social strata. This New Mexico town that initially did not appear on any map brings to mind Garrison Keillor's description of the mythical town of Lake Wobegone, Minnesota, "where all the women are strong, all the men are good looking, and all the children are above average." The women of Los Alamos were strong—they had to be to withstand the isolation, the secrecy, and strange living conditions; the men were not all that good looking; but most of the children could be safely called "above average." Academic achievement was respected, encouraged, and, to a large extent, expected. Particularly notable are the accomplishments of those whose parents had little education. The son of a heavy-machine operator who had not finished high school holds a prestigious job in the State Department. The son of a carpenter is a nationally known artist. The daughter of another carpenter is a university professor. Daughters of machinists and construction workers have earned doctoral degrees. A security guard's son is nationally respected as an authority in African-American history.

The children of the scientists had a harder road to follow, but they also have achieved. For some, their parents' level of achievement served as a goal, but it was a goal they suspected they would never attain. This predicament was particularly true of sons. Several are physicists—some even working at Los Alamos and other national laboratories. Some went into physics because it was all they knew of a profession: all their parents' friends seemed to be physicists. Others deliberately chose professions where they would not feel they were competing with their fathers.

Daughters of scientists (with some exceptions) generally felt less pressure pulling them to a scientific career and appear to have had an easier time finding their own path. A common theme in their reminiscences is the sense of intellectual excitement they recall from the conversations of their parents and their parents' friends at Los Alamos. Several say they have never again experienced anything quite like that intellectual zest.

Most of the children of wartime Los Alamos left the town, either when their families moved away at the end of the war or, for those whose families remained, when they went off to college. Many have since returned, either because they knew they could get a job at the Laboratory or because of an attraction to the land and the area's cultural mixture. Many have chosen to live not in Los Alamos but in the surrounding villages or Santa Fe.

A surprising number of those who spent only a couple of years of their childhoods at Los Alamos say they think of Los Alamos as home, more so than places at which they lived much longer. And they keep returning for visits. Those who now live in California, Chicago, Boston, or New York have taken a bit of the culture of northern New Mexico with them. One is likely to meet a now-grown Los Alamos "child" in Chicago or Pittsburgh wearing her favorite New Mexico Indian jewelry. And it's not unusual to walk into a colonial home in Virginia or a Manhattan apartment and see New Mexico landscapes on the wall, an adobe incense burner with piñon sticks on the mantle, or some of the famous black pottery from the San Ildefonso pueblo.

Along with this connection to the culture is a connection to the people. The children of Los Alamos know and care about one another even if they haven't seen each other for more than 40 years. They know about one another's work, triumphs, and difficulties. The scientists who were together at Los Alamos during World War II frequently had known each other previously, through their university research or their graduate study. And they would continue to interact over the years, coming together at physics conferences or when they returned to Los Alamos, as many did for a summer or a semester. The families became extraordinarily close.

Discussing the project that brought Los Alamos into existence—the development of the atomic bomb—the children have a variety of responses. In general those whose parents returned to universities grew up immersed in liberal ideas and are likely to have participated in antinuclear campaigns and given serious thought to the idea of pacifism. The children who remained in Los Alamos, whose parents continued to work for the Laboratory, tend to be more staunch defenders of the Lab and its work. But almost all believe that, given the circumstances of World War II, the threat of Hitler, and the likelihood that Germany was working on atomic weapons, their parents made the right choice. And they are proud of their parents' contribution to ending the war. Their pride, however, is often qualified. As Henry Bethe, son of physicist Hans Bethe, puts it, "It's not a pride that says, 'God, aren't we great.' It's more of a pride that there was this thing to be done and they did it."

What follows is the story of what it was like to be a child in Los Alamos in its first decade, 1943–52. It is not a history of the atomic bomb or the nuclear age but the story of a place, the town of Los Alamos, as seen through the eyes of its children.

KEEPING THE SECRET

I

THE SECRET PROJECT

In the spring of 1943 strangers started appearing in Santa Fe, New Mexico. They came from all over America and even parts of Europe. They had traveled to Santa Fe as part of a secret project, and all they knew was that they were to report to 109 East Palace Avenue. This influx of strangers continued for the next couple of years. Among these people was Jeannie Parks, a vivacious young woman who had grown up in New York City and gone to college in Texas, where she had taught school. In August 1944 she got off the train in Albuquerque, boarded a bus, and arrived in Santa Fe on a hot Sunday morning. She walked across the sun-drenched plaza with its grassy square surrounded by adobe buildings that seemed to grow out of the red-colored earth. In one corner of the plaza was a Woolworth's, but its adobe building wasn't like any Woolworth's she had ever seen before. It was all so different from the skyscrapers that meant home to her that she began to wonder what kind of a place she had come to.

Spotting some soldiers in uniform, she asked them to direct her to 109 East Palace Avenue, and they led her around the corner and through a wrought-iron gate into a courtyard. A huge elm tree took up most of the open space, behind which was a two-room adobe building. Seated at a desk inside was Dorothy McKibbin, a pleasant, round-faced, rosy-cheeked woman with a small white dog at her feet. Officially McKibbin was the personnel director for the secret project on The Hill; unofficially she was the welcomer and morale booster, the bit of cheer when cheer was needed. She directed Jeannie to a military bus parked out back and told her to come to the office whenever she came to Santa Fe, to think of it as a home away from home.

The bus was full of soldiers. As it wound its way up the steep slopes, making hairpin turns on the rutted-out, one-lane dirt road, the GIs did what they often did—played on the fears of newcomers. "There goes the back wheel off the road," one called out, as Jeannie, accustomed to subways and city buses, covered her eyes. Summoning the courage to look out, she saw that the road hugged a steep cliff and that there was no barrier between it and the drop off to nowhere. One more jerky, skidlike turn and she began to wonder why she had ever listened to Dr. Cook's advice that this was "too good an opportunity to pass up."

Actually, Jeannie had already passed up this advice once. The previous fall she had received a mysterious telegram offering her a teaching job somewhere in New Mexico. She had been tempted, but the information was vague. Her housemates told her it was probably in a mining area and would be desolate. Although she was intrigued, she decided to stay put. Occasionally during the year she had wondered about the strange telegram, but she hadn't given it any more serious thought until June of 1944, when she arrived at the University of Minnesota for her second summer of graduate work in education. Almost immediately, her professor of the year before, Walter Cook, approached her and said, "Why didn't you take that job in New Mexico?" "How did *you* know about it?" she asked. Instead of answering, he told her she had turned down a good job where there were encyclopedias in *every* classroom, lots of library books, lots of art supplies, and a wonderful view from the classroom window. It was the part about the encyclopedias and the art supplies that got to her: her Texas school district had no money for art supplies, and she had dug into her own pocket to buy crayons and paper. This sounded like some kind of utopia.

Dr. Cook had said he could arrange an interview, and now here Jeannie was, on a remote hilltop, in an army bus that had just stopped at a small guardhouse where a soldier was checking passes. Jeannie did not yet have a pass, so the soldier summoned the school superintendent to vouch for her. The superintendent then drove her to her first dinner in the town that would become her home for 50 years. It was a dinner she would never forget.

The three-story building Jeannie entered was made of 800 ponderosa pines. The logs were placed vertically rather than horizontally, for a stately appearance of columns. The dining room ceiling was 19 feet high, with second floor balconies running along two sides and a massive stone fireplace at one end, the head of a New Mexico elk mounted above it. Most of the diners, seated family-style at long tables, were young men in civilian clothes, many of them bespectacled, with a distracted air. The letter Jeannie had received describing living conditions had stated that she would live in a dormitory and eat in a mess hall. Looking around the room, with its rustic charm and its colorful Navaho rugs decorating the walls, she said brightly, "This isn't such a bad mess hall." "That," she recalls half a century later, with a girlish giggle, "was the wrong thing to say. That was Fuller Lodge and it was *the best* place to eat in Los Alamos. That's where all the high-ups ate."

As she ate, Jeannie looked out the windows at fantastic rock formations that were like nothing she had ever seen before. "Are they collapsible?" she asked. The men sitting around her stared for a moment, then burst into laughter. What she was looking at was a millennia-old mountain ridge. "I had never seen such formations because I grew up in New York City," she

4

explains. "They looked so fragile compared with tall buildings. I thought the first wind that comes will blow them down. A big rain will get them for sure."

The next stop was at her dormitory room, where everything was green—the GI bed, the blanket, and even the towel. "This is strange," she thought, but even stranger was the school, which was also green. "I thought at least there would be a little red schoolhouse," she exclaimed to the superintendent. "This is like being in the army!" "It is the army," she replied.

From the start, Los Alamos was a unique—and uneasy—combination of military and civilian. It was a town with one mission—to work out the technical feasibility of an atomic bomb. It was controlled by the army as part of the Manhattan Engineering District. Other Manhattan district sites were Oak Ridge, Tennessee (which produced the uranium); Hanford, Washington (which produced the plutonium); and the Metallurgical Laboratory (known as the Met Lab) at the University of Chicago. In army lingo, the town of Los Alamos was Site Y of the Manhattan Project. But while the army controlled the town, the Laboratory was administered by the University of California under contract to army. The scientists who came to work at the Lab came as civilians. The technicians, machinists, and other staff were a mixture of military and civilian.

From the beginning there was tension between the military and scientific approaches to problem-solving. For the scientists, the goal was to discover new information about how the world operates by open investigation and sharing of ideas through all-inclusive discussion. The army, on the other hand, saw its job as safeguarding the nation by completing the project in secrecy, best accomplished by compartmentalization, hierarchy, and classification of information.

The two philosophies were embodied by the respective military and scientific leaders, General Leslie R. Groves and J. Robert Oppenheimer. General Groves, a career military man, stocky and sturdy, had studied engineering at West Point. In 1942 he was 46 years old and already had proved himself an extremely capable administrator. As deputy chief of construction for the entire U.S. Army, he was able simultaneously to think big and to make sure that the little things got done. He was also adept at working with Congress. At the time of his selection for the Manhattan Project, he was completing construction of the Pentagon and hoping to go overseas. He was in the halls of the Capitol when a superior told him the overseas assignment was not coming through, that he had been chosen for another job—one that, if done well, could win the war. "Where?" he asked. "Washington." Groves's less than enthusiastic response, he remembered years later, was simply, "Oh."[1]

Robert Oppenheimer, the man Groves chose as the scientific head, was a thin academic with a tendency to hunch. By the end of the war he would be emaciated—his clothes hanging, his ever-present porkpie hat set at a jaunty angle, a pipe poised somewhere between hand and mouth. General Groves had chosen Oppenheimer as the civilian head of the project for his reputation both as a theoretical physicist and an inspiring teacher. Groves needed some-one with an intellect sufficiently wide-ranging to grasp all aspects of the scientific problems, the imagination to suggest solutions, the leadership ability to form working teams from a group of strong individuals, and the charisma to keep up morale. The 38-year-old Oppenheimer met the qualifications. Soon the two were working together to find a location for the experimental research installation.

The number-one site requirement was isolation. Other prerequisites in-cluded a location far from any coast, with a sparse population within a 100-mile radius; controlled access yet sufficient roads and preferably a railroad for moving in people and material; land already owned by the government or able to be acquired in secret; enough space for testing grounds and for separation of various Laboratory sites; water and power supplies in place or conveniently developable; and housing in place for the first arrivals.[2]

Focusing on the Southwest, army officials zeroed in on Jemez Springs, New Mexico, about 20 miles from present-day Los Alamos. When Groves and Oppenheimer met there one day in the late fall of 1942, Groves voiced some misgivings, particularly about the possibilities for expansion should the project exceed the 30 scientists plus support personnel then envisioned. The steep cliffs would make construction difficult. Oppenheimer said he knew a place nearby at Otowi, a ranch school for boys.[3] The school was located on a relatively flat plateau between two mountain ranges, the Jemez and the Sangre de Cristo. Much of the land around it already belonged to the govern-ment. With the United States now in the war, a number of the teachers had been called into the service, and the school was having a difficult time finan-cially. A government takeover for the "duration" might be welcome, or at least tenable.

In late November 1942 A. J. Connell, head of the Los Alamos Ranch School, received a letter from Secretary of War Henry Stimson that said,

> You are advised that it has been determined necessary to the interests of the United States in the prosecution of the War that the property of the Los Alamos Ranch School be acquired for military purposes.
>
> Therefore, pursuant to the existing law, a condemnation proceeding will be instituted in the United States District Court for the District of New Mexico to acquire all of the school's lands and buildings together with all personal property owned by the school and used in connection with its operation. Although the acquisition of this property is of the utmost impor-tance in the prosecution of the war, it has been determined that it will not be necessary for you to surrender complete possession of the premises until

February 8, 1943. It is felt that this procedure will enable you to complete the first term of the regular school year without interruption.

You are further advised that all records pertaining to the aforesaid condemnation proceeding will be sealed, by order of the Court and public inspection of such records will be prohibited. Accordingly, it is requested that you refrain from making the reasons for the closing of the school known to the public at large.[4]

Connell promptly canceled the Christmas break and intensified classroom instruction to finish the school year by 8 February. Meanwhile, the army machines were already digging deep into the earth to turn a quiet ranch school into an army base that 50 years later would be a thriving one-company town, its economy centered on "the Lab."

A much-quoted comment on the whole Manhattan Project is the observation Groves is said to have made to his assembled staff as he watched the turmoil of construction and listened to the demands of the scientists and their wives: "At great expense we have gathered here the largest collection of crackpots ever seen."[5] Groves knew that one way to keep his "crackpots" happy was to allow them to bring their families, a decision that added a whole new element to the secret post. The base/town now needed a school and maternity and pediatric medical care. The army found itself in the business of arranging for maids and a nursery school so that wives—who were taking up scarce housing—could lend their talents to the project. And the MPs patroling on horseback had the unusual role of confiscating a ham radio that teenage boys had hidden in a treehouse in the woods or watching children climb through a hole in the fence and deciding when to look the other way and when to tell their parents.

In January 1943, when the army began converting the former Los Alamos Ranch School, the town had a population of 1,500, mostly contractors. All that spring large army trucks crawled up the hill, and the Indian boys from the nearby pueblo of San Ildefonso watched them in wonder. By early summer the army buses were making regular trips to Santa Fe and the nearest railroad station in Lamy, New Mexico, to meet new arrivals. At the end of 1944 the community originally envisioned as 30 scientists and support personnel had 5,675 residents.[6]

The winter and spring of 1945 was a particularly tense period in Los Alamos. Almost all the residents had relatives in the war. They knew that the secret work in which they were engaged was something to shorten the war. But as they received letters from family members in Europe and the Pacific, they wondered whether the project would be completed before the start of the invasions for which their relatives were destined. Even though the lights burned much of the night in the Tech Area, time still seemed to be running out.

Along with lack of time came lack of space, water, housing and other facilities. The water level was dangerously low. Headlines in the community newsletter circulated by the army warned, "CONSERVE WATER." Power shortages became more and more common. Women complained that every time they were scheduled for an Indian maid the power was sure to be shut off. The commissary was crowded with women lugging heavy metal-handled baskets (along with a toddler or two), enduring long waits to buy whatever happened to be available. Dormitory rooms built for one now had two or three; the apartment buildings were full. Housing had intentionally been kept to a minimum because each new family increased the needed services— and because of the limited water and electric power. Family housing consisted of two-story apartment buildings, housing four or eight families; duplexes; and prefabricated single-family houses. Housing types were named after the contractor who built them. The apartment buildings, for instance, were built by the M. M. Sundt Construction Company and called Sundts. The duplexes constructed by Morgan and Sons were known as Morgans. Many of the single-family houses were built by Robert E. McKee and called McKees. Prefabricated homes trucked in from the town of Hanford were known as Hanfords. There were also 16-foot by 16-foot hutments. The majority of the families lived in Sundts. By the end of 1946 there were 332 families in Sundts, compared with 56 in Morgan duplexes, 100 in McKees, and 107 in Hanfords.[7]

There was a strong hint of utopian collectivism. Every head of household had a job and a place to live, constructed and maintained by the army. Rent was determined by salary. The more one made, the more he paid. In 1943 those earning less than $2,600 a year paid $17 a month, while those earning $3,400 to $3,800 paid $34 a month, and those earning more than $6,000 paid $67 a month.[8] But housing was also extremely stratified. The top scientists were given housing in the old log houses of the Ranch School. Dubbed "Bathtub Row," these houses were prized both for the luxury of being able to soak in a bathtub and for their prestige (the rest of the housing included showers but no tubs). Martha Bacher Eaton remembers a party given for her mother when it was announced that her family would be moving to a recently vacated Bathtub Row house. Jean Bacher's friends each presented her with a towel, some of them embroidered with scenes showing her enjoying her splendid new bathtub. Robert Oppenheimer and his family lived on Bathtub Row, as did Kenneth Bainbridge, the Harvard physicist who directed the Trinity test, and William "Deak" Parsons, the navy officer brought in to direct the expanded Ordnance Division. Enrico Fermi, the Nobel laureate from the University of Chicago, was offered a Bathtub Row house but chose instead the more democratic life in a Sundt.

Sundt apartments came in one color, green, but two sizes—two bedrooms or three bedrooms. Generally there were two downstairs apartments and two upstairs units. The upper units were reached by an outdoor stair, ending at a balcony, from which several children remember watching army men and women marching by in formation during the war years. Two features almost everyone remembers are the heating system and the Black Beauty stoves. Each apartment building had its own furnace, which burned either coal or wood and was regularly stoked by men who seemed to spend their nights in the furnace room drinking coffee and talking merrily in Spanish, which could be heard throughout the building. Children also discovered that they could talk to those above or below them through the heating pipes. It was through heating-pipe conversations that Enrico Fermi's daughter Nella formed a friendship with Gaby Peirels that continued for 50 years. The Black Beauty was another matter. It was a massive stove, fueled either by coal or wood, upon which women were expected to cook meals. Many took one look at it and cooked most of their meals for the duration on an army-issued hot plate.

Quonset huts and trailer parks were hastily thrown up—not just for single men doing temporary heavy construction, but for the electricians, machinists, and technicians who were pouring in, bringing with them families in prewar cars stuffed with household goods. Often they were assigned to half a quonset hut. It included a kitchen area but no bathroom. To get to the shared bathrooms they walked on boardwalks, past rows of laundry hanging on the line. During the summer of 1944 the army took over the cabins at the nearby Bandelier National Monument, a 50-square-mile park, to house the overflow, and at least one intrepid family spent the summer of 1945 in a shepherd's tent pitched in Bandelier.

The town hospital also became overcrowded. Shirley Barnett, wife of Los Alamos pediatrician Henry Barnett, recalls her first glimpse of the hospital on a sunny day in the summer of 1943. There was then one other doctor and a staff consisting of "a medical secretary and two small Indian boys acting as hospital orderlies, messenger boys, and general local color."[9] "The hospital," she recalls, "had six beds, an operating room, and a few small rooms and a large room for a pediatric nursery." The nursery was kept busy. Barnett recalls that "eighty babies were born during the first year, and about ten a month thereafter."[10]

In June 1944 medical corps officer Stafford Warren wrote a memorandum to General Groves recommending expanding the hospital to a 50 to 60 "sick patient" capacity, to include 16 cribs for pediatrics. He based the recommendation on the observation that "approximately one-fifth of the married women are now in some stage of pregnancy" and that "approximately one-sixth of the population are children, one-third of whom are under two years of age."[11] A widely told story has Groves asking Laboratory director J. Robert Oppenheimer to do something to curtail the high birth rate. Oppenheimer's reply, if any, is not known. But such a request would have put him in an awkward spot, as he himself was one of the proud fathers standing on packing boxes to look through the window at their babies when his daughter Toni was born in December 1944. The high birth rate—and the general's displeasure—were soon celebrated in a verse making the round of the town:

> The General's in a stew
> He trusted you and you
> He thought you'd be scientific
> Instead you're just prolific
> And what is he to do?[12]

The job of treating the illnesses of the Los Alamos community was in many ways unique. There was the ever-present need to get people back to work as soon as possible. In addition, the unusual layout of the town and lack of communications made house calls an adventure. The apartment houses had numbers but the numbers seemed to follow no sequence. Moreover, very few of the streets had names. At least at first, the doctors knocked at a lot of wrong doors.[13]

Telephones were few and far between. The doctors each had one, but hardly any other residents had them. So instead of calling a doctor in the middle of the night, family members were likely to run to the doctor's house. As Shirley Barnett recalls,

> On these occasions, we would be awakened by the noise of someone stumbling around in our living room, cursing softly. The first time this happened I was frightened enough to want to pretend that it was all a bad dream and there positively was no one in our living room. However, I was forced to accept reality when a male voice at our bedroom door inquired if this was Dr. Barnett's residence. . . . The one thing we had to remember before going to bed was to close the top of the piano in our living room. One nocturnal visitor tripping around in the dark, had inadvertently come down rather heavily on the keyboard of the piano, throwing himself and us into a state of wild confusion.[14]

The commissary had opened in March 1943, buying out the merchandise of a Santa Fe merchant who was going out of business.[15] By July 1944 it was clear that it was barely meeting the needs of this growing community. On 12 August 1944 Lieutenant Colonel Whitney Ashbridge sent the following memorandum to Manhattan Project headquarters:

> Because of the peculiar nature of the project at this Post and the necessity for maintaining good morale among the civilian population, it is considered necessary to carry in stock at the Commissary more items than are authorized by Army Regulations. The isolation of this Post and the security regulations

are also contributing factors which prevent Post residents from access to civilian sources of supply. . . . It is considered by the undersigned necessary to carry a large variety in order to satisfy civilian personnel and so they may put forth their best efforts for the furtherance of the project.[16]

Lab employees got a day off a month for a shopping trip. The army supplied bus rides to Santa Fe. Old-timers recall starting off with long lists and high hopes—sort of like a day off from school—and returning with many items simply carried over to the list for next month. Clothes were often ordered by catalog. The story is told of one catalog delivery arriving with a note, "You folks at Box 1663 do buy a lot!" A similar tale is of a letter sent to P.O. Box 1663 by a mail order company sternly stating, "We don't know what you are doing to our catalogs. We have sent more than 100 catalogs to this address and will send no more."

With its youth and isolation and spectacular scenery, there was a tendency to think of Los Alamos as a Shangri-La. Some people even called it that when they first arrived. But it didn't take long before they began thinking of it more as a pioneer outpost and of themselves as pioneers. They had left established communities, often university towns, to travel over treacherous roads to live near Native Americans in a veritable wilderness. As one physicist's wife later wrote, "I felt akin to the pioneer women accompanying their husbands across the uncharted plains westward, alert to danger, resigned to the fact that they journeyed, for weal or for woe, into the Unknown."[17]

Babies born at the little military hospital inside the gates—and there were a lot of them—were born at P.O. Box 1663. Car titles and licenses—along with insurance policies and food and gasoline rations—were issued to numbers rather than names.[18] Since the town did not officially exist, its inhabitants could not vote—a fact that rankled, especially as the elections of 1944 approached. (In 1948 Los Alamos residents voted in the New Mexico state elections, but the state Supreme Court invalidated their votes because people living in Los Alamos were not New Mexico residents.) The town's nonexistence created other anomalies. If it did not exist, its schools could not very well be part of the New Mexico school system, so they were administered instead by the University of California, which also administered the Laboratory.

Letters were censored. One dropped them unsealed in a special box. The censor would read them, returning them to anyone careless enough to give any hint of where they lived. The story is told of a high school student whose letter was returned because in a description of a biology class she had sketched amoebas. The censor reasoned that since amoebas reproduce by fission, this was giving away too much.[19] Another child received a letter from a relative saying that she was enclosing a package of chocolate-covered raisins—a rare treat. But there were none in the letter. "What do you think happened?" the girl asked her mother. "I think the censors must have eaten them," replied the mother.

The secrecy extended to names and occupations. Enrico Fermi was known, officially at least, as Mr. Farmer (no one was ever "Dr."), and the Swedish physicist Niels Bohr became Nicholas Baker, or Uncle Nick to the children. Several children recall their confusion when, meeting up with Uncle Nick after the war, they discovered that he had a "new" name, Niels Bohr. Fearing that people might guess the nature of the work at Los Alamos if they knew the professions of its residents, the army discouraged words like *physicist* and *chemist*. Dorothy McKibbin, the personnel director who oriented newcomers, occasionally could not control her curiosity. "If there was no stranger around and I was feeling very wicked," she later wrote, "I would glance in all directions, examine the empty air, raise an eyebrow, and whisper tensely, blowing through my teeth like a suppressed wind instrument, 'Are you a phhhhht?' "[20] Some of the wives quickly formed their own code names for their husbands' occupations—physicists were "fizzlers" and chemists were "stinkers."[21] The place where the fizzlers and stinkers worked—and in a very real sense the center of town—was the Laboratory. The green Lab buildings—hastily built and nondescript—were designated by letter, originally from T to Z. As the project kept expanding, all 26 letters of the alphabet were soon used as names, along with a number of Greek letters and mathematical symbols.

Men and women disappeared behind the gates of the Lab promptly at eight each morning, six days a week, emerging again for lunch at noon and then in the evening. Many would return after supper to work into the wee hours. As Ruth Marshak later recalled, "The Tech Area was a great pit which swallowed our scientist husbands out of sight, almost out of our lives. . . . They worked as they had never worked before. They worked at night and often came home at three or four in the morning. Sometimes they set up army cots in the laboratories and did not come home at all."[22]

Sunday, the official day off, was spent by most Hill residents exploring the terrain. There were picnics to Frijoles Canyon at Bandelier National Monument, with those who owned a car—or had use of an official one—stuffing in family and friends like sardines. For the children of scientists, these picnics had a predictability. The women would set out the picnic lunches and watch over the babies, leaving the older children free to roam the ruins or wander to a refreshingly cool pool of mountain-stream water trapped in a rock ledge. The fathers, meanwhile, would walk apart, seemingly oblivious to their surroundings, deep in discussion of the physics problem they had come to this remote spot to solve.

The same pattern emerged in the mountain climbs that were another popular Sunday outing. Many of the scientists had either grown up or studied in Europe, becoming avid hikers. But as they reached a sought-after summit, they often seemed not to even notice the stupendous view but to be preoccupied instead with "the gadget" and how to make it work. Children of scientists and nonscientists alike learned not to ask about their fathers' work. Fathers went to work behind the gates of the Lab each morning, and that was it. You didn't ask about anyone else's father either. It was something you simply didn't discuss—at home, at school, or at play.

2

ARRIVING AT P.O. BOX 1663

The children arriving in Los Alamos in its early years were a motley bunch. They came by train and car from all over the United States and parts of Europe. Some had traveled extensively—often out of necessity, as they fled from fascism. Some families had been in the United States just a few years. Others, particularly the Spanish Americans from the towns surrounding Los Alamos, traced their New Mexico ancestry back several hundred years.

Many of the parents came to Los Alamos out of patriotic duty. This was a job to help the war effort. For others, there was also a strong economic motivation. Jobs had been scarce in New Mexico for some time, worsened by a long drought. The new army base needed carpenters, construction workers, and heavy-machine operators, and the pay was good. For those who knew the secret of Los Alamos, the problem the scientists and technicians were trying to solve, there was sense of urgency. They believed that Hitler also had scientists working on an atomic bomb. They felt an enormous commitment and determination. At the same time there was great scientific interest. They were about to gain new insights into how the world worked. If their "experiment" succeeded, they would unleash a terrifying new energy with far-reaching consequences.

In subliminal ways this intensity was conveyed to the children living in Los Alamos in the early years, giving them a feeling that they, too, were bonded by something exciting and unusual. But as they arrived, they responded individually, according to the particular backgrounds and experience. A boy whose father had worked in agriculture and who knew of internment camps from hearing about workers rounded up worried that his family now was about to be interned. A girl separated from her parents by illness as she arrived came to Los Alamos feeling abandoned. Another, who had been on a series of travels since fleeing Italy, took the journey in stride, especially as she did not particularly like the city where she was then living. Still another remembers a long train ride from Montreal and a WAC driving fast over unpaved roads in a landscape very different from Canada.

Secundino Sandoval

In the fall of 1943 Sam Sandoval drove his family up the winding road to Los Alamos. Like many of his neighbors, he described his heritage as "Spanish American," but while most of New Mexico's Spanish Americans were Catholic, Sam was Presbyterian. He and his brothers and sisters had been educated at a Presbyterian boarding school in Albuquerque. A skilled craftsman despite having lost two fingers in an accident, Sam found work hard to come by in the early 1940s and had moved his family around the state and even to Arizona in search of better jobs. By 1941 he was in Arizona, working first as a miner in Superior and later as a farmer in Phoenix. When he registered his children for school, his eight-year-old son Secundino, who was light-skinned, was placed in a class with whites, while his seven-year-old daughter Clara, who was darker, was placed in a class with "Mexicans"—a segregation that opened Secundino's eyes to the idea of discrimination.

An observant child, Secundino was also aware that an Italian family they had known in Superior had been "taken away" and that some Japanese families in Phoenix had been sent to camps. He never asked about it, but the idea that a family could be sent off like that frightened him. So when his father stopped the car at a gate with an armed guard and surrounded by army machines, Secundino hunched down in fear. The wait was several hours long—at least it seemed so to the nine-year-old. As he sat there, listening to dynamite blasting in the distance, he was sure that his family, too, was entering a camp. "[When we] had to wait five hours and hear the dynamite going off and rocks blasting at the edge of the canyons, I'm scared to death. 'Why are they taking us to this concentration camp?' I didn't tell my father, [but] I thought we were being confined to a concentration camp for no reason at all." Once they entered the town, Secundino was struck by the smells—the "odor of coal burning—sort of grim, sort of strange. But there was the beautiful smell of pine trees, wet pine trees.

"In the rural community of Northern New Mexico [that I had known] we played marbles. We stole apples from the convent. We had fights. Boys and girls did not play together, and games were not organized by the classes. You just went out on the playground and played by yourself. [In Los Alamos] we went out to the playground and played Ring around the Roses, boys and girls holding hands. My gosh—unheard of! I never heard of holding a girl's hand in fourth grade. So I wouldn't do it. . . . A Halloween party and bobbing for apples—that was all new to me. Valentine's Day the kids in the class would buy valentines and send them to all the kids in the class. I would go home, say to my father, 'Can I buy some valentines?' 'What for?' 'To send to all the kids in the class.' 'No. A valentine is something you send to one person.'

"I had never seen blue eyes or blond hair. So you have to understand how difficult it was for me—like being dropped in a different environment, not knowing the language, not knowing the people around you, and it caused a lot of problems. It took many, many years for me to overcome my own prejudices. . . . There was a definite distinction. You were a scientist, you were in an upper echelon. Your father was a carpenter, you were in a lower echelon. . . . It caused me a lot of fights. . . . We did have incidents in school. We had people who were coming in from, say, Oklahoma or Texas to work in construction. In Texas or Oklahoma, back in those days, if you were of a different race, dark skin, dark hair, you were Mexican. They categorized everyone under the name Mexican, whereas my father always said, 'Hey, we're Spanish.' Spanish American, that was the term used then. It caused some problems in school. Kids come in, call you Mexican. Call him Okie. Call him something else, hillbilly. There was this kind of tension.

"To a certain extent we were prejudiced maybe against the children that were very brilliant, [children of] scientists. I would pick on a kid in the class, beat him up after school. It was like moving into a different country, all these different cultures. And seeing the GIs marching with weapons. We played war games during the war. Everybody had a wooden gun or pistol we made. There used to be a saw mill here in Los Alamos. They had a lot of remnants left over. We used to take the boards and build forts."

Sam Sandoval had been hired to do construction—he was particularly adept at flooring and roofing. While most construction workers were assigned quonset huts, he was able to get a Sundt apartment. "I remember the first time we came into the Sundt," recalls Secundino. "Of course the Sundt was empty. You used to have to call some number, tell them how many children you had, and they would bring so many army bunk beds and the refrigerator and the stove. Everything was army-issued. All the houses were maintained by the U.S. government. They had a priority list. The higher up you were the easier it was to get your house painted or the linoleum changed.

"My father encountered difficulties when we moved from a double unit to a triple unit across the street. He had permission to move the refrigerator, and he moved it in. The gentleman who was going to move in [to the apartment we had vacated] came in, and he cursed my father out. I will not repeat the words. My father was a good fighter. My father punched this man and knocked him down on the floor. I was scared. . . . That night we were sitting at the dining-room table eating, and the provost marshall drove up to our house with a couple of MPs. They were going to arrest my father. We were all scared that my father was going to go to jail. He [had] hit this man. The provost marshall knocked, said, 'Mr. Sandoval, did you strike this gentleman?' He said, 'Yes, I did.' My father said, 'What would you do if I called you this name?' And he repeated everything. [The marshall] said, 'I would be very angry.' My dad said, 'Exactly.' And he closed the door. That was the end. They drove away."

Both of Secundino's parents were artistic. During the rare times when Sam wasn't working, he would pick up a pencil and draw faces; Secundino also loved to draw. His parents encouraged him with coloring books or a set of watercolors for Christmas. In school he learned that through his drawing he could compensate for his insecurity with the English language and—in his own way—compete with the children of scientists.

Martha Bacher Eaton

Somewhere between Boston and Lamy, New Mexico, Martha Bacher came down with the chicken pox. It was July of 1943. Martha was seven and riding trains crowded with soldiers to join her father, Robert Bacher, at his new job. Bacher was a Cornell University physics professor who most recently had been working on a special, war-related project at MIT. Now he was at a secret place in the desert. Martha was traveling with her mother, Jean, and her four-year-old brother, Andrew, who was called Sandy. While Martha's chicken pox was an itchy nuisance to her in the hot, dusty railroad car, it was a potential disaster to the Los Alamos community. An outbreak of chicken pox could sweep through the town, keeping people away from work, delaying the all-important project.

When they arrived at the small depot in Lamy, Martha clambered out excited to see her father. But he barely greeted her as he whisked his wife and son into a waiting army jeep. Shocked, hurt, and full of fear, Martha was taken to another jeep with three soldiers and driven separately. All alone, not knowing were she was going, she watched the strange soldier driving fast up steep hills. Once inside the gate, the soldier took her directly to the small hospital that had recently been completed. The shock of her arrival in Lamy is still powerful in her memory.

"There were two jeeps with soldiers and MPs in them. My father came over and greeted my mother and my brother and took them into one jeep. They left me to go in the other jeep all alone with the MPs because I had the chicken pox. I was very hurt because my father didn't even say 'Hello' to me. That was part of being quarantined. They didn't want the scientists getting the chicken pox because then they wouldn't be able to work. . . .

"The hospital was just built. I was the second patient. The nurse's name was Sarah, and I screamed all the time. She kept trying to get me to be quiet. I was terrified. . . . My parents weren't allowed to come see me because they were afraid the chicken pox would break out all over. . . . I had no idea where my parents and my brother were. After a while my brother came [down with the chicken pox], and he was in the same hospital room, so I could ask him where we were living and what the furniture was like, because we had left everything behind.

"I felt abandoned when we first arrived, and I felt abandoned when both my parents went off to work. . . . My mother is an artist, but they employed some of the wives to work on the computers. [Because] both my parents worked at the Lab, I didn't see them [much]. The people who looked after my brother and me were Indians. My experience with Indians was just incredible. I just found them very fascinating. . . . The only time I remember really seeing my father was when we'd go off hiking practically every Sunday. We did the hikes with the Fermis. . . . The men would all go off and talk physics, the women would all sort of linger back . . . and then the kids were left to sort of scramble along and keep up. The mountain that we used to climb most of all was called Rabbit Mountain. It was a very difficult mountain to climb down, and it was one of the Fermis' favorites.

"Once we got accustomed to [Los Alamos], there wasn't much we could do that would hurt us. We saw this fence outside. Stuart Smith [son of metallurgist Cyril Smith and his wife, Alice] and I decided we'd dig under the fence and go investigate what was outside. A couple of weeks later we heard our parents talking about the fact that people were sneaking into Los Alamos under the fence. And we tried to tell them that the kids were the ones who were sneaking out and then back in. . . . They wouldn't believe us. They were convinced that the Japanese or spies or somebody was coming in under the fence. So [the military] put the fence way underground, then they put barbed wire and radio stuff around the top, so that ended our escapades going out under the fence.

"Then there was the time that I wasn't allowed to have any [new] shoes because Stuart Smith and I had, in one of our escapades, decided to trap the MPs who, we noticed, walked around this triangle exactly the same way every single day and every single night. So we dug this mud hole and camouflaged it. Every morning before school we'd go out to see whose [shoe] we caught. There was one time that we did catch a shoe, and it turned out to be [Edward Teller's wife] Mici Teller's shoe, so we had to skip one of our shoe rations. That was the end of our mud traps.

"The bad thing about this secret place [was that we could tell] absolutely no one where we lived. When we went to Santa Fe and we were approached by anybody, we'd have to just tell them that we lived at P.O. Box 1663. I remember feeling quite scared because I would have to lie about where I lived and I wasn't allowed to say what my name was. So there were a lot of things that I learned that were secrets. It took me a long time to talk about Los Alamos with friends later. And there was one day that some men did come up to me and sort of loomed in on me in Santa Fe and asked me where I lived and what my name was, and I wouldn't tell them. They started insisting that I tell them. But I didn't. I was really scared. And they said things like, 'How can anybody live in a post office box?'

"The place [in Santa Fe] that we could go that was really safe was Dorothy McKibbin's office. . . . I remember meeting her when we first got to Santa Fe before we went up the hill. Even though I did have the chicken pox, she did say 'Hello' to me. And I remember her saying very carefully that this was our home when we were in Santa Fe. So after these two men loomed in on me, I ran over there. I think [the men] were the FBI testing kids, because I think they did it to some other kids too.

"That was the negative—that there were certain things about me that were secret and people weren't supposed to know about. I remember when we went back to Cornell one of the things the teacher said in introducing me was that I had come from New Mexico where they built that bomb. She said, 'Isn't that right?' And I said, 'Oh, no. I didn't live there.' I still couldn't say anything about it."

Nella Fermi Weiner

The soldier waiting at the Lamy depot that summer day in 1944 looked hard at the woman who had just disembarked with her two children—a girl, Nella, about 13, and a boy, Giulio, of eight. When he approached her, she misunderstood his question, replying, "Yes, I am Mrs. Fermi." The soldier frowned, and said, "I was told to call you Mrs. Farmer."[1] Whenever the woman's husband, Nobel laureate Enrico Fermi traveled on Manhattan Project business, he used the pseudonym Henry Farmer. But no one had told Laura Fermi that she was now Mrs. Farmer.

The arrival was memorable in another way. Unlike other families, where the husband often preceded his wife and children to Los Alamos, Laura and her children were coming to live in Los Alamos before Enrico did. It hadn't been planned that way, but at the last minute Enrico had been called to help solve an urgent problem in Hanford, Washington, where the plutonium was being manufactured. Having already sublet their Chicago home and received by messenger railroad tickets on the Santa Fe Chief, Laura decided, egged on by her children, not to wait for Enrico.

The idea of Site Y, a mysterious place in the wilderness, had struck the children's imagination. When the train tickets arrived, Giulio had jumped up and down saying, "I want to see them. Let me have them!"[2] Boarding the train to Lamy, Laura shared her children's excitement. She knew very little about her destination except that it was surrounded by a fence and that children could roam at will within that fence. She knew also that it was a place where hiking boots would come in handy, as would an electric roaster. And she knew the precise measurements of her windows—thoughtfully measured for her by one of the physicists so that she could buy curtains in Chicago.[3]

The trip from Chicago to Lamy was one more piece of a journey that had begun in Italy four and a half years earlier. On 6 December 1938 Laura and Enrico—accompanied by Nella, then seven; Giulio, then two; and a nursemaid—had boarded a train in Rome bound for Stockholm, where Fermi was to receive the Nobel Prize for Physics. They had told their friends that they were then going to the United States for six months while Fermi was a guest lecturer at Columbia. Actually they were going for good—to escape fascism and the reprisals that might come upon them because Laura was Jewish. There had been tense moments on the train, especially when a German guard came to inspect their passports and had slowly and deliberately flipped through the pages over and over again. Laura remembered that even her husband, the family reassurer, had watched with his lips so pursed that they disappeared inside his mouth.[4]

After some months in New York, the family bought a house in Leonia, New Jersey, and set down roots. One of Fermi's colleagues at Columbia lived close by. The children began to think of Leonia as home. When Fermi's job with the Manhattan Project moved to Chicago, the Fermis took another long train ride. After the wonderful feeling of settledness in Leonia, Chicago was an uprooting for Nella and Giulio. Nella especially wasn't very happy there. So the next stage in the journey—to a secret place in the wilderness—seemed particularly appealing.

Nella Fermi Weiner recalls that "back when we were in Italy when I was really small, I remember the grown-ups huddled around the radio, and there was talk of anti-Semitism. I didn't even know what that meant. But I was scared—not because I understood what was going on but because I understood that the grown-ups were scared. I remember when France fell. The was when we were . . . in Leonia. Coming from Italy, France is big. The fact that Poland or Czechoslovakia fell didn't impress me so much. But France was really big. I thought [Hitler] had gotten the whole world. I think everybody expected Britain to be next.

"By the time we were in Los Alamos, the tide had turned quite a lot. Besides, we weren't always thinking about the war. . . . My father was very cautious. When we were traveling from Leonia to Chicago, he said it would be best not to speak Italian, which we spoke at home. [He said] that people might get hostile [because the United States was then at war with Italy]. . . . So we kept on speaking English until we got to Chicago, by which time my brother had forgotten how to speak Italian—or so he said. For years we carried on these conversations where the rest of us spoke Italian, and he would answer in English. So he still could understand it very well. . . .

"I went to seventh and eighth grades at the Lab School [of the University of Chicago]. I was very unhappy there. It was an awfully snobby school. I felt shut out, so school at Los Alamos was a big relief. I had some good friends, and I felt accepted. I also felt on the top of the heap, which never really hurts.

"My mother, my brother and I took the Super Chief [to Los Alamos]. . . . The first thing that happened was we were fingerprinted and probably photographed for our passes. . . . When you look at it from the point of view of a 13-year-old, that's an adventure. One of the things that was intriguing about going to Los Alamos was that we could write letters to our friends but the letters came from Box 1663, and our friends could write to us through Box 1663. For most people it was Box 1663 Santa Fe, but for us it was Box 1663 Chicago. I think we had the Chicago address for security. It was obvious that it was a code, but during the war, people kept quiet.

"My father had a bodyguard [both in Chicago and at Los Alamos]. We were on friendly terms, which was lucky because it would have been an awful thing if you didn't like your bodyguard. If my father was traveling, the bodyguard would go with him. But at Los Alamos he didn't have much to do, so they put him to work in the censor's office. My father had always worked very hard, but there was more intensity in Los Alamos. I remember one time when my mother had to drag him out of the Lab on Christmas Day. But Los Alamos was also the place where I began to get closer to my father. Toward the end of our time there I was getting to an age where he could talk to me on his level.

"I was very interested in the adult society around me, partly because there was a scarcity of kids my age, but also because the adults were a lot more interesting than the kids at school. I knew nothing about what was going on. I had read in my science book that sooner or later we would have ships powered by nuclear power. I figured that's what they were doing. You see all these scientists disappearing into a black hole, and you read that in your science book—it seemed likely. But I kept it to myself. I never thought of a bomb."

Joan Mark Neary

In July 1945, during the final tense months of the war, a Canadian woman with four small children boarded a train in Montreal, bound for Lamy, New Mexico. During the change of trains in Chicago, she was greeted by a soldier who had been assigned to help with her children, who ranged in age from seven to just a couple months.

The children's father, mathematician J. Carson Mark, was already at Los Alamos as part of the British delegation sent by Winston Churchill to help the American scientists. His wife, Kay, would later write about first seeing the town: "Trucks stood in orderly rows behind wire fences, along with jeeps and tractors. Next, there were sheds painted green. Then suddenly we were in the midst of a conglomeration of small buildings, army trucks, wire fences, and people. As we drove rapidly through it my impressions were mainly of green paint and lack of height, for there were no trees and no large buildings at this point."[5]

Then they came to the trailers, standing "on each side of the road, lined up side by side with very little space between them—and painted green." It looked as if "some orderly soul with a penchant for filing had sorted them all out and arranged them in groups of a kind. I found the result unbelievably funny."[6]

Farther on was their destination—McKeeville, a series of small, white, single-family houses that, Kay remembers, seemed "like small apartments which, owing to some disturbance in their development, had grown up separately instead of all together in a compact single building and had never therefore acquired a seasoned outer shell.[7] The house assigned to the Marks looked like all the others but had a distinct advantage: it was next to the laundry. Kay was relieved: "If I could find my way to the laundry, I'd always be able to get home."[8]

Joan Mark Neary, who was six when she first saw Los Alamos, recalls, "I was born in Winnipeg in 1938. A few years afterwards we moved to Montreal. I believe it was there that [my father] got involved with the Manhattan Project through the British Mission, which was the parallel effort in Canada. In 1945 my mother had a baby, my second brother [Graham]. He was a tiny infant when my father came to Los Alamos [in the spring]. Sometime in the summer the rest of us came down. . . .

"[In Chicago] some army person came out of the crowd, knew us from description, took care of us all day, and put us on another train. We ended up in Lamy, where a WAC met us. I remember looking out the window and being impressed by the landscape. It was completely dry, with these tiny trees all over it. It was such a change from Canada. I didn't like it at all. The WAC drove us to Los Alamos. She was quite a driver. The roads were not all paved. You had to go from Santa Fe to Espanola, then along a road that was filled with dips like a roller coaster. She drove very fast, drove up the windy little roads there. . . . Maybe my mother knew where we were going, but we kids had not been told.

"We got to Los Alamos and had a house that doesn't exist anymore. . . . It had no bathtub, just a shower and a little stove in the center of the house, no sidewalks. We were on a muddy street. . . . I remember my mother taking me down into the canyon when she and I were out on an adventure together. It was very steep.

"It was a military town at that point. You needed a pass when you were six to get in and out of town. People at the guard gate looked into the trunk, checked everybody's passes. They were very careful about security. . . . I knew it was secret. I guess I never had any curiosity about why it was secret. It just seemed something reasonable to me. . . .

"We had commissaries that had cans that didn't have pictures and labels on the outside. There were ways to identify them, I guess, by code or labels on the shelves, but the cans themselves were army-colored cans. We had water that occasionally had worms in it. They had to bring it up in a truck. Once we got to take a bath. Rose Bethe lived in Bathtub Row in one of the four or five houses over there that had real bathtubs. She invited us all over for a bath. It was a big event. We didn't have a telephone when we first moved there because there was hardly any telephone system in Los Alamos. . . .

"My father worked six days a week for a long time. I don't know when he stopped doing that. He went on trips. He worked late. The work was very intense. It really never slackened up. He had colleagues dropping in and out. It was a very small town. The Lab was a three- or four-minute walk from where we lived. Work was everything for the men, I think, and the women had to do everything for their families. . . .

"For a long time it was pure socialism. [When] anything went wrong with your house, you called and somebody came and fixed it. You didn't own your house. Rents were incredibly tiny. . . . I remember my mother and her friends dashing back and forth to each other's homes, helping each other with the kids, having a very open sisterly sort of friendship with each other. The feeling of 'whose house is better than whose' [and] 'who's got a new this or that' wasn't part of life at all. It was very unmaterialistic. . . .

"The four-family apartment [had] lots of kids in it. [We'd] go into each others' homes, play in the yard together. There wasn't any traffic. We played across the street, which was hilly. . . . [We] didn't wear shoes. . . . The lack of interest in material things applied to clothing as much as anything else. Nobody got dressed up or stayed very clean. . . . We had lots of picnics. We used to go to Bandelier a lot. It was easier to do in those days in a way because it was a fairly undiscovered spot, never crowded. On the other hand, the roads were not paved and it could be a problem at certain seasons.

"My husband is always saying that my outlook was formed by living in a town with a fence around it. There were no crimes in Los Alamos that I knew of. There were no strangers you had to be wary of. We never locked the doors or worried at all about theft or being hurt or anything like that. . . . I grew up trusting people, liking people. It may not be realistic, but it's nice.

"There was no talk about what was going on there. Everything was completely secret. I wish, looking back on it, that I had had a camera and kept notes or something, because in my childhood so many of the towering figures of the age passed through the dining room."

3

THREE NAVAL OFFICERS AND A CHILD'S SECRET

The Parsons

As William "Deak" Parsons drove up the winding mountain road to Los Alamos, he was, in a sense, coming home. His father, a Chicago lawyer, had brought his family to New Mexico in 1909, believing that the rugged frontier of the West was the land of the future. The son had grown up in Fort Sumner and Roswell, New Mexico, and then gone east for college, graduating from Annapolis in 1922. He had worked on early radar development and in field-testing the proximity fuse. He was a career officer at the Navy Proving Ground in Dahlgren, Virginia, when General Groves tapped him to head the expanding Ordnance Division at Los Alamos. This important division was to bring together scientists, engineers, explosives experts, and those experienced in ordnance.[1]

Groves wanted a military man to direct it. Told that the best candidate for this army position was a naval officer, Groves agreed to interview him, and liked him at once.[2] Parsons was the first navy officer assigned to Los Alamos[3]—a fact that caused some confusion on his initial visit there in the late spring of 1943. Because of the ever-present worry about spies, the guards at the gate had been told to scrutinize the uniforms of all military personnel and report any that deviated from the norm. Because the army guards were not familiar with the navy uniform, as Captain Parsons appeared at the gate the guard called into town to say, "We've really caught a spy. . . . He's wearing the eagles of a colonel, and claims that he's a captain."[4] Confusions would continue throughout Parsons's two and a half years at Los Alamos. His daughter, Peggy Parsons Bowditch, remembers that at least once when her father called for a car and driver he was told that a captain was not a high enough rank to requisition a car.

Peggy was eight when she arrived in Los Alamos. Accustomed to the lush vegetation of Tidewater Virginia, she took a while warming up to the landscape. "It seemed like a god-awful place where nothing would grow," she recalls. Not long after they arrived, her mother took her on an outing to Santa Fe. Suddenly Peggy "got all teary-eyed," and her mother asked, "What's the matter now?" "I'm thinking of all these people who have never seen Virginia," Peggy responded. "Then I did an about-face and absolutely adored it," she remembers. "I played outside all the time, rode horses. . . . I liked being able to ride anywhere and feel a kinship with the layered land- scape. . . . There were wonderful places to play. . . . The only thing people worried about were rattlesnakes, and I never saw a rattlesnake the whole time I was there. . . . There was a tremendous sense of freedom. We were fenced in, but you knew where there were holes under the fences."

The Parsons family settled into the Bathtub Row house next to the Oppen- heimers. An avid horsewoman, Martha Parsons soon was taking long rides with Kitty Oppenheimer. Because Kitty did not enjoy entertaining large groups and Martha loved it, Martha soon became the official hostess, and the two families developed a lifelong friendship. As Peggy recalls, "We had a large house with a downstairs bedroom that we didn't use and a porch off of it, so my friends and I could [play] there. At times we had an MP walking around our house 24 hours a day, and one walking around the Oppenhei- mers'." From her vantage point of living in the town's social center, Peggy remembers "a frantic social life. When these people relaxed, they really [let off steam]. There was a great deal of music, chamber music groups. . . . My mother was always giving parties. . . . I remember the night Niels Bohr came, only we had to call him Nicholas Baker for security."

Like everybody else, the Parsons family spent many Sundays picnicking at Bandelier National Monument. Peggy's mother would pack old newspapers to light a fire, but "before she lit the fire Daddy would reread the old [issues of the] *New York Times,* so we always had to wait while daddy read. . . . The *New York Times* and the encyclopedia were his Bibles." Peggy recalls that her father was not enthusiastic about the Los Alamos assignment: he "thought Los Alamos would sidetrack his navy career, that it would be a dead end. But he did what he was told." The Los Alamos assignment did indeed affect William Parsons's career in ways he never envisioned. Two years after his arrival he sat in the cockpit of a small plane as a scientific observer to the first atomic bomb test at Alamogordo, and three weeks later took off from the island of Tinian, charged with the job of assembling the bomb to be dropped on Hiroshima.

The Bradburys

A year after the Parsons family's arrival, another family took the same cross-country trip to Los Alamos. Before the war Norris Bradbury was a physics professor at Stanford University. He was in the navy at Dahlgren when he was transferred to Los Alamos, where he would later serve as Laboratory director for 25 years. As the two Bradbury boys—nine-year-old Jim and seven-year-old John—bounded out of the car, they began exploring their new home. "From a 10-year-old's point of view," Jim recalls, "it was an adventure, and I think that the scientific adventure that was going on behind the fence somehow translated to us as an adventure.

"It was a makeshift town with lots of service people, lots of hustle and bustle, lots of seemingly contradictory types of activities ranging from the most secret—you weren't supposed to ask questions about what was happening over here—to the not-so-unusual. . . . I think we sensed the urgency, the differentness of it all. I don't know that we felt special, but we certainly realized we were different from the surrounding communities. . . . There was a sense of mission and also a sense of isolation. The stress, the pressure, the urgency associated with that whole project was certainly passed down to the kids [although] we knew nothing about what was going on there. The rumors were that it was an advanced submarine—the most unlikely thing—being built. But we were kids. We were just kids growing up, and we did the normal things kids do.

"Another aspect that I now . . . look back upon as being a positive value was the fact that we did not have any strong awareness of ethnic differences. Very strange. I think our parents did. . . . They were more conscious of Indians, Hispanics, Anglos who had lived here before versus the Anglos who came in from all over the world. [But] the kids experienced none of this.

"I think another thing that must have had some effect was the uncertainty about the future. If you could be certain about one thing, it was probably that you weren't going to be here very long. . . . Most of the people had a hard time accepting Los Alamos as their home. They all had homes somewhere else, and they were at Los Alamos for a while. . . . Parents will say, 'We're going to go back to California or to Utah, that's home.' But kids can, in a very real sense, say, 'This is where we are.' It's more living in the present. . . . Then it did become home, in a larger sense, for a great many people."

The Wilders

In March 1945 Norris Bradbury made a trip to Oak Ridge to recruit personnel for the explosives division. One of those he chose was Ed Wilder, a navy lieutenant with a degree in chemical enginering. Wilder was told simply that he was being sent to the Southwest and that he would be developing procedures for "machining a material that had never been machined before."[5] Wilder drove west with a fellow engineer, Bill Wilson. That May, Wilson's wife, Betty, suggested to Duddy Wilder that "we go visit the fellows." Together the two women packed up their four young children—Ellen Wilder, not quite six; her brother, Marshall, three; and the Wilson children, aged two and three—crowding into the Wilders' "big old Buick Roadmaster." They arrived in Albuquerque, almost 100 miles from Los Alamos "but as close as they would let us come," recalls Duddy.

There was no housing available in Los Alamos, where their husbands were living in military dormitories. So the families remained in an Albuquerque motel, and the two men made the 200-mile round trip twice a week to visit. "Finally the guys said they thought we could stay at Bandelier, so we got a shepherd's tent, and we camped there for 10 weeks, if you can believe that," says Duddy. It was shortly after they moved into the tent a few miles from the back entrance to the Laboratory that Ellen discovered the secret of Los Alamos.

Ellen and Marshall were playing in the Frijoles Creek near their tent site, throwing rocks into the water. Marshall accidentally dropped a large rock just as Ellen was reaching down to pick up another. Ellen's thumb was smashed, and her father drove her to Los Alamos, where there was a doctor. Ellen remembers arriving at the back Site S gate—the one nearest Bandelier—and "they wouldn't let us in." The problem was that Ellen did not yet live in Los Alamos so she did not have a pass. They waited what seemed a very long time while the MPs looked at Ellen and said something about a "secret." "An MP gave me some little mints with jelly centers," Ellen recalls. "I didn't want to eat them, but I didn't want to hurt his feelings, either."

Finally, Ellen was allowed in to see the doctor on duty, who happened to be an ear, nose, and throat specialist. After the thumb was bandaged, Ellen remembers, "Somebody took me to see the ducks on the pond, probably to get me to stop crying. I looked at the ducks and decided they must be the secret. I knew there had been this hoopla about getting me in, and I hadn't seen anything else that was very interesting. So I counted the ducks [there were 11] and thought, 'OK, I've got it.'"

In the fall, shortly after the war's end, the family moved into a McKee house not far from the fence that encircled the town, and Ellen frequently would go to the edge of the fence in the hopes of finding someone on the other side to whom she could tell the secret about the ducks. The problem was that no one came, and "I got bored." The solution, she decided one day, was to get her brother Marshall to crawl through the culvert that went under the fence and find someone. (Ellen was too big to crawl through.) Marshall wasn't keen on the idea, so Ellen "started him in backwards." When he decided he didn't want to play and tried to come out, he found that his leg was jammed against the pipe, and he couldn't move. He started crying. Neither Ellen nor her mother could get him calm enough to move his leg, and they had to wait for Marshall's father to come home and do it. For Ellen, the afternoon was turmoil. "Marshall was crying, and I was thinking, 'I'm not going to get a pass when I turn six.'"

Duddy Wilder suspects that some of Ellen's fascination with spying may have come from the worry that her father and Bill Wilson had expressed during one of their visits to Albuquerque. They had said they thought the FBI were following them. That was one of the reasons they wanted their families to leave the motel. "Somehow it got impressed upon me that something extraordinary was happening here," says Ellen. "I knew it was not normal to keep a little kid with a broken thumb out. . . . Something was out of sync or special. I was tuned into it."

4

DIVERSIONS AND SAFE HAVENS

Robert Y. Porton

For the children of Los Alamos during the war, the military presence was pervasive. While most of the soldiers appeared simply as long legs in uniforms, one soldier—a Florida native with music in his soul and unusual responsibilities—stands out. Robert Y. Porton was one of two soldiers in charge of recreation. His duties ranged from handing out baseball bats and gloves to supervising the ice-skating rink deep in a canyon and scheduling basketball games in Theater 2, the community building that served as movie house, gymnasium, dance hall, and church. Porton also ran a small radio station heard only within the confines of Los Alamos—a name he was careful never to mention on the air. At noon and during the evening, he broadcast classical music by playing records borrowed from the scientists. Sometimes the entertainment was "live"—either a scientist playing the piano or Edward Teller reading fairy tales. These broadcasts helped knit the community together. Eagerly anticipated by both children and adults, they are vivid in many of the children's memories. "At noontime they used to have a program called Music at Lunchtime," recalls Secundino Sandoval, now a renowned artist. "They played the theme song, 'Leapfrog.' I'll never forget it. I used to run from school to get to the house to listen to that song."

In the late fall of 1944, 27-year-old Bob Porton had just finished basic training in the army's combat engineers division at Fort Leonard Wood, Missouri. At the University of Florida he was drum major with the Fighting Gator marching band; later he led his own dance band in Tampa. He had also served in the Air Corps (which later became the Air Force) for three years. At Fort Leonard Wood, he remembers, he was interviewed for several possible jobs in the army: one was with a "supply outfit" that was going overseas; another was "in a place out west where the living conditions are very rugged." A week after the second interview, he recalls, he was asked into the office of a rather puzzled lieutenant who wanted to keep him at Fort Leonard Wood. The lieutenant said, "I just found out that you're either

33

going overseas or you're going to Santa Fe, New Mexico. If you're going overseas I can pull you out because I want you to teach military supply here. But if you're going to Santa Fe I can't touch it with a 10-foot pole, and I don't know why."

Porton was headed for Santa Fe, and he wouldn't know why for almost a year—when the bomb was dropped on Hiroshima. He was soon chugging west to New Mexico on a train crowded with soldiers. The train ride ended in the tiny town of Lamy. Porton alighted at a remote adobe building facing a mountain dotted with sheep. The place struck the many GIs who would land there during the war as the end of the world: one could look in any direction and see only hills and clumps of trees. Once installed in his green dormitory, Porton often found himself working seven days a week. But the work was varied and enabled him to use his musical skills. In fact, he believes that it was "the best assignment I could have ever asked for as a military individual in the entire United States."

The radio station, he recalls, was, like most everything else in Los Alamos, unorthodox and secret. "The scientific personnel—electronics people—had put together a transmitter and everything and coupled into the high power lines of Los Alamos as an antenna, and at the edge of the project we had a capacitor cutting it off so our signal was only heard up here. We kind of had a captive audience. Because of all the transformers and electrical lines and all the equipment up here, outside radio hardly got in at all. . . . I'd always been fascinated by radio, and so this chap [also assigned to the recreation department], Tom Fike, he operated the controls, and I did the announcing, and people would call in with requests. . . . It was called the Community Radio Station. . . .

"Later, I got permission from the post commander to establish call letters. He finally agreed, and I just picked KRS, Community Radio Station. We were not licensed by the FCC . . . because it was all secret. . . . We never used the words *Los Alamos*. We never used the word *atomic* or anything. . . . We'd only go on the air [over the noon hour] to provide requests and music and local news items. . . . In the evening some civilians came in, and most of it was classical music programs for the scientists. As time went on, many times we'd go to a famous scientist's house and borrow an album of classical records and play it that night and then the next day return it. . . .

"We started a program . . . called Music of the Masters, and it went for years. . . . Many scientists used to tell us that after working in the Lab all day long and concentrating and working on difficult scientific projects [they especially appreciated the Music of the Masters]. . . . Edward Teller used to tell Hans Christian Andersen and stories of that sort on the radio for the kids. . . . [He was] kind of a grouchy old son of a gun . . . [but he] always had a soft spot for kids."

Porton also played drums with two combos. The larger group was called the Keynotes, and the smaller group was known as Sad Sack Six, from a popular comic strip. Because the 15-member Keynotes played for most of the big Saturday night dances, Porton often got very little sleep on the weekends. Early Sunday morning he had to be back at Theater 2, helping to transform the dance hall to a church: "[We'd] go to the barracks, get a few hours sleep and then come back. The custodians lived in an old dilapidated barracks next to the place [Theater 2]. I'd have to go wake them up—most of them had hangovers. . . . After church was over around noon we had to turn all the pews around, and Sunday afternoon and evening we had an army motion picture [screening]. In the wintertime, two, three, four nights a week, it was a gymnasium. We had basketball games there."

For a while Porton also had the job of teaching physical education to the high school boys. This was perhaps his greatest challenge: "I had 37 boys, five days a week, and I had never done anything like that in my life. The kids couldn't participate in athletics around northern New Mexico. . . . When I took them over, [they] were a very diversified group: sons of famous scientists, maintenance [men's] kids, Spanish kids. . . . They did not have discipline. They would throw stones at houses, use profanity, cause all kinds of trouble. One of the things I did was form a military company to instill discipline. . . . I was kind of dressing them down in front of Fuller Lodge, and one kid said, 'You can't talk to me like that. Do you know who my dad is?' I told him I didn't care. . . .

"The strange thing is they used to gripe about some of the things they had to do because I gave them close order drill, everything, never figuring they would have any use for it. But by the time they all got out of high school, the Korean War had started. Most of them went in the service. And there were several of them that used to write me letters with great pride in saying, 'I told them that I had ROTC.' I even became a counselor because there were a number of these kids who, again, due to shortage of skilled clerical workers and everything [had both parents preoccupied with war work]. Many of the wives of scientists worked, and the kids didn't have anybody to talk to. Their dads wouldn't get home until late at night. And everything was rush, rush, rush. They'd say, 'Sergeant, can I come in and talk to you about something.' So it was interesting for me."

Porton remembers that there were four distinct military units at Los Alamos: the Provisional Engineering Department (PEDs), who "operated all the heavy equipment and the maintenance and everything a normal county does—the big tough guys, the truck drivers, and you name it"; the Military Police (MPs); a WAC detachment ("telephone operators, secretaries and finance [personnel]"); and the Special Engineering Detachment (SEDs), whom Porton describes as the "fair-haired boys." They "had some college or had a degree or were technical. They worked in the Laboratory. And there was one big difference. The PEDs and the MPs were like regular military when it came to having to do KP and all that, but the SEDs, because of their technical ability, were given all the better things." At first the soldiers in charge of recreation were part of the PEDs; then they were transferred to the SEDs, and "everything improved. We went into a different barracks and started getting promotions."

Of all Los Alamos's peculiarities as a military base, the overriding one was secrecy. "Back then," marvels Porton, "the secret was just so well-kept. . . . We could never have a Manhattan Engineering Project today like we had back then. Somebody would get ahold of it. . . . When I arrived here, I was given a security lecture that impressed me very much. . . . [The officer] said, 'What these people are doing here can shorten the war by at least a year. My advice to you is do the job to which you are assigned. Don't ask questions. Don't talk.' . . .

"Over the years I've had one question thrust at me by 100 reporters, 'Did you know what was going on?' And I've been very, very honest in saying, 'Not really.' Now I knew generalities. I knew it was explosives. All that sort of stuff. But I never asked any questions. . . . I got a letter from [my] mother, and she [asked], 'Where are you, and what are you doing?' And I wrote back and said, 'I'm out in the West. The scenery is beautiful, and the weather is fine.' She wrote back and said, 'You didn't answer my question. What in the world are you doing? And where are you?' I wrote back and said, 'I'm out in the West. The scenery is beautiful, and the weather is fine.'

"The only difficulty I had was when I went home on my first furlough. . . . I went out to visit my [former] colonel [in Florida]. . . . He said, 'Where are you? What are you doing?' And this is what saved me: In Santa Fe they had something called Bruns Hospital. It was a hospital for tubercular military personnel. And I dated the first sergeant in the WAC detachment so I knew [a lot about it]. Bruns had a little hospital military radio station. And this was one that just broadcast through the wards—it didn't go out at all. They got special services transcriptions of shows, Jack Benny, big band stuff. I talked them into loaning us some, and we'd play them. And when this colonel asked me, I said, 'Oh, I'm operating a little in-house radio station in Santa Fe, New Mexico, for the military.' He said, 'Why didn't you say that in the first place? What are you trying to put on, like we got a secret base somewhere?' "

Dorothy McKibbin

Dorothy Scarritt had come to New Mexico to recuperate from tuberculosis. A native of Kansas City, and a graduate of Smith College, Dorothy was in her mid-twenties when she was diagnosed with the disease. Her parents sent her to a sanitarium in Santa Fe, and despite her illness, she greatly enjoyed her two years in the Southwest. A warm, outgoing connoisseur of both people and art, she made many friends, particularly in the art community.

In 1926, cured of tuberculosis, she returned to Kansas City, met and married Joseph McKibbin, and moved with him to his hometown of St. Paul, Minnesota. Their son Kevin was born on 6 December 1930. Ten months later Joseph McKibbin died of Hodgkin's disease, and Dorothy and Kevin moved back with her parents. But Dorothy was too independent to remain there long.

She remembered how much she had enjoyed Santa Fe, and in April, 1932, she loaded Kevin into her Model A Ford and headed west. She got a job as a bookkeeper at a place called the Spanish & Indian Trading Company, a job that suited her well and fed her passion for Indian arts and crafts.

World War II put an end to what had become a comfortable way of life—and catapulted her into the center of the Manhattan Project. When her boss closed down the business to join the war effort, Dorothy was out of a job. She was crossing Palace Avenue one day when a friend came up to her and said, "I hear you're looking for work. I know of a job as a secretary, but it's so secret I can't tell you any more." The secrecy appealed to Dorothy's sense of adventure, and she said she was interested. She was soon at work at an address that no one associated with the Manhattan Project's Site Y will ever forget—109 East Palace Avenue, Santa Fe.

Located kitty-corner from Santa Fe's main plaza, 109 East Palace Avenue today is a gift store. The only thing connecting it to its past is a small plaque that says "1943–1963 Santa Fe office, Los Alamos Scientific Laboratory, University of California. All the men and women who made the first atomic bomb passed through this portal to their secret mission at Los Alamos. Their creation in 27 months of the weapons that ended World War II was one of the greatest scientific achievements of all time."

The reason people remember 109 East Palace Avenue is not because of the building. What they remember is the warmth, the smile, the patience, the optimism that radiated from Dorothy McKibbin as she assured them that they had not come to the end of the world and that whatever problems they put before her—travel, housing, lost furniture—could be solved. As head of personnel, she issued passes, found places for people to live, and arranged their transportation from Santa Fe to Los Alamos and for the shipment of their furniture. She sympathized, encouraged, advised, and soothed frayed nerves.

During the war Los Alamos residents were not allowed to talk to or visit with anyone living in Santa Fe (or to say where they lived, other than P.O. Box 1663), but they could visit Dorothy's office. When the Los Alamos residents came to Santa Fe to shop, Dorothy's office was their headquarters—

the place where they arranged to meet, where they stored packages, changed diapers, or just rested. Many of the children remember particularly the warm fireplace and the smell of burning piñon logs.

Hill residents could also visit Dorothy's home. It was an especially popular destination for the single young scientists, GIs, and WACs holed up in overcrowded dormitories. On their frequent overnight visits, the young scientists and soldiers would unroll their sleeping bags on the patio, look out at the Sangre de Cristo mountains, breathe in the scent of roses, and relax in a feeling of normalcy. During these "sleep-outs" Dorothy's young son, Kevin, was pleased to discover that the scientists could be down to earth and friendly. "You'd never know they were young Ph.D.s and post-docs," he says. "When they were staying around the house, they took an interest in things that I was doing."

Dorothy had had her house built in 1936—after four years of traveling throughout northern New Mexico with a camera and sketchbook, gathering ideas. Her goal was to re-create a traditional rural New Mexico home of the late nineteenth century. The result is a U-shaped house, with the back patio and garden inside the "U." "It was delightful because it was private—and it was a wonderful place in the summertime," recalls Kevin. Day lilies, piñon pines, and rose bushes grew there; when the roses bloomed Dorothy held an annual "party for the roses." Kevin thinks it was partly the adventure of taking a secret job that drew his mother into the Manhattan Project. "My mother was a risk taker. She had no fear of the unknown. When she was told, 'There's a job but I can't tell you what it is,' that was the bait that got her. Then she met Robert Oppenheimer . . . and was really enthralled with him. She liked his spirit."

In the summer of 1944, when Kevin was 13 and fascinated by military machines and ancient relics, Dorothy was asked to spend several weeks at the campgrounds of Bandelier National Monument, the 50-square-mile park that backs up to the Los Alamos Laboratory. There was very little housing at Los Alamos, and new people kept arriving. They were being lodged temporarily in cabins at Bandelier, and Dorothy, who could make a lost and thirsty traveler feel comfortable in the desert, was called upon to do just about that. For two months she left an assistant in charge of the office and moved into cabin Number One at Bandelier, with Kevin next door in cabin Number Two.

"I was living in Heaven in Bandelier," Kevin recalls. "There were no tourists. I had my run of Frijoles Canyon. The whole Pajarito Plateau here is covered with Anasazi ruins, . . . and I was all over the place. My mother had a government car and she would go to Los Alamos on a daily basis from Bandelier. Frequently she just let me out somewhere on the road in an area where I knew there were ruins. I would arrange to meet her a few hours later by the road, and I would go and explore."

Sometimes Kevin would go with his mother to Los Alamos: "I got a real thrill out of this bustling, booming thing that was going on up here. I had known Los Alamos as the Ranch School before the military project was thought about. I had friends who went to school up here. . . . In 1942 and 1943, when they brought the bulldozers in and it was all going up, it was an amazing thing to see. I'm mechanical, and I enjoy seeing things like that, all the equipment and the military vehicles and the people working like beavers."

"There were some military personnel who came through my mother's office," Kevin recalls, "but for the most part they went through another office. I can remember one time when I went to her office after school. There were three or four or five WACs in there and they were sobbing their eyes out because they had come to this place that was the end of the world and here was this lady telling them they still had 45 miles to go. . . . Many of the military who came were all geared up to go either to the European theater or later the Pacific theater. Instead they found themselves here in what they termed God-forsaken country.

"We had over the years—starting during the war—a number of weddings at my mother's house. There were close to 30. The first weddings were people from Los Alamos who didn't want to get married up here [in Los Alamos] but couldn't go anywhere else. . . . The weddings were usually in our back yard or in our big living room. My mother knew everybody in Santa Fe so she could get a judge or a minister. . . . Those weddings have always stood out in my memory. They were fun. The last wedding at that house was my daughter's."

Kevin studied at the University of Colorado and the University of New Mexico. During the summers he worked at the Los Alamos Laboratory, where he returned once he had earned his degree in geology. In 1964 he left the Laboratory for the National Park Service and was stationed at parks in Utah, Arizona, and Arkansas before coming home to Bandelier. There, until he retired, he shared with visitors from around the world his fascination for the geological and archaeological history of the canyon-slashed plateau, with its remains of cliff dwellings gouged out of volcanic ash compressed for thousands and thousands of years.

Kevin remains "truly amazed" that he grew up "right in the midst" of one of the century's most far-reaching developments. In the summer of 1945 he and his mother were following the course of the war closely, plotting the sites of various campaigns on large maps. On 6 August, he remembers, "My mother came home for lunch . . . and we had the radio on as we always did, and that's when Truman announced the dropping of the bomb. My mother looked at me and said, 'That's what we've been doing.' I thought, 'Wow.' I was . . . kind of flabbergasted by this whole thing, that I had been right in the midst of this."

"When we were employed we were told to ask no questions, and we didn't—much," Dorothy wrote about six months after the war ended. "We worked with pride. We sensed the excitement and suspense of the Project, for the intensity of the people coming through the office was contagious. . . . Our office served as the entrance to one of the most significant undertakings of the war or, indeed, of the twentieth century."[1]

Edith Warner

Edith Warner, who had taught high school in Pennsylvania, had come to New Mexico for her health. In 1921 she suffered some kind of breakdown, and her doctor recommended an extended outdoor vacation. She sought a quiet place where she could be at peace with nature. A friend suggested a guest ranch at Frijoles Canyon, and in 1922 she stepped off the train in Lamy, greeted by invigorating air and a stark, desert landscape about which she later wrote, "I know that no wooded, verdant country could make me feel as this one does. Its very nudity makes it intimate. There are only shadows to cover its bareness, and the snow that lies white in the spring. I think I could not bear again great masses of growing things. . . . It would stifle me as buildings do."[2]

When her year ended, Edith returned to Pennsylvania, with the goal of saving enough money to return to New Mexico. A few years later she was back, anxiously looking for a job. She found one—as caretaker at the Los Alamos Ranch School's small freight house on the railway line near a bridge across the Rio Grande. The slender, shy spinster seemed an unlikely candidate for the job, but she needed a place to live, and the school needed someone to stay in the house on the edge of the pueblo. In addition to unloading and guarding the school deliveries, Edith opened a small tearoom—providing lemonade and her special chocolate cake to boys from the school and to the intrepid tourists who drove the winding dirt roads up the hillsides. By 1942 gas rationing had all but eliminated the tourists, and with word that the school would be closing in early 1943, Edith wondered whether she would be able to remain in this land that she loved. But as it had in the past, fate intervened—this time in the form of Robert Oppenheimer.

Because of the urgency of the project and the tenseness it was likely to engender, Oppenheimer thought it would be a good idea to have a place where people could get away for a while—for an afternoon visit or a quiet supper. He knew that the serenity of the little house by the bridge had a calming, centering effect on many who visited there. He asked Edith Warner if she would expand the tearoom to serve suppers. As she described this stroke of fate in a 1943 letter, "Stranger even than the army's choosing this locality was that the civilian head [Oppenheimer] should be a man I knew. He had stopped years ago on a pack trip, come back for chocolate cake, brought a wife, and now was to be my neighbor for the duration.[3] . . . That beginning has increased until there are one or two groups on most nights for dinner. They come in through the kitchen door, talk a bit before leaving, and are booked up weeks ahead. Because they are isolated and need even this change for morale, I feel it is definitely a war job for me. In addition they are mostly interesting and so solve my need for people."[4]

Among those who came to dinner was the physicist Philip Morrison. Years later he told Peggy Pond Church (the daughter of the Los Alamos Ranch School's founder, Ashley Pond), "Edith Warner stands in the history of those desperate times as a kind of rainbow . . . a sign that war and bombs are not all that men and women are capable of building."[5] Lois Bradbury, wife of Norris Bradbury and mother of three young boys, was a frequent visitor to the little house by the bridge. "Sometimes you wanted to get off The Hill," she recalls. "The men were just so involved. People needed to get away from the tension. It was a very common feeling among the housewives. . . . Edith wasn't interesting as an intellectual, but she was interesting in her devotion to her ideals. What was right and wrong was very definite to her, and that attracted a lot of people here. . . . [Edith was] a very strong person and an idealist in a spiritual sort of way. . . . She was very quiet, very reserved. . . . She was such a relief after all the hubbub [of The Hill]."

Alice Smith, who taught high school history while her husband, Cyril, worked on the project, remembers, "Edith was really a focal point. . . . One didn't just drop in on Edith. We wouldn't have been turned away if we had, [but] you knew that she valued a certain amount of privacy. Too much intimacy would have been rebuffed." Alice, who later edited Oppenheimer's letters, believes that Oppenheimer reacted to the steadying inner strength that Edith quietly radiated. "This comes out in his . . . letters," she says. "[The adults] would go have dinners [at Edith Warner's], and it was a major occasion," recalls Martha Bacher Eaton. "It was [a place to go] out of Los Alamos. It was sort of like Dorothy McKibbin's—it was safe. We used to stop by and see [Edith Warner] on the way back from Santa Fe."

Children, too, responded to the special atmosphere of Edith's little house. "I'm trying to think what the equivalent is," ponders Catherine Marshall (daughter of physicist Samuel Allison and his wife, Helen), describing visits to Edith Warner's. "It was like going to the opera, something that's very special. It was not quite like a birthday because it occurred randomly and more frequently. But the prospect of a dinner at Miss Warner's, especially one that a child would be allowed to go to, was something to be anticipated with joy [and] a little apprehension because it was clear that these were adult occasions and children were taken on sufferance and required to be virtually silent."

Julian Martinez, who grew up in the pueblo, also remembers a peacefulness surrounding the little house near the bridge. "The atmosphere was nice there at Edith Warner's," he recalls. "Our people were admiring as to what [she] was doing. She lived in a regular adobe, nothing fancy. She kept to herself, but she was accustomed to our people and our ways." Julian's cousin Gilbert Atencio, who also grew up in the pueblo, remembers enjoying cold milk and chocolate cake at Edith Warner's after a fishing trip to the Rio Grande. "People accepted Miss Warner because she was good to people," he recalls. "Sometimes she would have dinners for special, older people in the pueblo."

Edith Warner died in May 1951 at age 59. Among the scientists who wrote to her family was Niels Bohr, a man admired by his Los Alamos colleagues for both his scientific genius and his humanity. During his frequent visits to The Hill, he had often joined a group dining at Edith Warner's. A passionate advocate of sharing nuclear knowledge, Bohr recently had sent an open letter to the United Nations, urging openness and cooperation and sharing of scientific developments. After Edith's death, he sent a copy of his United Nations' letter to Edith's sister, Vel Ludlow, with the inscription "in gratitude for the friendship of your sister."[6]

Tilano

Edith Warner had not been in her house long when an Indian in his fifties, with long black braids came to build her a new fireplace and help with the chickens and gardening. His name was Tilano. After walking over daily from the San Ildefonso pueblo for a time, he eventually came to live at the little house. In his youth Tilano had traveled with friends from the pueblo to New York to perform Indian dances. From there he had gone on to perform dances in London, Berlin, and Paris, coming home by way of Edith's hometown, Philadelphia.[7] This travel had given him a broad outlook but it also made it hard for him to return to the communal life of the pueblo.

As Peggy Pond Church has written, "In his own way [Tilano] was as much alone as Edith. His wife had died in childbirth, in the second year of their marriage. Because of his long absence as a young man from the pueblo he was in danger of becoming rootless. . . . She must have given him the peace and security he needed. . . . She found in him the masculine strength and wisdom that kept her own life in balance and a spirit of playfulness that had been lacking in her own serious upbringing."[8]

Lidian King, daughter of physicist L. D. P. King and artist Edie King, remembers, "My first memories are when [I was about four and] my family was one of four or five families who went and helped Edith Warner and Tilano build [a new] house [across the road from the old one]. [My] memories begin . . . [with] Edith, her personality and Tilano—[a] sense of respect. . . . We would ride his horse, help him shuck corn. There was a . . . sense of closeness [to the land]. . . . There was something very deep about that connection."

Tilano liked sharing his world with children. He was always giving them small gifts and pointing out natural wonders like a beautiful feather or a newly laid egg. He presented them with arrowheads he had found, miniature moccasins he made, and a postcard-size picture of himself that he mailed to children all over the country in the late 1940s. Both Robert Oppenheimer's son Peter, and Edward Teller's son Paul grew up with this picture of Tilano. Joan Bainbridge Safford, daughter of physicist Kenneth Bainbridge, says her younger sister Margaret's only "memory" of Los Alamos is the small black pottery bowl with a red tomato on it that Tilano gave her shortly before the Bainbridges left Los Alamos in 1945. Going to Edith Warner's was how Martha Bacher Eaton got to know Tilano: "At first I was kind of scared of him because he was a big man. But he was so gentle and so present. This made my Indian connection a lot stronger." She received a going-away present of two arrowheads and a little pair of moccasins.

Kim Manley, daughter of physicist John Manley, remembers Tilano as a gentle man who "had wonderful stories": "I just loved Tilano. . . . He was so quiet and gentle. He would take us for walks . . . and give us feathers from the turkeys. He made a pair of moccasins for one of my dolls. He made a feather headdress for me to wear. I have a picture of him on my wall in a ceremonial costume and he carved the frame himself." Catherine Allison Marshall remembers "sort of hanging out with Tilano, as they would say now." She also recalls that "Tilano loved comics books. Was it Superman? There was some particular comic book. Whenever we drove into Santa Fe . . . we would stop off, and my mother would visit with Miss Warner and Tilano, and we would always make sure we had the right comic book to give to him." Joan Mark Neary recalls that "Tilano had a horse called Chicko. He told me I could have the horse, that he would give it to me but keep it there. We could ride it when he was there. I was always convinced it was mine."

Remembered by the children of Los Alamos as gentle, patient, and giving, Tilano served as a bridge between cultures. From the time he came to stay with Edith Warner and help her with the heavy work of hauling water and wood and coaxing a garden to flourish, he lived somewhere between the worlds of the Native Americans and the newcomers. Edith Warner's house was well away from the pueblo proper, but still on the edge of San Ildefonso. Through his actions as much as his words, Tilano conveyed to the children of the scientists the sacredness of the natural world, the joys of living in harmony with nature and the peace to be found in sharing these joys.

Among his own people, Tilano bridged generations, passing along the traditions of his generation to the those growing up during World War II and going off to fight in Europe and the Pacific. "I used to help Tilano work in the garden at Miss Warner's and help him with the horses, the cows, chickens and geese," says his nephew Julian Martinez. "I learned a lot from my uncle. He had big responsibilities at the pueblo. After he started aging a bit, he came to take part in those responsibilities. . . . He was a good horseman and a great hunter, too. He showed me how to make traps to trap rabbits, quails and birds." Almost four decades after Tilano's death, Julian speaks of his uncle as if he were still alive. "Uncle Tilano is like a storyteller," he recalls. "He gets along with kids, is very giving in what he has taught me—how to hunt, how to track, how to survive."

5

THE LITTLE GREEN SCHOOLHOUSE

Dorothy Hillhouse was teaching elementary school in Santa Fe in the spring of 1943 when she looked up to see a thin man with a porkpie hat standing in the back of the classroom. Later she was called to the principal's office and told that the man, Robert Oppenheimer, had asked to have her released for a special project to help the war effort. Dorothy's husband, George, operated a butcher shop in Santa Fe. He had already signed on as a meat cutter at the wartime project on the mesa. He left Santa Fe in April, returning in June, when school let out, to bring his wife and daughter, Barbara Jean, to their new home. Barbara Jean, who was seven, remembers her first glimpse of her new home, an apartment in the midst of a jumble of quadraplex apartment buildings, all green, all alike. One of the first things her mother did, she recalls, was to set a pot of red geraniums by the front door so they could recognize their home.

When the Hillhouses arrived, construction for the new school had not yet begun. The task of organizing the school system at Los Alamos fell to Walter Cook of the education department of the University of Minnesota. The original plans had called for using the two-room, log and stone schoolhouse where the children of teachers and other employees of the ranch school had had their lessons. But by June 1943, with families pouring in almost daily, it became clear that a new school must be built. The school that finally opened in October was, like most everything else, painted army green. It housed kindergarten through twelfth grade in two wings, an elementary school wing and a high school wing. One climbed a series of long steps to walk from the grade school to the high school. The first year there were four classrooms in each wing, with the elementary grades doubled up. New rooms were added in the fall of 1944 and regularly thereafter.

Barbara Jean Hillhouse Wilson, like many of her contemporaries, remembers the school fondly: "The rooms all faced to the west. We could look through huge windows out onto the mountains. The trees were close. It was almost like going to school in the out-of-doors. . . . The classrooms were still not completely ready for occupancy when we went in. There were large picnic tables for us to use as desks, with communal pencils and rulers and erasers and workbooks . . . down through the center of the table. Each room had an area at one end of it that was designed as a stage area. It had . . . a small area where there was a sink so you could prepare various and sundry things and wash up. There were curtains there, and it was one of the highlights of the day to be in a play that we staged for our classmates or for other classes in the building."

Although the school was public, it could not be part of the New Mexico school system because of the secrecy of the town. So, as with the Laboratory, the University of California agreed to act as paymaster, with the federal government ultimately footing the bills.[1] Building the school, even though it involved drilling into solid rock, soon proved to be the easy part. What to teach—and who would do the teaching—were far more difficult. First thoughts had gone something like this: with all these brilliant scientists and their equally brilliant and educated wives, it will be easy to set up a school that will be something of an educational experiment for all these extraordinarily bright children.[2]

Bernice Brode, a wife and mother who worked in the Lab and taught in the high school, remembers the initial optimism: "Here was a chance of a lifetime to put our own ideas on education into practice. . . . Take any subject and there'd be some expert in that field . . . [to] teach our children." She remembers, too, the "completely unrealistic" assumption that "with all these thoroughly educated people to be hired, why wouldn't it be a cinch to set up and run a fine school?"[3] It wasn't.

For one thing, different people wanted different things—riding, German, piano, Russian. "[The] parents—they had strong views," recalls Jeannie Parks Nereson, who first taught a fifth-sixth combination and then only the sixth graders. "They all wanted the school to have everything. . . . [They] would want tennis and horseback riding. We even had piano. And they wanted a lot of languages in the high school, even if there were only three students. [The parents would say,] 'We want our kids to have German,' so they'd get up a German class. It was amazing! But they had people . . . who knew things. Some people would come from the Lab [to give a talk or teach a class]. . . . We were allowed to order extra books for reading in addition to the textbooks. We had a library in our classroom, one whole wall with lots of shelves. We could order six copies of any books we thought were worthwhile for children to read, so we had lots of reading material."

Another difficulty was the skewed age distribution. With an average age at Los Alamos of 24, the children were young. The largest group was infants and preschoolers. There were a hefty number of elementary school children, but very few teenagers. Of the 178 children enrolled in the schools in 1943–44, only about 40 were in the high school, eight of them the children of scientists. The senior class numbered two. (The school population grew each year, necessitating regular additions to the school. By 1949 the number of students had grown from the initial 178 to a whopping 1,554.)[4]

Within the original teenage group, backgrounds varied widely. There were children of Nobel laureates, like Nella Fermi, and children of construction workers, who had gone to many schools as their parents moved from job to job. While the differences did not prevent their being friends, they did cause difficulties in teaching. "We had children of such different backgrounds," remembers Alice Smith, who taught history in the high school. "Some of the children had come from some of the best schools in the country, but there was such a spread of qualifications."

Alice, who had a doctorate in English history, was, like other teachers, both overqualified and unprepared for the job she had suddenly been asked to tackle. Presented with a beautiful new building but no teaching materials, she sent away to Yale University for a set of American history films. They turned out to be outdated and "caused a great deal of merriment and amusement so we didn't stick to those very long." Jane Wilson, wife of scientist Robert Wilson, taught English; another scientist's wife, Betty Inglis, taught mathematics, at least for a while. (One Monday morning she walked into her classroom to be greeted by a strong odor, opened her desk and discovered Limburger cheese. She turned around and walked out for good.)

One of the ironies about the school was that science was one of the weaknesses, according to several students. The scientists were fully engrossed in their work, and the wives with scientific training were also working on the project, so it was a struggle just to cover the basics. (After the war ended, several of the scientists did give lectures to the high school students, well remembered by those in attendance.)

In the high school, discipline was a problem. By the time the school finally opened, many of the teens had been roaming the mesa on their own for weeks. They recognized that "the school was new and the management uncertain, and they made the most of it," recalls Bernice Brode, who filled in for Betty Inglis for a time.[5] Discipline was easier to maintain in the elementary wing, but the teachers faced the same disparity of experience among the students. Mary Jeanne Bolan Nilsson, a Kansas native who arrived in the summer of 1945 to teach fourth grade, remembers the lesson she learned as she presented a social studies unit called "Across the Lincoln Highway."

"Here I had children from all over the world," Mary Jeanne recalls, "because I had some scientists' children, from universities on the East Coast, and they had been many, many places and were very worldly. So we were trying to make it extremely exciting going across the Lincoln Highway and the United States. We built the highway, drew it as a mural around the room. We'd stop in Chicago; we'd stop in Kansas City; we'd go on to Salt Lake. At the end of the unit, I said, 'If you were going to plan your trip, where would you start and how would you get across the Lincoln Highway? You can start anywhere you want, but you have to take the Lincoln Highway.' I figured they might start in Albuquerque and go to the West Coast and then come back across to New York. Some of the kids had fabulous ways of getting there.

"I had a little girl whose father had been with the ranch school and her whole life had been in Los Alamos. This student, in her telling, had no concept of this highway. None. I learned a great lesson as a teacher—that you preassess. All along I'd assumed she had a visual sense of the Lincoln Highway. She had none whatsoever. I said, 'Tell me about all the places you've been.' She had been to Espanola. She had been to Santa Fe. One time she thought she might get to Albuquerque, but she hadn't been there yet. Here was this little girl who had a concept of the ranch school, Espanola, and Santa Fe, attempting to go across the Lincoln Highway with these children from around the world!"

6

TWO VIEWS FROM BATHTUB ROW

Joan Bainbridge Safford

Joan Bainbridge Safford was not quite seven when she arrived in Los Alamos in the summer of 1943. Her two and a half years in Los Alamos are vivid in her memory because they are framed time, different from anything before or since. Joan is the middle child of Kenneth Bainbridge, the Harvard/MIT physicist who directed the Trinity test, and his wife, Margaret, a Quaker, who was later a mainstay of the Cambridge, Massachusetts, Friends Meeting, and active in peace movements until her death in 1967. Joan believes the time in Los Alamos heightened her political awareness. Like her mother, she has spent much of her adulthood committed to public service, including working for peace and civil rights and against nuclear proliferation. Nevertheless, her memories of Los Alamos are of a happy, almost magical, place where children played in the woods, used their imaginations, and met some wonderful people, including the nearby San Ildefonso Indians. Now a lawyer, she serves as deputy U.S. attorney for the Northern District of Illinois and lives in a Midwestern Victorian house full of Southwestern art and pottery.

"There's no question I was politically and historically more aware because of my experience at Los Alamos," she says. "When we went back to Cambridge, this Los Alamos experience was the thing that distinguished me. It is such a bracketed time. I think that's why it is so vivid in my memory. It's not like anything I experienced before or afterwards—the physical quality and the sense of freedom and independence. . . .

"My father and brother had preceded us out there in the 1939 Dodge. I got the chicken pox [just as we were ready to leave] so that delayed the departure for my mother, my sister, who was just past one, and me. We went by train. I have a clear recollection that somewhere between Chicago and Lamy, New Mexico, my sister learned to walk.

"We arrived in Lamy on a hot and dusty day [in 1943]. My father picked us up and we drove to Santa Fe. [The scenery] was so entirely different from anything I had ever seen before that it's very vivid [in my memory]. We went to the plaza and the office of Dorothy McKibbin. We started up [the Hill]. I was sitting in the back seat. I felt very, very car sick. But I also remember these incredible views. I remember when I was back in 1983, driving in a rental car, being struck again by these incredible views.

"Anyway, we arrived late in the evening. It was summertime, and I think we went directly to our house, one of the original Bathtub Row houses. The house had stone and wood walls, big, thick walls. There was a big stone fireplace and a small kitchen with a coal stove, which was hard on my mother, who had never dealt with a coal stove. There was a kind of side porch which had been glassed in that became my room.

"I think my father got the house we did because there were three children. Most of the physicists had two children or fewer. My father had gotten involved in war work in September 1940. It was his cyclotron that they dismantled and brought from Harvard to Los Alamos. He had been a graduate student, traveling in Germany when things began to get bad. Then he had been at Cavendish [in England] when Jewish scientists were arriving. His feelings about Germany were very, very strong. He was short and blond and was constantly being taken for a German which he found very, very upsetting.

"[At Los Alamos we children] were cut off almost entirely from a sense of the war. Looking back, that seems curious. One heard about the Germans and the Japanese. But our fathers were not off at war. We weren't playing war. It was play of a more innocent sort—more oriented to where we were.

"[When we arrived] the school was not yet ready. They were just constructing it. School was fun. Classes were small. There were children of construction workers. There was a girl named Theresa who was Hispanic. I had a teacher, Mrs. Hillhouse, in second grade, the wife of the butcher.

"There was construction going on all over—houses going up. There were small houses across the street being constructed. Down a street of six or seven small houses was a circle of four-family houses. They looked back into the woods. Those woods became for us a wonderful thing. The woods were different from New Hampshire, the only woods I was familiar with. There were these tall pines. We immediately took to the woods. The boys [my brother Pidge, and his friends Jack and Bill Brode] built a treehouse behind the house and eventually had a ham radio out there which got them in some trouble with the Los Alamos guards, who couldn't figure out where it was coming from. We created our own kinds of imaginary world there. There was no danger to it at all. It gave us a great freedom. You walked down behind the housing, through the woods, to the school. I can remember tramping through snow above the knees to go to school. . . .

"I remember you could go over to the mess hall on Friday nights and have steak, which we hadn't had for a long time in Cambridge. Steak, corn, and baked potatoes, which was an amazing thing to me.

"The Indians made an enormous impression. The women were working as cleaning women. The men were working construction. Popavi Martinez [son of the renowned potter Maria Martinez] was working with my father. I don't know in what capacity. [He] did a buffalo dance at the school. My sister, who was in nursery school, saw him go into the school. When she came home that afternoon she was very excited. She kept talking about how she had seen a 'buff-ee-o.' My parents couldn't figure out what it was, and she couldn't explain. But I had seen the buffalo dance.

"We had a wonderful woman who worked at our house named Juanita Gonzales, who was married to a San Ildefonso Indian. She was from Taos, I believe. Her husband had been injured in the war. She was a potter, made beautiful pottery. She had won a prize at Santa Fe for a bear-paw bowl. She would invite us to San Ildefonso. That's vivid to me, the dancing, the sound of the chanting, this black bread—kind of like ash. The other thing that made an impression is this kind of powder they put on faces and bodies for some dances.

"I remember that we wanted to go to Santa Fe for an Indian market, but there was polio. Polio at the time was the great striker of terror into the hearts of parents. So there was this thing—you couldn't go to Santa Fe in the summer. There was a square dance group, which had a party at San Ildefonso. And Bernice Brode had started a square dance group for children. I remember my mother made me a gingham skirt with a flounce. And we square danced over in Fuller Lodge. . . .

"The school expanded. By the fall of 1944, it seems to me it was a bigger school. I remember going to Edith Warner's for my brother's birthday. She would cook wonderful chocolate cake. You had to have a reservation. It was a special treat.

"I remember the arrival of my beloved friend Martha Bacher, who was a year older than I. And I remember buying our clothes from catalogs. Martha and I were insisting that our parents buy duplicate dresses from the Montgomery Ward catalog. So we had several pairs of dresses.

"My mother, who had been born in New York State and never traveled in the United States beyond Chicago, just loved New Mexico. She was not athletic. But she took to the hiking and Indian side of it. My parents had no excess income, but she bought a bowl from our cleaning woman, Juanita. She bought a few Indian rugs [and took them home to Cambridge].

"My father directed the Trinity test, so he was gone most of the time from January 1945 on; then after the test [in July] he went fishing for a few days. Right after the test, what was striking was that it was the kids of the construction workers who knew the most about it.

"[During the rest of our stay in Los Alamos] I really do have clear memories of my brother and me doing things with my father. My father made us fishing rods, wrapped them with silk himself, and gave them to us for birthdays or

Christmas. We fished in the Valle Grande with him. . . . My father was not really political. I can't conceive that he would have worked on weaponry after the war. He was anxious to get back to teaching and research.

"Weekend entertainment was climbing and hiking around. I can remember going camping in the Valle Grande. I can remember Martha Bacher and me standing in the Rio Grande and singing 'The Acheson, Topeka, and Santa Fe' while we kicked as if in a chorus line."

Martha Bacher Eaton

Like her friend Joan, Martha Bacher Eaton felt defined by her experience at Los Alamos, but in a different way. Martha's father was a physics professor at Cornell, and when the family returned there after the war she didn't dare admit to having been at Los Alamos. That was a secret part of her experience that she wasn't supposed to tell. Again like Joan, Martha was affected by the Indians. She traces her spirituality and to some extent her interest in psychology to experience with Indian caretakers with whom she communicated nonverbally.

Martha's memories are less positive than Joan's, in part because of her dramatic experience coming down with chicken pox on the train and being separated from her mother and brother and driven alone to the mesa; but perhaps also in part because she has lived with a feeling of guilt for her father's role in developing the bomb. She expiates it, she says, with membership in environmental groups working to heal the earth.

"After we'd been there about a year and a half we moved from the apartment to Bathtub Row. When it was announced that we got to move up to Bathtub Row, everybody put on a shower for my mother and gave her towels. They were planning to come take a bath. Some [of the towels were decorated] with rick rack, [sketches of] a bathtub, and somebody slipping. Alice Smith gave [my mother] one with [a depiction of] Alice getting into her shower and Jean [my mother] getting into her tub with bubbles. [My mother] must have gotten about 20 towels.

"I got to know some very, very interesting people. All the kids that I knew really liked Robert Oppenheimer. He was really friendly. We'd be playing around before school when the men would go to work. He would have to walk up the street through Bathtub Row to get to the Lab. We liked his hat, and he would stop and say Hello. We were afraid of Edward Teller, by the way. He had mean eyebrows and everything. Nick Metropolis [one of the young physicists] was a fascinating person. Kids liked him. I was once bored and said I didn't have much to do. He said, 'I'll tell you what: See this picture of this man and this woman [newspaper picture].' He said, 'If you're very careful, you could erase the clothes and see them naked.' Well, that kept me busy for about two weeks.

"Niels Bohr—Mr. Baker—the kids were always set up for [his arrival]. If he was coming to town, it was a big deal. His son was fun, too—he wasn't too much older than the kids. It was really kind of interesting when I met Niels Bohr in Washington to find out he was the same man I had met as Mr. Baker.

"When the adults had parties, they really had parties. They started early and went to the next morning. They usually had them on Saturdays. There was a lot of drinking at those parties. They were loud. Today they would be called drunken brawls. My memory is that they didn't have them [regularly] —maybe once every two or three months.

"I remember the day [president] Roosevelt died. I was having a piano lesson. I was over at Kay Manley's house, and this woman came down from upstairs and said something, and Kay Manley said I had to go home. I remember my mother was home, and she was vacuuming and she was crying. My mother practically never cried, so I knew this must be really serious. So I asked her what in the world was wrong. She said the president had died. I knew it was a tragic thing.

"My mother's younger brother was a lawyer, and after we'd been there six months to a year, Oppenheimer decided that he needed to have some kind of legal person. My mother really made a big pitch for getting my uncle there. That was really nice for me because my aunt stayed home because she had a baby, so I used to go over and see her.

"I remember when the word would get out that the PX was having steak everybody would line up and try to get a piece of steak before they ran out. I don't know where the word came from. It was usually on some obscure night like Wednesday. That was a big event. The whole family would end up lining up. I don't think my father was [home] much. That's what was so good about steak night: he'd be there.

"When I was in the third grade, my teacher took the class to San Ildefonso on a field trip and we watched Maria [the potter Maria Montoya Martinez] making her pots. It was just captivating, just marvelous. She wasn't famous then. She was just somebody who made pots, black pots. She taught us how she did it, sitting on her dirt floor.

"When a lot of people were leaving [at the end of the war], the Indians put on a party. We sat around and got some of this [colored] water. It turned out they had tried to give us Jell-O, but they didn't have any way of cooling the Jell-O. What they had tried to do was give us things we liked like Coca-Cola and Jell-O. That's what they would do—give you something that they thought you would like, not what they liked. . . .

"I'm a very spiritual person, and I don't think that I would have been this kind of a spiritual person if I hadn't run into the Indians. My family wasn't religious at all. I picked it up from the [Indians]. There wasn't any way to talk to them, so I had to relate to them on a different kind of dimension—which was possible to do. A lot of times when I was down at the pueblo I noticed they didn't necessarily talk to each other either, even among themselves. . . .

"We left in January or February of 1946, [going to] Cornell where I [had been] born. When we went back to Cornell, I just felt like I didn't belong. It was pretty awful. I gained a lot of weight so that made me feel even worse. I felt kind of freakish. There was something protective about being in Los Alamos—all those MPs walking around. It was a tight-knit community, and the kids really all got along together.

"After a year at Cornell, we went to Washington, where my father was on the Atomic Energy Commission. By the time I moved to Washington, I had put [it] all together and realized what a terrible thing [the bomb] was. I was told that that's why my father was on the Atomic Energy Commission—they had to find peaceful ways of using all this dangerous stuff.

"I remember [that] after the Alamogordo test, a lot of the scientists brought back this wonderful green sand [solidified into jewel-like rocks] that we kids used to play with a lot. I remember playing with it for years, even when we lived in Washington, so that was two or three years later. All of a sudden, one day it was all gone. I asked my father what happened to those beautiful rocks. He said , 'Those beautiful rocks are dangerous. They are full of radioactivity.'

"So I sort of put it together: They came from the bomb, and that's what did all those things to those people in Hiroshima and Nagasaki. [My father] has some of this green sand encased in plastic but that's the last I saw of it. Also, my aunt died of leukemia about 1949, and my uncle, up to the time he died, was convinced that she got leukemia from the waste that they used to take from the Lab right past their apartment building. I have a certain kind of breast cancer, and I can tell you that the doctors are really interested in it. When I first went to this breast cancer center they were very careful to find out what experiences I had had with radiation [and] those rocks.

"[Another] way that I think I was really deeply influenced by the whole [experience at Los Alamos] was once I realized what they had been doing building this bomb and killing all these people. This might have entered into my not wanting to talk about Los Alamos, too, because I felt so guilty. I consider myself a peace person. . . . I do believe my father when he says it had to be done. I still don't think it had to be used. There could have been a demonstration or something.

"I don't think I was ashamed of my father, but I really felt guilty for their doing that. For years afterwards, up until I was about 20 or 21, I would ask my father, 'Don't you feel guilty having done that? You know, you built this machine and it killed all these thousands and thousands of people?' And he kept saying, No, that it was absolutely essential that they build this bomb or the Germans would have built it.

"I believe that. But I'm not sure I would be as politically conscious as I am now [if he had not been involved]. I'm not sure I would belong to as many Environmental Defense Funds and things like that as I do. It just gave me a feeling for life and how valuable that is."

7

FATHERS AND SONS

Severo Gonzales

Severo Gonzales, who graduated from Los Alamos High School in 1948, is one of a relatively few teenagers during the war years who had not come to Los Alamos from somewhere else. His grandparents and great grandparents are among the earliest homesteaders of the Pajarito Plateau. In 1891, his paternal grandfather began farming an area of Los Alamos that is now one of the Lab sites. Six years earlier, his great-grandfather on his mother's side, Antonio Sanchez, had begun a summer homestead on the Pajarito Mesa. Severo's father, Bences Gonzales, was a bean farmer hired to staff the Los Alamos Ranch School.

Bences knew not only how to survive in this rugged terrain, but how to thrive on it. He was a specialist at outdoor cooking. On the long pack trips that were a regular part of life at the school and especially the summer camp it ran, Bences served up dishes ranging from fresh meat baked in stone ovens to *sopaipillas* (similar to doughnuts), boiled in kettles of fat. At the school he also took care of the trading post, handled the mail, and ordered the groceries that had to be shipped in. When the army took over the school, Bences Gonzales signed up with the Manhattan Project, working in the commissary and later at the Lab until his retirement in 1959. Then he moved to the valley, and lived in Espanola into his ninety-seventh year.

His son Severo, now retired from a state government job in Santa Fe, was a teenager when the army took over the ranch. He recalls, "Dad was born in San Ildefonso [on the pueblo]. There were a few Spanish on the outskirts. [The Indians] didn't want anybody to live too close. They had secret ceremonies that they didn't want anybody to see or watch. . . . My dad knew Tilano very well. He was friendly with all the Indians in San Ildefonso, especially Maria and Julian Martinez, the famous pottery makers. Dad bought a lot of their pottery and sold it to the boys at the Ranch School. They, in turn, would mail it to their families around the world.

"My general impression of people coming in the early parts of the Manhattan Project is that [they thought] they were going [to a place] where everything was wild, [where] you might be shot with a bow and arrow by an Indian. [In fact], there's been people visiting Los Alamos from all over the country [since before the Manhattan Project]. Rich people from all over came to see their sons graduate. No airplanes then but all kinds of limousines. . . . We were surprised in the old days [that] there weren't any kidnappings because there were some pretty famous kids in Los Alamos whose parents had money.

"We were poor, but we always had everything we wanted. A lot of the students, [when] they were graduating, they'd give us their tennis rackets, balls, skates, hockey clubs, pucks. . . . I had a complete set of shin guards for playing hockey. Boys that were going back East, they had money—real nice jackets these boys would give us.

"You'd see the boys out there at six o'clock in the morning exercising. You'd see them every Saturday morning riding. Exercising, good living, good eating. When they'd leave, some of those kids really put on that weight and height. This fresh mountain air—I won't say that for Los Alamos now. You read in the papers about 'Acid Canyon' and all that stuff that's going on up there—but then that was wild country. . . .

"It was very peaceful, very quiet [in the days of the school]. The Manhattan Project brought in a lot of things. . . . When the army first started going up there, and Mr. Oppenheimer and those people were looking for a site, the first person they had contact with was my dad. . . . In the evenings when we were having supper, he would tell us that the general had come. . . . My dad was one of the first persons Mr. Connell told what they were up there for. . . . He was trying to figure out how he could block them or discourage them. . . . Then he told my dad, 'They're only going to be here for the duration. They'll give it back after the war is over. They need it for some special project for the war.' . . . Then all of a sudden they had this gate. . . .

"When the army took over, since he had all that experience in the store, [dad] immediately went to work for what they called the commissary [for] the GIs. . . . [In the beginning, before the individual passes] . . . they issued one letter and that was a pass to get in and out of Los Alamos. My dad had this one letter with all his family listed in there, just one letter. I can remember borrowing the letter to leave Los Alamos with some friends. I've often wondered what would have happened if [my parents] would have had to leave Los Alamos. Seems kind of funny and awkward that they would only type out one big letter. . . .

"My mother became a professional babysitter. She babysat for some of the big shots of Los Alamos. These ladies loved my mother. They liked an older person to take care of their kids. . . . She was bilingual and had six children of her own. . . . I wish I'd kept the names of everybody she babysat for. . . .

"My brother took care of the Oppenheimer horse. . . . I can still see Oppenheimer most of the time walking, with his hat and walking with different people. With Fermi. From the Tech Area to where they lived they had to go almost in front of our house. Some of the biggest people are the nicest. They go about their business and treat you nice. . . .

"They used to do a lot of blasting, up there. They would fire away, fire away. Everybody knew they were testing explosives, but nobody knew what was going to come of it. . . . If Los Alamos wasn't what Los Alamos is, this whole valley would be about a fourth of what it is. Santa Fe would be half of what it is. It would be selfish to say I wish I was still homesteading."

Bill Jette

In December 1943 Bill Jette, the son of metallurgist Eric Jette, came home from fifth grade to find all the furniture in his house except the beds packed in boxes and ready to go on a "lift van" the next day. He had been told nothing about a move and demanded to know what was happening. His mother said only that they would be spending Christmas with her relatives in Denver and hinted that maybe they would move there. The expression on her face told him not to ask any more. Still mystified, he reached into his pocket and took out the sealed envelope his principal had told him to give his mother. The envelope contained his school record.[1]

Early in the evening of the next day, 7 December 1943—two years after Pearl Harbor—the family walked out of their home in Croton-on-Hudson, New York, for the last time. With Bill in the car were his mother, Eleanor Jette, who had grown up in Denver, studied mathematics, loved horses and intellectual puzzles, and was the family driver; his father, Eric, who had taught metallurgy at Columbia University; and the family cat, Mikey, who immediately stuck his head under a rug in the back seat and started to yowl, not letting up until he finally reached his new home.

After a long visit in Denver, the family set out again. Now Bill realized that they were not moving to Denver after all and asked just where they were going. His parents didn't tell him until they were nearly there. By this time the roads were mostly dirt, turned to mud and frozen to slippery ice. When they rolled into Los Alamos, after stopping in Santa Fe to pick up passes, it was late afternoon. Eleanor got her first glimpse of the green Sundt apartment buildings and decided they "looked like hell."[2]

"I hadn't the foggiest idea [where we were going]," recalls Bill Jette, now an architect in Albuquerque. "My parents told me what they thought I needed to know. I guess I shut up after that. . . . We got [to Los Alamos] . . . and I literally thought I'd come to the end of the earth. It was snowy and gray and dismal, and the first impression I had of the place we were going to live in [a Sundt apartment] wasn't very good.

"It was hard to get close to my father. I swear the day we got to that place he walked into those laboratories and I just rarely saw him. . . . When I finally figured out what the old man was doing, I was proud of him. . . . It bothered me [that my father was reticent]. It got to be a real family issue, and it hurt. Why, hell, he never did tell me much even after that. . . .

"One time one of my buddies and I went around the back [of the town] between the edge of the canyon and the fenced areas [near the technical area]. My father was in his office. I didn't even know which building he worked in, but he saw us. He opened up the window. . . . And he was just screaming, 'Get out of there.' . . . We weren't doing any harm to anybody. To this day, I don't know why he was so upset. . . .

"I was sort of off in my world [as a child]. I guess when it got tense [between my father and me] was after the war was over. I was growing up and, you know, I kind of wanted some answers, and I wasn't getting any answers. Eventually, when I was in college, I spent summers working in those laboratories. After the first summer, I kind of had an idea about why he couldn't talk about what he was doing because I couldn't talk about what I was doing. . . . I learned up there you didn't ask too many questions about what you did."

Despite the communication chasm that was growing between him and his father, Bill soon began to enjoy his new home. "Los Alamos was a fun place to grow up. . . . There was all sorts of mischief to get into. They had rules. One of the rules was that you could not go beyond the fence. I don't think I was there a week before I went through that fence, along with my newfound friends. . . . We went under most of the time; the holes were big enough. And we'd play in the canyons, just explore. It was a great place to just wander around and see things.

"[Being from] New York, I've never seen any country like this. The place was full of deer, chipmunks. I look back on it now and I can only remember one case of outright juvenile delinquency. A couple friends of mine stole a couple of jeeps and just rolled them off the edge of the canyon. They dropped about three hundred feet. . . . The first summer we spent [at Los Alamos] we got a horse. We got one horse, then another, then another one. We had our own little private stable out there that we built ourselves. . . . It was my task every day to go out there and feed the horses. The stable was outside the fence. I went under the fence to get [there] because I wasn't about to go a half-mile out of my way [to go through the guard gate]. My mother and I rode through those gates, took pack trips, fished. It was just magnificent, incredible, like the original settlers—we rode all over those mountains. . . . Christmas was fun. We would go out and cut our own tree, literally in the back yard."

Bill says that growing up in Los Alamos "had everything to do with" his decision to become an architect. "From the day I got there to the day I left, they were building something, usually houses. They never had enough houses. I spent some summers working on construction." The excitement of making things was further prompted by the availability of scrap materials in a "dump on the east side of town" where the Lab would deposit scrap materials. "There was just all sorts of stuff in that place to fascinate a boy. Machine parts and shiny bits of metal and all sorts of stuff. . . .

"I don't think I was more than 12 or 13 years old when I decided I wanted to be an architect. I got in a drafting [class] at the Los Alamos school. And I found out I had talent. I could draw. I made up my mind then and there, and I always stuck with it. . . . My father wasn't very proud of the fact that I wanted to be an architect. . . . My dad thought my being an architect was kind of artsy. I think that's why he objected. . . .

"We had one experience together [that gave us mutual respect for our professions]. My dad was running the chemistry and metallurgy division when they built a new laboratory. It was his laboratory, and it was his building. It was the biggest building ever built up there at Los Alamos. And it was very, very technical, highly specialized. Those guys were dealing with radioactive materials, airborne contamination, and God knows what else. If you knew half of what they did in that building you'd leave town. . . . He was dealing with Skidmore, Owings, and Merrill, a very, very fine [architectural] firm. . . . I think he got a glimmer . . . of what I was into and my interests. And we understood each other a little bit better after that. . . . I was in the school of architecture [at Rensaleer Polytechnical Institute] at the time. . . . I could sit down and talk to him intelligently about a mechanical system in the building. I think he was kind of impressed. . . . Before he died, I think maybe he realized that I picked the right career after all. At least, I hope so."

Of his response to the work of Los Alamos and his father's part in it, Bill says, "I don't think I was ever consciously overwhelmed by the fact of what my father was involved in until people started asking me about it and I had to sort of tell them a story. . . . I've always defended what they did. I've never pushed it, . . . [but] I always remember what my mother said in [her book *Inside Box 1663*]. I had an uncle, a doctor in the South Pacific. That letter my father got from him after the war was over. That's my last line of defense. That letter thanking him for ending the war, that's a significant letter in my judgment. The stories he tells about being a doctor in the South Pacific and how grateful they were when that war ended. They were all set to jump off and invade the Japanese [mainland]. . . . So I think the upshot of it was it certainly created a new age in this work. But I've got to believe the benefits outweigh the bad side of it. . . . During the 1960s it seems like I spent half my time defending what they did up there. . . . It sort of calmed down after the 1960s. . . . One of my sons is a child of the 1960s. He has a problem with what his grandfather did. We don't even discuss it. What's the point?"

8

TEENAGERS' PERSPECTIVES

While the elementary-school-age children recall the freedom to wander and explore a fascinating natural world, those who came to Los Alamos as teenagers between 1943 and 1945 were more aware of the upheaval in their lives and the restrictions placed upon them. Most of the teenagers in the early years were children of machinists, technicians, and support personnel. Many had come from Texas; others came from the Midwest, and still others were from the neighboring towns of New Mexico. Those whose parents had construction jobs were accustomed to living in a town a short time and then moving on. Others had lived all their lives in one town and felt wrenched away from familiar surroundings and expectations and plunked down in a strange land.

As they recall those early years, they say they noticed right off that Los Alamos was different, but were so caught up in teenage concerns that they gave little thought to the particulars. They missed the activities available in most towns—the high school was too small and too secret to offer activities like team sports, cheerleading, a band, or a yearbook club. They appreciated the youth center, opened not long after the war ended, and they took advantage of the recreational facilities left over from the Ranch School—the skating rink, tennis courts, and stables. Boys were fascinated by the military trucks and machines but disliked the military drill that passed as physical education. Girls similarly disliked the drills that "their" WAC put them through but enjoyed opportunities to explore classical music records and such magazines as the *New Yorker* while babysitting in the homes of the scientists. Several who babysat for the Tellers remember Mici Teller with fondness—for broadening their horizons and reinforcing their ambitions.

Some felt the town was repressive, too strict; others delighted in finding ways to get around the rules and, often, sneaking out of the town. As they look back on the intensity of war years, they remember a close community where everyone was pulling together and there were few class distinctions—a town where "everyone was in the same boat." Bill Fox, who came at age 12 in 1943 when his father took a job as a fireman at Los Alamos, recalls,

"One of the big things that was different about this town is that there has never been a distinction. As I understand it . . . if you lived in a university town, it's 'My daddy is Dr. So and So.' Here they might be a Ph.D. in physics but they were 'Jim.'"

Betty Marchi, who also arrived in 1943 when her father, a chef, ran the dining room at Fuller Lodge, remembers, "We were on the basis, 'We're one people up here at Los Alamos, trying to get a thing done.' It didn't matter if you were the janitor, or the street worker, or the scientist. We all got along." The class song that Betty Marchi remembers succinctly conveys the plight of teenagers. Sung to the tune of "You Are My Sunshine," it goes:

> The other day, dear, as I lay dreaming,
> My dreams were full of thoughts of home.
> The gates surround me, and peace confound me,
> And I fear I cannot roam.
> Los Alamos, Los Alamos, we find its comforts all too plain.
> In spite of sunshine, our favorite pastime
> Is complain, complain, complain.

Johnnie Martinez and Anita Luttrell Martinez

In the 5 June 1947 issue of the *The Hilltop Echo*, the first issue of the high school newspaper to be actually printed, a reporter gazed into a crystal ball to foresee the future of the class of 1947: "Flash!! 1986—Forty years from now, Anita Luttrell and Johnnie Martinez have decided they have been going together long enough and have decided to get married." Anita Luttrell Martinez treasures that copy of *The Echo*, even though the writer missed the mark by several decades. Johnnie and Anita were married in 1948. By the 1990s they were grandparents several times over. Johnnie had retired from the Lab, where he worked in the weapons division for 40 years, and Anita had retired from her job as a school secretary. They had lived in the same house for 35 years, having bought it in 1965 when the government finally made home ownership possible in Los Alamos.

Anita arrived at Los Alamos in what should have been her senior year in high school in March 1946. Johnnie had arrived in 1943, following his father, who had gotten a job as a janitor at Los Alamos and soon moved up to a stock clerk, making a lot more money than he had been making in various jobs in Santa Fe. By the end of June 1944, with the draft hot on their heels, several of the high school boys, including Johnnie, decided to enlist. Johnnie opted for the navy to "see the world." He was in the middle of the Pacific Ocean when the bomb exploded at Hiroshima, and he realized "what they were doing up here." Johnnie and Anita met when he came home after the war and started working at the Lab. Johnnie and Anita remember a town that presented opportunities in their youth, followed by steady employment, stability, and security.

"When my dad said we were moving up here," recalls Johnnie, "we didn't know where it was or what was going on. We just packed up and moved, and really enjoyed it. We couldn't figure out what the big secret was—why you had to sign in and stuff like that.

"The jobs my dad used to have in Santa Fe were in a shoe store and pool hall. Jobs that didn't make much money. When he got this job here as a janitor he near tripled his salary. Then he went to the Lab and made more money than he thought he'd ever make. . . . My mom and dad and my younger brother and my third brother Gilbert, they moved up here, and my second brother and myself, we stayed in Santa Fe until the football season ended, then we came up here. . . .

"You could hike in the canyons. You could go fishing. You didn't have to worry about 'These people don't like you and those people do like you.' When we moved up here I tried to get my friends in Santa Fe to get their parents to move up here.

"[On Sundays], I remember all the Protestants would go to church at nine o'clock in the morning. They'd have an hour. And all the Catholics are sitting outside waiting for them to come out. . . . Everybody knew everybody. Then the Catholics would go in and have their church services.

"[When we went to Santa Fe] everybody would ask you, 'What are they building up there?' And we'd say, 'Windshield wipers for submarines.' This is what everybody was saying they were building, so this is what you'd tell them.

"I came while he was gone [in March 1946]," recalls Anita. "We brought our own house—we lived in a trailer. There was a trailer park. I went to about 18 different schools in five years or so because my dad was a heavy-equipment operator, and he moved around. Sometimes I wasn't in one school long enough to get a grade. When I started trying to gather up [credits, I came out short], but I really didn't mind all that much because I wasn't in any hurry. So I didn't graduate that year [1946].

"To me it was [just] another school. That's it. I didn't know how long I would be here. I wish I had taken more notice about what was going on around me. I would know a lot more. When you're that young, you're just busy doing. You don't pay attention. You could be sitting in class, and there was this big, loud boom, and the windows would shake and rattle, and you just sort of [shrugs]. I don't remember ever saying, 'What was that?'

"I think parents felt good about the fact that we could not get off The Hill without passes. And if my mother felt like keeping my pass in her purse,

I'd have to have permission to get that pass. Otherwise stay home. We couldn't go anywhere. My mother was a matron—took care of certain dorms. . . . [The teenagers and the soldiers] never seemed to get in each other's way."

"Every once in a while they'd have a new GI come in and he was going to go get on the girls," says Johnnie. "But the guys would get together and tell him, 'Cool it.' And if he wanted a fight, we'd fight. But they left people alone."

"Every year that I stayed it was the longest I'd ever been anywhere since I left Texas [as a youngster]," says Anita. "Because of the fact Johnnie didn't finish school he was lucky [in the job he got]. Not only lucky because of the job he had, but he liked it. He was satisfied. He was fulfilled. He was happy in doing it. For 40 years. That's saying a lot. An awful lot."

Bill Fox

In March 1943 a young widower from Santa Fe sold off his furniture and brought his 12-year-old son and 14-year-old daughter to a new life in a new community. He had taken a job as fireman in the secret town that was going up on the mesa. The family was given a three-bedroom home in a Sundt apartment building, furnished with army cots and tables. To make ends meet the father worked two jobs—adding an evening job at a snack bar. His long hours left the children on their own, but they were taken care of. The son, Bill Fox, who loved sports, learned, to his delight, that he could go to the movie theater that also served as the gymnasium and shoot baskets whenever it wasn't being used by the GIs.

In the summer, at least for a time, there were swimming and canoeing at Ashley Pond (named for the Ranch School's founder); in winter every afternoon after school, Bill rushed to the outdoor rink in the canyon where you could shovel off an area and skate. There were tennis courts, too, and he got good enough that one summer he was asked to teach younger children. After an afternoon's sports Bill could meet his father at one of the cafeterias around the town. For a motherless boy from a poor family, it was not a bad place to be!

Not long after they arrived, Bill Fox's father got a new job working for the University of California in one of the laboratories. And as soon as he turned 18, so did Bill. His best friend's father helped him get an apprenticeship in glass blowing. He became expert at fabricating the variety of equipment required for the Lab's sophisticated experiments, and took pride in the art. He met his wife, Charlene, in the cafeteria where she was working as a cashier. After more than 40 years at the Lab, he retired.

"[That first spring, 1943,] we went to school in a log building from the Boys Ranch," Bill recalls. "There were probably 30 to 40 people in there from the first grade to the twelfth. As I recall, there was one teacher, and most of the time was recess. We did read a few books, but seems like it was a passing thing till they could get Central School built. I don't know if they graduated them or not—maybe they did—but three or four boys who were old enough left to go in the army. . . .

"We'd go to the skating pond in the winter. You didn't pay anything. You just went. You took the shovel, cleaned the ice and went skating. I myself did that about every day in the winter, as well as probably 10 other kids. We did swim a little bit in Ashley Pond. One of the boys got killed, drowned, and that took care of anybody swimming there. We had canoes. There was a canoe rack out there [from] the Boys Ranch. . . . You could just go get one, put it on the water and use it. Then this kid got killed. . . .

"They [had] put a fence around the place and were patrolling it on horseback. As kids, if you wanted to ride a horse, you'd go down there, go get you a horse in the corral, throw a saddle on it and go riding. . . . Some of these boys—there was a couple of boys that were here at the time of the ranch—they knew how to ride [well]. . . .

"I don't think for an adult it would have been all that pleasant, but for a kid, if we wanted to play basketball in the middle of the day, they had an old theater where they showed films in the evening, but in the day you could just go take a ball and play. . . . They had a sergeant [who] . . . had control of the gymnasium. . . . When it was not being used [by the military], the kids could go play. You could go charge out a baseball or anything you wanted—baseball bat, glove and a ball. . . .

"The man who lived next door to us was the wood keeper for Los Alamos. At first the stoves that you had here were the old wood stoves. [It was] a very short time before they converted them to coal. But a lot of furnaces around Los Alamos were all run on wood. He was in charge of getting this many acres of wood.

"It seems like the time we came there were a lot of Sundts under construction, but . . . I don't believe there were over about 13 that were up at the time I came. . . . It was amazing how many workers were working on every building. You would have maybe 50 or 60, something in that neighborhood, people working on a fourplex. They were like ants, so the buildings went up in a hurry. Two- and three-bedroom apartments, with hardwood floors and fireplaces. . . .

"During those early times the mud was awful. One of my first jobs—which didn't last too long—but anyway, they had a barbershop, and I shined shoes for a little while. Not too many people wanted their shoes shined. Things were so dirty you'd walk outside and get dirty again. It was dusty in summer, mud in winter. . . .

"I remember one year . . . they had to put in a big water tank. The population must have been growing a little bit more than [the water supply could handle]. They put in a big tank in the middle of town. They dug some pits on this side of the Rio Grande. . . . They had big trucks go up and get the water and bring it here, and they'd put it in that tank. I remember they had so much chlorine in it, that you took a silver spoon and it turned black."

Bette Peters Brousseau

In the fall of 1943 the Peters family arrived from Amarillo, Texas. As Rex Peters, who would head up a large machine shop, maneuvered the hairpin turns, his wife noticed the gloom surrounding their older daughter, Betty. At 15, Betty had anticipated attending Amarillo High School and cheerleading for the football games. To boost her spirits, her mother suggested, "Why not look at this as a new adventure? Do something different. Change the way you spell your name or the way you wear your hair." Betty thought about that and decided that from now on she would spell her name like her favorite movie star, Bette Davis. So as the car chugged up the final incline, it was Bette Peters who stared at the mountains, the guard gate, and all the military machines and wondered if this new place would ever feel like home the way Amarillo did.

Except for two years away at Stephens College in Missouri, Bette Peters Brousseau has lived on the mesa since 1943. She has worked at the Lab in various capacities, principally in the travel department and in the supply and property department. She married a man who was on Guam when "the weapon" was released and later came to work at the Lab. She has raised six children and now divides her time between volunteer work for the Los Alamos Historical Society and a docent's job at the Norris Bradbury Science Museum, where she shares her enthusiasm for Los Alamos, while also finding herself frequently called upon to defend the part it has played in history.

"The way I felt, and a lot of other kids felt in those days, you lived and died in the same town," Bette recalls. "I had gone through grade school, through junior high with the same group of students . . . so it was a little traumatic. . . . [Now] I feel that coming here changed my whole life. . . . Lots of times you don't realize it at the moment. But as time goes by, and you get gray hairs . . . you realize the opportunities you had. . . . Just meeting people from all over the . . . world and the country. And seeing different backgrounds and cultures."

She remembers sensing that the community was different: "I think most of us who came here knew off the bat that this was not a normal community we were in. Because of the war. . . . [But] nobody really gave it an awful lot of thought." And she clearly remembers instructions not to talk about where she lived, especially on excursions to Santa Fe: "When somebody told you, 'You don't talk about this. Keep your mouth shut,' people did. . . . They did not talk. Every time you went off The Hill you were cautioned by your parents. One time I was in Santa Fe, and my father happened to come down. He was going to go hunting. And he was in this hardware store. . . . He says, 'I'm getting a license.' . . . And he says, 'Now I'm putting down that I live on a ranch out here. If anybody says anything, that's what you say.' . . .

"I have had people come into the Bradbury [museum] . . . who've been away for years and came back. . . . I get talking to them and they say, 'I never told anybody.' One man came in and said, 'I tore up all my pictures. I tore up everything, because they told me not to tell, and I didn't want anybody to know.' . . . This particular man had been a soldier. And I talked to his wife, and she said, 'He's said so little.' . . .

"For a while, the big thing was to see if you could sneak off The Hill. . . . [You] would get somebody's daddy's car, wait till real late at night and sneak out of the house. . . . Not everybody had their passes. Some parents would hold the teenagers' passes just [to be] on the safe side. So if you didn't have a pass to get out, what they'd do is put you on the floor of the car and cover you up. . . . The main thing was the challenge. . . .

"There was a record store in Santa Fe, and we'd go down there and play all these records and maybe buy one or two records. . . . There was a drugstore and we'd go over there and have something to drink and just kind of kill time, and then we'd come back on the bus. And we'd sit on the bus and we'd sing. Some people used to get upset about that. We'd sing 'Ninety-nine Bottles of Beer on the Wall.' "

The war ended just before the start of Bette's senior year, and she began campaigning for a "regular" graduation with all the trappings—caps and gowns and a yearbook and a class ring. "We decided we wanted to have a regular graduation . . . caps and gowns and everything. The principal, Mrs. Crouch, she just didn't think we could afford it. We wanted a yearbook. . . . There were six in the class [of 1946], five girls and one boy. . . . Up to the time we graduated there had been two other graduations [just handing out diplomas; no ceremony]. . . . So when we decided we wanted all this stuff, I went over to the photography group [at the Lab] . . . and said, 'We want somebody to come and take pictures for our annual.' . . . It was too expensive [to get the annual printed] for such a small group. So what we did was buy some nice scrapbooks. . . . We even designed a ring. . . . There used to be—you'd see [ads] in these pulp magazines, in the back: 'School rings. Have your school ring designed for $5.95.' Well, we sent them a design and they did it up. . . .

"We had a baccalaureate. . . . We tried to made the graduation as normal as possible. It came to a point we had to give the school an official name. This Mrs. Crouch [the principal], she wanted to name it Alpha. . . . It sounded too scientific. We said, 'What's wrong with having it Los Alamos?' . . . We all voted on it. The name was going to be Los Alamos. [We called] ourselves the Hilltoppers. That was logical to us. We lived up here on top of this hill, on the mesa top. . . . And we chose the colors of green and gold—gold for the aspens and green for the pine trees. We ordered caps and gowns, had a 'skip day.' We all took off, had a picnic on our own. . . . The night we graduated, somebody [had] got hold of a man who was an anthropologist. And he came and talked. . . . The large theater here . . . was filled to the rafters. This principal didn't think anybody would come. But everybody wanted to hear this man talk. . . . People had been away from normal things, graduations, lectures and things. They wanted to see something like that again."

Betty Williamson Peterson

Betty Ann Williamson arrived in Los Alamos—over her protests—when she was 15, in 1945. She had lived most of her life in a small Texas town, where the family had roots. Her father left his pharmacist job to sign on as an electrician. At first they lived in a kind of quonset hut. Then they moved to a Sundt apartment. While observing that "this place was different," Betty was primarily caught up in the business of being a teenager—seeking out amusements and ways to get off The Hill. She graduated from Los Alamos High School in 1947, the year after Bette Peters. The number of graduates had jumped from six to 20, but the class still did not have an official yearbook. In its place the 5 June edition of *The Hilltop Echo* listed such information as mottoes and "last will and testament." Betty Ann left her "ability to skip school without getting caught" to an underclassman. Her motto reads, "Let the world slide, let the world go; / A fig for care, and a fig for woe."

"We followed a couple cousins up here [in 1945]," she recalls. "They said, 'You'll love it. It's a lovely town on a hillside.' . . . I didn't really want to come up here. [It was] one more place where I didn't know anybody. . . . I was 15 when I came. . . . I wasn't terribly interested in sitting home and studying or going to the library. . . . I wanted to go back to where I had spent my early years—in a little tiny town in Texas.

"There were all sorts of wild rumors [about what was going on here]; I'm not sure it made any difference [to me]. I was here under protest. And, if we were not getting into mischief of some sort, I had a horse that I could go out and ride. In these early stages I was riding military horses and later Mounted Patrol horses. [We lived in] I think they were called the National Huts [similar to quonset huts], a square box. You had a boardwalk to go down to the one big restroom. The clothes lines were all in the middle . . . in the mud. [Later] we did move to a Sundt. We lived over [my friend] Mary Alice. Mary Alice's mother was very, very strict. She kept her pass. The only time she could get off The Hill was when she was with her parents.

"My mother worked so I had the car, [and I'd drive off The Hill]. There were usually several kids in the car. We'd put [Mary Alice] in the trunk when we got near the guard gate. We'd go plowing through. When we got far enough away, we'd stop and take her out of the trunk, let her back in the car again. At night we'd frequently put her on the floor, put a blanket over her and just go out that way. So her mother had no idea how many times she was in Espanola or Santa Fe. Or just off. It was nice to get away. Because there wasn't a lot to do. And it was very confining. . . . All the housing belonged to the government. If you lost your job or if you retired or quit, you were out. I don't know if they gave you two weeks or what. But you had to leave The Hill.

"My grandmother had lived with us in Texas. When she got here she was not allowed in. She was given a 24-hour pass to find a job or get off of The Hill. So she found a job clerking, running the cash register [at the Spanish American Club].

"Our [phys-ed] teacher was a WAC. . . . She didn't really want us or anything to do with us but she had to, so we marched. We marched from Central School to the Big House. We were really quite good. [But] we were tired of marching. Some of us got together and decided we didn't want any more of it, and the next time she did this to us, we were going to refuse. So we marched down to the field with our books. And when she said, 'Fall out and in,' one by one we just dropped our books. She turned livid. She couldn't punish the whole school, so, I think, we got away with that. . . .

"Lots of our mail was censored. And that was not something that I was certainly used to. . . . So much of our stuff was Trans-shipped. We'd get candy bars in here, chocolate candy bars. You know how they get white when they get too old? A lot of ours were that way. They had been overseas and back trying to get to us [to the commissary]. . . . We were pretty well aware that we were in a different place."

Neale Byers

Like a lot of families arriving in 1945, Neale Byers's parents brought their home with them—a 14-foot trailer. Looking back, Neale wonders just how the three of them managed to live in that trailer for a year. His most vivid memories from that year are the "military aspect" of the town—the guard gate, fences, security, and soldiers everywhere. In 1946 the Byers family moved back home to Illinois, but they were in Los Alamos again a year later, still in a trailer, although a larger one this time. Neale spent his sophomore and senior years at Los Alamos High School, graduating in 1948. In his senior year he was a teen announcer for the radio station that Bob Porton ran and was elected as vice president of the class first semester and president second semester. He took some drafting classes at which he excelled. He came back to the Lab after college, intending to stay just long enough to make the money to buy a car and finance graduate study—and ended up working there close to 40 years.

"During World War II, my father was working for the Rock Island arsenal [in Illinois]," he recalls. "[The Manhattan Project] was scouting the country for machinists, and in June 1945, after I'd finished my school year, we came out. . . . They had told us we had better pick up a house trailer. I don't know how the three of us lived in this 14-foot trailer. It was like camping. There were no [paved] streets, no sidewalks, just boardwalks the army had built and mud everywhere. There was a water shortage at times and a lot of military police. . . . We stayed for a year. Then I was probably 15 or 16—almost 16. . . .

"Back there in 1945—that first summer was terrible. Nothing but mud and rain. A lot of places the water pipe was above ground, insulated and wrapped. But it froze up this one winter [1945–46]. I remember everybody in town building fires to thaw it. You could see bonfires from clear across the mountain. They kept those bonfires going all night long. They had to go to the Rio Grande and haul water. You were allowed a pail. They treated it just like you did in the army with the army pills. It was a dirty brown color, but it was water. . . .

"[The town] was very secret. People weren't . . . allowed to go anywhere for a while. It was like being in the service really, even for the civilians. . . . There were fences everywhere. . . . There were so darn many soldiers. . . . Nobody had an idea what was going on even after the first bomb [Trinity test] was [exploded]. After the bombing of Hiroshima, a lot of people knew what they had worked on—what it was all about.

"In high school it was like one big class. There was no separation between seniors and freshmen. If they were taking geography they all took it, and there weren't too many. [Back in 1945] every afternoon about three or three-thirty a sergeant would march us all the way from our high school over to a field, and we'd do nothing but march, march, march. The WACs took care of the girls, and they did the same thing—the WAC would march the girls around. That was our physical education. . . .

"Bob Porton, he was the [sergeant]. One day he called attention and I didn't come to attention. And his face got red. He thought, 'What's going on here? We got some little rebellious kids?' Another guy—I can't remember his name anymore—he and I both refused to come to attention. . . . We weren't soldiers, and why be treated as soldiers? We said we wanted to do some other activities like other kids do in high school—basketball, football. Just anything else other than being treated like a soldier. So the principal— I guess he felt real bad. So the next day when we all lined up . . . back at . . . the field for marching activity, here comes Bob Porton with another fellow. He was in service, too—a younger fellow. He took over and, by golly, he had us playing football on a dirt field. . . .

"They had there two theaters primarily to help the soldiers. The guys in the high school [asked] could we use the gym. So after a while, the boys got to use the gym for basketball. Then pretty soon the girls said, 'Well, my gosh, we want some activities, too.' So the girls kind of got started. The two theaters were really being used continually—all afternoon for high school activities to late in the evening for the soldiers.

"I used to go to the movies all the time. . . . Younger children . . . were kind of restricted. We used to go to the military PX, but it wasn't a good place for young kids. They were serving beer as well as ice cream. . . . And you had a lot of GIs sitting around drinking beer. For the kids, you could get a Coke or ice cream, but you just didn't feel comfortable, especially the girls. [We used to say], 'Let's go to the PX and get an ice cream.' The PX was clear on other side of the pond. We'd have to walk all the way around [the pond and the motor pool] to get to the PX. . . . So rather than walk all the way around, we'd climb up over the fence, in through the motor pool, up over the fence on to the other side. . . . Naturally there were MPs guarding things all over the place. Man, we'd get chased by the MPs! We'd run like crazy, up over the fence. They knew we were kids. What could we do? We weren't doing any damage. . . .

"A lot of machinists came from Texas, but they [also] came from all over the country. Quite a mixture here. After a while you realized it didn't make any difference where you were from [or] whether you were Jewish or Polish or German or French or Spanish or whatever. . . . I think at first it was a little bit hard, because you were used to coming from communities where certain things were felt. . . . [But here] nobody was better than anybody else, and you didn't get any special treatment. . . . Well, [the scientists] did . . . , but you can understand why they had to have a little bit of special treatment. . . . To get them here you had to provide some housing for them. . . .

"The thing that I appreciated later on—I think a lot of other people did, too: you were in the same boat. You didn't have this class distinction. . . . You didn't have this snobbishness going on between classes of people. . . . You were all treated the same, and nobody could brag about being better in any way. I thought that was pretty neat."

Betty Marchi Schulte

Betty Marchi Schulte's memories of her high school years in Los Alamos bring into focus certain negative aspects of life on The Hill. The small number of teenagers created a bonding, but it also produced a pressure to go along with the gang. Betty, who at age 15 considered herself more mature than some of the other teenagers, did not take part in many teen escapades. As a result, she sometimes felt left out. While others saw the omniscient military presence as a challenge—How do we sneak through the fence? go for a joy ride in a military jeep?—Betty simply saw the town, the school, and her home as full of restrictions.

Graduating from high school in May 1945, one of the tensest times for Los Alamos, Betty recalls no ceremony—just the handing out of a few diplomas. Right after that nonceremony she started work at the Lab, later marrying a fellow worker, Stephen Schulte. They lived in Los Alamos most of his career, eventually moving to Santa Fe and then to Albuquerque to be near their only child.

Interviewed in the summer of 1992, Betty was distracted by worry. Her mother had died of cancer, her father had just died while battling cancer, her sister had been diagnosed with cancer, and her husband, who was suffering from cancer, had just had a stroke. She couldn't help but wonder about the connection of all this cancer to Los Alamos—and worry about whom it might strike next.

"We came from Santa Fe to Los Alamos," she recalls. "It might as well have been across the world, though. . . . My father . . . was a trained chef who came from Italy in 1922 or 1923. He went up to Los Alamos May 1, 1943. My father opened all the eating establishments up here. They brought in the GIs to help him cook. He was in charge of Fuller Lodge, and I remember when he opened a mess hall in the SED area. My dad used to carve, out of ice, gorgeous figures for their officers' banquets. He carved dolphins, castles.

"I think all of us had to grow up quickly there. It was hard. You had all these good friends you left back home. You couldn't find [a real friend] there.

[And] when you found one, it was hard because you knew they were going to move away. Then there were all these young GIs. They were wonderful men and boys. Some of them you could trust, some you didn't dare. Well, how did we know? My parents wouldn't go into detail, but they'd say, 'Be careful.' . . . I guess our parents were too involved with the war, and here we were on our own. We were helping each other. . . . And we were learning by experience, or by other's mistakes.

"We all had a hard time growing up there. No one had a place. No one knew where we belonged. Everything was army, army, army. It's strictness. We were strict at home, strict at school, there was strictness anywhere you went. . . . And regulation this and regulation that. 'You can't go here. You can't there.' . . . I don't know who got this youth center for us, which helped quite a bit. Then there was a big to-do about, 'Should we let the GIs in?' So they let the younger ones in. Then some of the parents said, 'If the GIs are going to be there, you can't go.'

"We had a three-bedroom Sundt. . . . Talk about torture: they were not soundproof houses. When these boys moved in above us with their clodhoppers—and they stomped. . . . Mud. It wasn't anything if it wasn't muddy. We wore our rubber boots that you pulled up over your shoes. To get our mail, we'd have to walk a quarter-mile maybe—in the mud. . . . We'd go several times a day to get our mail. We never knew when it was going to come, when a truck would bring it or what. Nothing was on schedule.

"We had these clothes lines out back . . . , and when it rained and poured, and all that mud, then the dogs would come. Mother had to redo all those sheets. It was a red clay mud. You didn't have any flowers, any trees. We missed all that because we had always had gorgeous yards. We eventually planted grass in our front yard."

But Betty also remembers material well-being. Los Alamos had "the best." It had the best food, the best school, the best teachers. "Everything was plentiful. We were never short of butter, meat, milk. . . . That's how Los Alamos started—they took the best of everything they could find: 'We need good food, we need good schools . . . we just need the best of everything.' So we did have the best. . . . We had wonderful teachers. It was like going to college or a private school. . . . It sounds like it might have been easy but it wasn't. . . . If there's four of you in the class, and the teacher's going to call on you, you're going to have to know the answer. If there's 25 in the class, you can get away with it sometimes. We were very bright—we had the highest IQs in the nation, at Los Alamos, at the time. Mrs. [Alice] Smith our history teacher was wonderful. Mrs. [Jane] Wilson [our English teacher] was very good to me. . . .

"We had no idea what was going on. We were just a bunch of teenagers. We didn't care. . . . They were good days really, but you left all your friends, your family behind. . . .

"A very interesting thing: there was what was actually called a dump site. They had copper. They had metal. They had wood. In fact, the wood had bins—separate bins, soft wood, pine, whatever. All the people were allowed to go and get what you needed. It was free.

"There were accidents. [When] my brother was four . . . it was an August day. . . . Boy Scouts . . . had been out walking the trails and they . . . brought [back] these bazookas. They thought they were duds. Big shells like this. They were pounding them on the ground. My brother was playing right here. We had a 1942 Cadillac parked right here. And those shells blew up, and the concussion knocked my brother way over here. We found him wandering. The shells went through the car. Cars were steel in those days. And the shrapnel went right through his hat. But just barely scratched him. He was deaf for about a week. . . .

"And then 15 years almost to the day . . . the same kind of accident took place. . . . [This time] it killed a boy, and they amputated about four or five legs [of other kids]. One little girl [who was] very close to our daughter . . . lost one of her legs. [It was] the same kind of shells. [The boys who found them] thought they were duds, and they were pounding them in the ground, and all these children were in a circle [watching]."

Some people in Betty Marchi Schulte's Los Alamos neighborhood later became concerned about an apparent unusual concentration of brain tumors among those who lived there. "[We lived] where the cancerous tumors seem to be concentrated. I didn't know we were sitting on a hot bed. . . . Mom died of cancer. Stephen [her husband who worked at the Lab all his career] had cancer. My sister's fought cancer. So far I haven't [had to]."

9

NELLA'S CIRCLE

Nella Fermi and her friends Jane Flanders and Gaby Peierls were three of the very few scientists' children in the high school—a fact that brought them together and set them apart as a group. All three were acutely aware of the differences in education between their parents and the parents of their high school classmates. They were also aware of the stratification of the town, made up of very distinct cultures. The school was one place these cultures came together. It was there that Nella made another friend, Emma Baca, whose father was a carpenter on the project.

The experiences of Nella's "circle" point up the variety of backgrounds and expectations among both the parents and the children. Nella herself was born in Italy, arriving in the United States through a trip to Sweden. Her father, Nobel Laureate Enrico Fermi, who had made scientific history when he achieved the first nuclear chain reaction, was one of the senior scientists.

Gaby Peierls was a year or so younger than Nella but so advanced academically that she took classes with the high school group. Nella and Gaby found they had a lot in common: each was the older child of a prominent, European-born physicist, and both had gone through a number of geographic and cultural upheavals. Nella had moved from Italy to New York to New Jersey to Chicago and now to Los Alamos. Gaby had moved from England to Canada to New York to Los Alamos. But while Nella had remained in the bosom of her family, Gaby had been thrust out on her own—she was seven when she was sent to Canada to get out of England during the bombings. She was still getting reacquainted with her parents when they moved from New York to this strange, new community.

Jane Flanders, daughter of mathematician Donald Flanders from New York University, was, as she puts it, totally WASP, from an old, established family in Chappaqua, New York. She felt uprooted and cut off from her comfortable social milieu, finding herself unprepared for the chaos and lack of decorum she observed in the classroom.

Emma Baca, born and raised in New Mexico, came to Los Alamos from Albuquerque. Her father joined the project as a carpenter, later working as a machinist. For her, the adjustment was to the switch from business courses and work at Woolworth's to classes in advanced algebra, where she thrived. Eager to listen and learn, she was soon taking walks with new friends who talked offhandedly of places she only dreamed of.

Nella Fermi Weiner

"Gaby had the room right under mine. So we used to talk to each other late at night through the pipes that were supposed to bring up the heat. That was great fun. . . . All the [Sundt] houses were alike. I remember one time when Gaby and I came home from school, we kind of wandered into somebody else's house. The streets had no names, and there were no street numbers. We walked in, and a strange lady came out. She was quite nice about it, and we apologized mightily. We assumed that no street names or numbers was done deliberately because of spies.

"We used to go hiking on Sundays, and in the winter we used to go skiing. Either Jane and I or Gaby and I would go on long walks. . . . It was the kind of place that invited walking. . . . Jane and I would take the bus and go into Santa Fe and go shopping. Heaven knows what we bought, if we bought anything. But we liked to go into Santa Fe. . . .

"Once Jane and I discovered a hole in the fence [that surrounded the town]. I was sort of inclined to let the whole thing go, but Jane was adventuresome. So we went through the hole and [outside the town] and came to the guard gate, showed our passes and came back in. Then we went through the hole again and showed our passes once more. We just went around and around. After the third or fourth time, I was beginning to get worried, afraid that someone would get mad at us. But Jane . . . didn't seem to have any fears about it. . . .

"There weren't many kids my age. Most of the [physicists] were younger than my parents, so there were a lot more kids in the elementary school than in the high school. . . . There weren't any boys our age essentially. So you're talking about a very limited field of boys our age and a practically unlimited field of boys five to ten years older, who seemed like men, mind you. . . . I had crushes on the GIs and all these guys who were a lot older than I was. . . . There were perils for girls [in this situation]. But at 13, I really was a child. The perils, such as they were, missed me completely. . . .

"High school was a mixed bag. [Los Alamos] was a very stratified society. . . . There was a real educational gap. . . . There were the kids of the physicists [and the other kids]. We were not necessarily more intelligent but we certainly had had more opportunities than these other kids. We put it down to our intelligence, but looking back I'm inclined to say we really had better chances . . . , not only having gone to better schools but also having parents who were, to say the least, literate. I remember my father teaching me algebra when I was nine. He didn't succeed exactly, but he tried. . . .

"So there was snobbery [based on the ways we had been educated]. . . . We could be pretty clubby, which we picked up from our parents who were just as clubby. . . . Some of our teachers were the wives of physicists. The two I remember particularly were Jane Wilson, who was teaching English, and Alice Smith, who was teaching history. I worshiped them both.

"We had a science teacher who really didn't know what she was doing, and Jane and I used to pick on her. That wasn't very nice but was probably par for the course for 13- or 14-year-olds. . . . The attitude of the class was, 'Don't do that. She's the teacher. She knows what she's talking about.' Well, she didn't. After the whole bomb thing went public—after Hiroshima and Nagasaki—somebody said, 'They've got a lot of [scientific] talent here. Let's get some of these physicists to give lectures to the high school kids.' Most of them weren't any good at it. There were two who were. One was my father. The other was Dick Feynman. . . .

"We used to go to the Indian pueblos a lot. My mother and her friends were interested in buying pottery. And, of course, you could buy it best by going to the potter's house. . . . We were part of the square-dancing group. And the square-dancing group sometimes danced with the Indians. One time we went to one of the pueblos, by invitation of course. They were teaching us their dances and we were teaching them our dances, and a great time was had by all, although we could not really talk to each other. . . .

"The war had been going on almost as long as I could remember, and it didn't seem like something that was going to end. So when it did end, it was very exciting—partly to know that it had ended because of something that we had done. Of course I hadn't done anything, but I was still excited. So it was very peculiar to get this letter from my aunt, my father's sister, saying that there were rumors that he had been involved in making the bomb and she trusted that they were not true. I couldn't figure out what the hell she was talking about until about 20 years later. . . .

"At the time, I think I was proud of my father's role in the making of the bomb. It seemed great that the war was over and the bomb had been built for good proposes. Obviously, your feelings change over a period of time and you get a different perspective on it. . . . Now I would say that a job that had to be done was done. . . .

"It would make life more simple [if my father hadn't been involved]. I feel rather in sympathy with pacifists. Wars are not good for children and other human beings. But at the same time, I can't quite be a pacifist because I have to ask myself, 'What could you have done besides fight under the circumstances of World War II?' Certainly you can say, 'If Germany had been handled differently after the First World War, maybe the war could have been avoided.' Once the war started, though, I don't know what else we could have done. But I haven't seen another war with this clear 'good guys/ bad guys' aspect. . . .

"The war was a very serious war. . . . I think everybody felt that way. . . . Most of the scientists would not have been working on an atomic bomb if they had not been really scared. . . . There was a real threat. . . . For quite a while it looked like Hitler might win. People felt it was unspeakably horrible to think that. The physicists were working very hard, and they felt pressured by the possibility that Hitler might get there first. I doubt very much if [the army] could have gotten a collection of physicists like that to [work on a bomb] if it had been a question of the war in Vietnam, the Korean War, or the more recent war [in the Gulf].

"After the war, it became evident that Hitler was nowhere near getting a bomb. What I've often wondered is whether some of the German scientists may have been dragging their feet. After the war, I read the Smyth report [the official report of the work done at Los Alamos]. It seemed to me that it gave away everything. My father said, in fact, it didn't because what was hard were the technical details [such as] how you get the pieces of bomb to come together at the right moment so that they will explode. He was of the opinion that the report was only saying the obvious. Of course he had peculiar notions of what was obvious."

At the University of Chicago, which she entered upon her return from Los Alamos at age 15, Nella studied art. Over the years she did painting, printmaking, jewelrymaking, and eventually ceramics. She was active in the civil rights movement and taught art for many years [including one summer at Los Alamos]. In her forties she returned to school to earn a Ph.D. in educational psychology. Her thesis topic resulted from one of her observations at Los Alamos years earlier—that she had seen an awful lot of pregnant women. "I had watched the younger women at Los Alamos all having lots of kids. What I was observing was the beginning of the baby boom. It interested me, and I did a dissertation on fertility patterns in faculty wives at the University of Chicago. I went around with a tape recorder interviewing women of two age groups: those born 1900 to 1914 and those born 1920 to 1934 and studied the differences in fertility patterns."

When college teaching jobs proved to be "shut up tight" she switched to the business world, doing tax accounting and financial planning. She believes that some people, like her father, have obvious clear-cut career paths, "but they are rather rare. . . . Most people fall into the accidents of what's going on." The "accident" of spending formative years responding to the scenery of northern New Mexico and the Indian artwork may have helped steer her toward a career in art. While she no longer makes of living at it, she remains staunch in support of "humanities education." Again responding to her experience at Los Alamos, she says firmly, "In the sciences we seem to be ten steps ahead. . . . We need more humanities education to learn how to handle the sciences."

Gaby Peierls Gross

When Gaby Peierls was born in 1933, her parents sought a name that would "be pronounceable in any language."[1] Then living in Cambridge, England—and about to move to Manchester—they had little idea where they were likely to settle and what nationality she would grow up. Her father, Rudolf Peierls, was a German refugee; her mother, Genia, was Russian. As they had thought likely, Gaby's early life involved a lot of moving around.

In 1940, when Gaby was seven and her brother Ron was almost five, the two children were evacuated to Canada. There they lived with different—but related—families. Gaby attended local schools and then a Canadian boarding school before joining her parents in New York City in December 1942. Arriving in Los Alamos in August 1944, Gaby, then 11, was two years ahead of herself in school, still getting reacquainted with her parents—and disoriented.

IQ tests taken at Los Alamos that fall showed Gaby to be the brightest of all the children there, recalls high school teacher Alice Smith. Gaby's mother directed her considerable energies toward making sure that her daughter would get the education she would need to compete in English schools. What Gaby remembers most about the year and a half is wanting just to be left alone. She also remembers feeling a strong need to keep separate her two worlds—the world of her parents, European-born scientists, and the new world of her American-born teenage classmates.

"It wasn't a bad time for me, but it was very mixed," she recalls. "I had had the feeling [that I was foreign and different] since I was seven. I was just very oppositional. I just wanted to stay home, be alone, and read books. . . . In school, I felt there was a cultural norm, and I was not part of it. For me that norm was the fire chief's daughter. She was the center of a group and went to church on Sunday, which we did not do.

"I was two years younger [than anyone else in my class]. That was hard in itself. My mother was always pushing. She kept worrying what would happen when we went back to England. So I did eighth-grade arithmetic by myself, then took ninth-grade algebra when I was in the eighth grade. I did Shakespeare with the tenth, eleventh, and twelfth grades. . . . I felt more comfortable with the tenth, eleventh, and twelfth grades because they were more secure.

"I remember coming back from ice skating with my parents and Hans Bethe in a car. Hans was driving, and we passed some boys in my class walking. He said, 'Shall we pick them up?' and I said, 'No.' I said it so immediately and loudly that they all criticized me.

"Each week we would bring money to school for war bond stamps. Mrs. Crouch, the principal, would give mental arithmetic tests to see who would count the money. Either Bill or Jack Brode [sons of physicist Robert Brode and his wife, Bernice] or I always won, so eventually we were not allowed to compete. I remember a debate in school, Roosevelt versus Dewey. It must have been at the time of the 1944 election. There weren't enough people for Dewey so I volunteered for that side. . . .

"Some of my strongest memories are the things I discovered myself: the Sangre de Cristo mountains, and sitting in school and looking at the hills outside the school and seeing a storm coming up around them. . . . We used to go to Indian dances at San Ildefonso. I remember being interested in the mixture of Catholic symbols in the dances. . . .

"One thing we used to do a lot of was babysit. I had never done that before. . . . When the women had babies, they would stay in the hospital for about a week back then. So we would stay with their other children. . . . I remember going to bed at night when my parents were having dinner parties, and I would fall asleep to the adults' conversation. Hans Bethe had a characteristic laugh. My mother had a very characteristic laugh. It was a wonderful time for my parents because there were so many people whom they had known in Europe. But they were also very serious about what they were doing.

"There were differences in status at Los Alamos that even a 12-year-old could see. There was Bathtub Row. There were the four-family houses, and there were the trailers and the quonset huts. I felt a concern about the differences, and I sort of had a fantasy of coming back and making the system fairer."

Trying to make systems fairer remains a strong motivation in Gaby's life. After a year and a half at Los Alamos, the Peierls family returned to England, where her father was knighted in 1968. Gaby graduated from Oxford University. She married an American psychologist and worked as a research assistant for an economist at MIT and later for a New Jersey branch of the American Civil Liberties Union. While raising her three children in Princeton, New Jersey, she earned a law degree from the University of Pennsylvania, specializing in family law. She worked for some years for the state of New Jersey, representing children being taken from their homes. Now divorced and in private practice in Boston, she represents families at risk of having children taken from their homes.

She describes her political leanings as "pretty far left . . . Social Democrat."

The Los Alamos National Laboratory Main Gate in the 1940s (after the name Los Alamos could be used openly). *Courtesy Los Alamos National Laboratory*

For many of the workers arriving in the hectic months of 1944 and 1945, the only available housing was Quonset huts that included a kitchen but no bathroom. Board walkways were the routes to the shared washrooms, and any laundry that fell from the line into the claylike mud necessitated yet another trip to the communal laundries. *Courtesy Los Alamos National Laboratory*

Dorothy McKibbin's office, at 109 East Palace Avenue, Santa Fe, was the gateway to Los Alamos. Dorothy helped weary arrivals with local transportation and information, but, most important, she exuded reassurance, which was the basis for the many lifelong friendships she formed. *Courtesy Los Alamos National Laboratory*

Housing was named for the contractors who built it. One of the most prevalent types was the four-family apartment house, with its two units on the first floor and two on the second. The second floor was reached by outdoor stairs and balconies. Built by William Sundt and Co., these units were known as Sundts. *Courtesy Los Alamos National Laboratory*

The stone and log cottages of the Los Alamos Ranch School became home to the top scientists and military personnel. One scientist's wife promptly dubbed them "Bathtub Row," as they were the only accommodations with bathtubs. Bathtub Row residents included the Oppenheimers and the Bainbridges and navy captain William Parsons and his family. *Courtesy Los Alamos National Laboratory*

J. Robert Oppenheimer was named director of the Laboratory because of his brilliance as a physicist, his charisma, and his ability to grasp all aspects of the scientific problems involved in developing an atom bomb. In the 1950s government officials questioned his loyalties because of prior Communist associations and his lack of enthusiasm for the hydrogen bomb, but most of his colleagues at Los Alamos remained staunch supporters. *Courtesy Los Alamos National Laboratory*

Nobel laureate Enrico Fermi was respected at Los Alamos as an elder statesman—and an avid hiker. He and his family chose a modest apartment over the Bathtub Row accommodations offered to the top scientists. *Courtesy Los Alamos National Laboratory*

Harvard physicist Kenneth Bainbridge directed the Trinity test, the world's first atomic explosion. "Now we are all become sons of bitches," he commented after the 16 July 1945 explosion at Alamogordo, then set off on a solitary fishing trip. *Courtesy Los Alamos National Laboratory*

In later conversations with his son, physicist Hans Bethe communicated the excitement the scientists felt in their search for knowledge about how the universe works, along with the intensity of their conviction that Hitler must not be allowed to get the bomb first. *Courtesy Los Alamos National Laboratory*

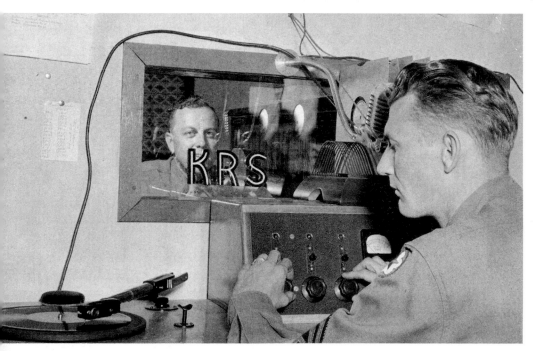

Robert Y. Porton (*seen through window*) prepares a wartime broadcast for the radio station heard only within the confines of Los Alamos. For one popular program, Music of the Masters, classical records were borrowed from the scientists. *Courtesy Robert Y. Porton*

When it opened in the fall of 1943, Central School had eight rooms: four for the elementary school (some grades doubled up) and four for the high school. Prominent in children's memories of the school are its large, west-facing windows and the views of the mountains. *Courtesy Gaby Peierls Gross*

Margaret Bainbridge, wife of Kenneth, visits the Puye ruins with her two elder children, Pidge and Joan, in 1944. *Courtesy Joan Bainbridge Safford*

Gaby Peierls (*right*), who was 11 when she arrived in Los Alamos, felt disoriented and somewhat of an outsider. She says that she "just wanted to stay home, be alone, and read books." *Courtesy Gaby Peierls Gross*

A picnic at nearby Bandelier National Monument (then known as Frijoles Canyon) was a favorite Sunday outing for Los Alamos families. *Courtesy Betty Marchi Schulte*

Because phys ed for girls was often conducted by a WAC, the classes were looked upon as something to be endured—and a reminder that the town of Los Alamos was run by the army. *Courtesy Gaby Peierls Gross*

Fishing near Los Alamos in the early 1950s. *Courtesy Betty Lilienthal*

"I was active in the Oxford University labor club. At one point I wanted to be a social worker. I think I've become very skeptical of authority, of business, of nuclear power. My brother-in-law is a philosopher, and I remember saying to him that 'all killing is wrong.' But I think I was more verbally contemplating an idea than stating a belief. [I have felt] anger that [the atomic bomb] was used, but I don't blame the people who were making it."

In fact, these people have a very special place in Gaby's memory: "Looking back, I have realized that you don't meet people like [the scientists at Los Alamos]. They were really nice as well as smart, really warm people. I've never come across [so] many adults like that in one place. They were quick at understanding, knew a lot and had wide interests. They had a sense of humor and an ability to admit it when they were wrong. I think I've had a sense since then that adults don't quite measure up."

Jane Flanders Ziff

For Jane Flanders Ziff, a mother and grandmother who teaches music in Amherst, Massachusetts, the move to Los Alamos was at first "the stuff that an adolescent dream is made of"—a trip to a secret place in the desert where the family could be reached only through a post office box. The adventure soon turned into "a big confusion" in which she felt alone, alienated, and frightened. Jane arrived in Los Alamos in 1943, a year ahead of Nella and Gaby. Although she was just Nella's age, she was socially precocious. At ages 12 and 13 she felt that she just didn't belong. She was full of hopes, longings, and confusion. The possibilities seemed so romantic—and so unreachable.

"We came in 1943 when I was 12, and the place was still new. . . . We came from Chappaqua, New York, where the schools were very good and everybody was academically oriented. It was a place where it was cool to be good. . . . My mother came from an old Quaker family in Chappaqua. My father was a mathematician at New York University. They were originally pacifists. My father had studied with Harald Bohr, Niels Bohr's brother, in Denmark in 1937. I remember when we were in Denmark, my mother wrote a letter to Roosevelt saying that we shouldn't start arming, [that] it was a bad precedent. . . .

"I think that [by 1943] my parents had come to terms with war. . . . The invasion of Denmark [affected them]. . . . My family was very WASPy from way back, but we had a great many close friends [who were refugees]. We had a German refugee staying with us. . . . And it was really believed that this was going to shorten the war. . . . My brother was at Harvard at the time. He was never allowed at Los Alamos. . . . Any [family member] who did not come originally was not allowed.

"I was very much looking forward to the desert. We took the train. It was terribly crowded. There were soldiers. In Chicago there was a big wait—it was hard to travel during the war, and we never did get breakfast, I remember that. I remember seeing the mountains suddenly appear. . . . The guardhouse was the most impressive thing. . . . And then we were fingerprinted, and that was very romantic. . . . I remember it was so impressive getting this pass. . . . I was fascinated by the landscape and did a lot of walking. My father got me into hiking. We climbed all the mountains around. . . .

"We had a Sundt apartment . . . facing the school. You could hear the bell and walk out. The school was quite a revelation to me. I had always been trying to keep up with some sort of mysterious, terribly respectable, and rather wealthy standard. To be in a place where the kids were undisciplined, not used to thinking in terms of school—I had never been in that kind of class before. . . . To Nella it was a big adventure. To me it was a big confusion—a big confusion, being presented with things that I couldn't handle. . . . It's not that I didn't feel it was a big adventure. I certainly did, but it was just beyond my ability to handle. . . .

"There was no social life of my age group. It did not exist. . . . In the high school there were one or two [scientists' children] in a class. The rest were technicians' children. . . . The Texas construction worker culture—that's who was in my class—and that's part of why school was so unfamiliar to me. It was not the white upper-middle-class like Chappaqua. In Los Alamos, at study hall if the teacher would go out of the room, everybody would throw things. In Chappaqua, they might have been reading comics, but at least decorum was observed. . . .

"I learned not to go to school. . . . I jumped out of the window after they called roll. They had this weird system of calling roll in the morning and the afternoon. I discovered that all you had to do was be there for roll call, then you could go to the bathroom and go out the window.

"[The year before Nella came] I had this wonderful friend Barbara who introduced me to flirting with soldiers. She left after a year. After Barbara left, I used to do it by myself. I used to neck with [the soldiers]. That was what I spent my time doing. It made me feel immensely guilty and filled with all kinds of desire. . . . It was an innocent enough age that the soldiers knew they were dealing with a young girl and were protective. . . . But I felt terribly guilty. I felt I was doing awful things.

"The Clines [friends of my parents] had a horse, and they encouraged me to exercise the horse. One of the things I used to do—I would go out and ride the horse and meet with the MP of the day, whoever it was. I had one I used to meet there all the time. There were MPs who came and did the inspections all around, sort of security patrol. I would lie in wait for them and flirt with them. . . .

"There was a bus that we could take into Santa Fe. I used to love to sit in the courtyard of the La Fonda [the main hotel in Santa Fe and a favorite gathering place of the scientists] and read. I would take the bus in, and of course the bus would be full of soldiers. I had read in *This Week Magazine* about a technique in which you look from under your lashes and how it's very come hither. And I found that it worked. It was very interesting. . . .

"Nella's father had a coterie of young scientists about him. . . . Nella and I would talk about with whom we were in love. But this whole undercurrent [of longings and confusions] didn't exist for her. She was happy to just be in love with somebody. I couldn't bear it, it was terribly painful for me. . . . I felt I was unable to belong to anything. I was too young to [socialize] with the scientists, though I fell in love and necked with them, too. But I realized they wouldn't take me seriously because I was so young. I also knew— because one was very conscious of social order—that the soldiers with whom I was necking did not belong to the right class, that I couldn't bring them home. It was a very painful time. . . .

"Had I been at home, I have a feeling I would have learned to be with the group. But to be displaced in this exaggerated romance of the science, of intelligence, of the glorification of smart people—and to be part of them, except that I wasn't; to be a child, except that I wasn't. It was a very, very hard thing. I knew my mother had no understanding [of what I was going through]. I was already quite alienated from her. I knew she couldn't help me. All she could do would be to be horrified. . . . I didn't want to be in this awful quagmire of longings that I didn't know how to handle. . . .

"I remember that the results of IQ tests in the school showed that Nella and I . . . had about the same IQ, but that Gaby was much smarter. . . . Gaby's mother was a terror. She used to tell Laura [Fermi] what to do. She was always giving Laura orders about how to handle me and Nella. . . .

"There was an interesting combination of really interesting teachers. Alice Smith was a terrific teacher. Jane Wilson was interesting and absolutely goofy. Jane had a big influence on me. She made us memorize all kinds of second-rate poetry. It's such fun because I have this memorized second-rate poetry in my head which I can go through in my mind.

"My family were musical. . . . I think we brought our piano. My father had a quartet, and my parents always had people in the house doing music. . . . The Indian culture was something that was respected and regarded as exotic. . . . Maria came to school and gave a pottery demonstration. . . . It had a big impression on me. I used to make pots by the coil method for a long time. . . . I'd never seen it before and it was very special. . . .

"[My stay in Los Alamos] was a concentrated time of being with people under rather special circumstances where the relationships and your experiences are separated from the rest of your life. . . . I've never been back. . . . I think . . . [about] . . . how strong the social classes [were] on who was smart and who wasn't, who was a scientist and who wasn't. And not being a scientist myself, never having been a scientist, I have the feeling if I went back there I wouldn't have any status at all."

Emma Baca Knowles

It was a cold night in April 1944 when the Baca family arrived at the guard gate at Los Alamos. "The reason I remember the cold," recalls Emma, who was 16 at the time, "is that our passes were not ready so we had to sit all night in the car." The family consisted of Emma, her four brothers and sisters, her father who had gotten a carpentry job at Los Alamos, and her mother, expecting her sixth child (who would be born 20 July in the small barracks hospital).

As she sat waiting for the sun to rise, Emma had little idea of the changes that this muddy hilltop would make in her life. Many years later Emma tells her story from her office in Santa Fe, where she works as financial specialist for the Emergency Medical Services Bureau of the New Mexico Department of Health.

"That brief time in high school made a big difference. It was a completely new environment for me, and I think it made a difference in whatever I did with the rest of my life. . . . There were a lot of things . . . that I didn't know were out there before I came to Los Alamos. . . . The thing about these brainy kids—and that's what they all were to me—was that they were generally pretty nice. Just because they had brains, they didn't have to be ugly. And they weren't. . . . What a breakthrough to see these other kids. . . . We were friends and we could talk. I couldn't talk about the things they did, but I sure listened. . . .

"Nella was younger. . . . I met her through school. . . . She was pleasant, and she wanted to be friends. . . . I remember her [in her baggy sweaters]. . . . Her mother must have knit her sweaters. . . . Nella read a lot and had so many interests and interesting things to talk about. . . . The [Fermis] had me over for dinner. . . . They lived in one of the nice houses—we lived in a terrible place. . . . I remember that was the first time I ever had artichokes. So, of course, I didn't know how to eat them. . . . [the Fermis] could have been snobs, but they were nice. . . .

"[The house we lived in] was called a hutment. It had two bedrooms for all these kids. At the time you don't think about it. Perhaps you're pushing it out of your mind. But later you think, 'How did we manage?' I don't know how I started babysitting for the Tellers. I think Nella had babysat for them. I would spend weekends there because Mrs. Teller went skiing, and Edward Teller never took care of Paul. He was busy. He went to the Lab on weekends. He slept, he ate, and played the piano. . . . It was nice to have all that good music there. . . . They had such nice silverware over at the Tellers', and cloth napkins. . . .

"I wish I had been one of the scientists, but I do believe I'm part of something. . . . My father was a carpenter, and he was doing defense work. . . . We lived in Albuquerque. That's where all of us kids were born. . . . We went up [to Los Alamos] in April of 1944 in one car loaded like *The Grapes of Wrath.* . . . I was in tenth grade, working some evenings and Saturdays at Woolworth's in Albuquerque. I had worked on the switchboard at St. Joseph's Hospital. . . . I had friends and a boyfriend. . . .

"At Los Alamos there was no typing, no secretarial things which I had been taking. But it wasn't so traumatic once I got into school. . . . Our teachers were the wives of the scientists. Jane Wilson—I learned so much from her. . . . She had Shakespeare records which she brought to school and played. . . . I hear [there was prejudice against the Spanish], but I didn't know it at the time. I didn't see any of it. . . .

"[I felt prejudice], but not against the ethnic thing, mostly against the uneducated. . . . Some people talk about how prejudiced things were, but I don't believe it. . . . The teachers knew that I had worth. . . . I took advanced algebra. There were such small classes, maybe there were five of us. We got individual attention. I remember getting an A + ... School was informal. Some of the teachers would take us outside. We wore jeans and sweat-shirts. . . .

"I got to do special things at a couple of programs like sing a solo. . . . I had played the violin in Albuquerque in fifth and sixth grades. So I guess I always had music. My grandfather and his brothers had a group, and they played at weddings and dances. When I was growing up I heard my grandfather playing the accordion on the front porch. . . .

"My father went to high school, but my mother didn't. . . . [At Los Alamos] . . . I saw how these educated people could do things. They could get so far in life because they had superior educations. I had planned to get one, and I didn't. . . . I was a good student and [the teachers] were going to help me [get a college scholarship]. Mrs. Crouch [the principal] got the head of the School for Inter-American affairs at [the University of New Mexico] to come to Los Alamos to interview me at Mrs. Crouch's house. He couldn't have come to our house. There wasn't room. . . . I got the scholarship. . . . Then I got married instead of going to school. . . .

"We were having our junior-senior prom. There weren't enough boys to go around. Bette Peters had a GI boyfriend. He said he knew a nice young man, so I said, 'OK, bring him.' . . . The prom was in June, then we did a lot of talking, and we went hiking a lot. He asked me to marry him in July. We got married in September at the Cathedral . . . in Santa Fe. Before we left to go to Michigan where he was from, I sent off my letter of rejection to UNM. I don't know why I didn't do both. People do these days. I've thought a lot about how maybe I was afraid."

Emma and her husband, Malcolm Knowles, spent the next several decades moving around the country—to Albuquerque, to Panama, to New York State, and to Austin, Texas—while Malcolm pursued a career in the Air Force and Emma raised their three children. When he retired they moved back to northern New Mexico, to be near Emma's parents. During that time Emma lost track of Nella but often thought of her, especially whenever she looked at the beautiful wine-colored bowl Nella had sent her as a wedding present. She would think back to the magic of those early years in Los Alamos. "Probably it was when I was in my thirties and had lived other places that I realized what a wonderful place [Los Alamos] had been. I learned so much. . . . I learned my capabilities."

10

THE CAT SCREAMED ALL NIGHT

When Germany surrendered on 2 May 1945, the threat that the Nazis would develop a bomb before the Allies—the threat that had motivated most of the scientists to work on the bomb—was removed. The army lost no time, however, in telling the scientists that they must continue. On 4 May, Robert Oppenheimer circulated a memo to project employees from Undersecretary of War Robert P. Patterson that stated in part,

> The importance of this project will not pass away with the collapse of Germany. We still have the war against Japan to win. The work you are doing must continue without interruption or delay, and it must continue to be a military secret.
>
> We still have a hard task ahead. *Every worker employed on this project is needed!* Every man-hour of work will help smash Japan and bring our fighting boys home.
>
> You know the kind of war we are up against in the Pacific. Pearl Harbor—Bataan—Corregidor—Tarawa—Iwo Jima—and other bloody battles will never be forgotten.
>
> We have begun to repay the Japanese for their brutalities and their mass murders of helpless civilians and prisoners of war. We will not quit until they are completely crushed. You have an important part to play in their defeat. There must not be a let-up![1]

When Germany surrendered, the uranium bomb was nearly ready and the scheduled test of the plutonium bomb was just two months away. Its planning had been in the works for many months. The experiment was the ultimate test of the scientists' work and would show whether human beings could harness this incredible energy and direct it at a target of their choosing. Lights burned longer at the Lab; security seemed to tighten. Bette Peters was walking home from babysitting late one night when a light suddenly beamed in her face and an MP demanded, "Halt. Who goes there?" "It's me. I've been babysitting," she said, in a startled voice. This was the first time she had ever been questioned by an MP.

Along with heightened security came rumors. One of the most worrisome was that a test was about to take place that had the possibility of setting the atmosphere on fire. George Hillhouse, the town butcher, heard this rumor and got permission for his wife and daughter to leave The Hill to visit family in Kansas. He and Dorothy had worked out a code by which he could let her know when it was safe to return. When she received a postcard with the cryptic message, "The cat screamed all night the night you left," she knew that it was OK to return home.

Robert Bacher, head of the bomb physics division, was also worried. Although the test site was some 200 miles from Los Alamos and the latest calculations had shown that there was little chance of igniting the atmosphere, Bacher did not want to take any chances with his family and sent his wife and children to stay with relatives in Michigan. Martha Bacher Eaton remembers, "When they had the test, my father and my uncle had sent my mother and my brother and me and my aunt and her two kids to Michigan to visit my grandmother. I woke up one morning and I heard my mother and my aunt say, 'It's happened. We've got to get back to Los Alamos.' We got to Chicago and somehow got on a train, the six of us in one drawing room. I think my parents told me that they had tested something big."

All that spring the scientists had been taking mysterious trips off the mesa for a day or several days, telling their wives only that they needed a bag lunch and a thermos of coffee. Once when riding horseback together, Deak Parsons's wife, Martha, and Eleanor Jette, wife of metallurgist Eric Jette, compared notes about the times their husbands left and returned and where they ate their meals. They deduced that the destination must be about six hours away, probably to the south. Eleanor got out a New Mexico map and pinpointed the spot exactly.[2] The destination was a remote and barren desert about 200 miles south of Los Alamos. The area is known as the *Jornada del Muerto*, Journey of Death. Its name is derived from the experiences of Spanish wagon trains heading north: they would be left to perish if they ran into difficulties in this stretch of land since there was no water or settlement for 90 miles.[3] It was there, on 16 July 1945, that the first atomic bomb was exploded.

Bob Porton was preparing for the noon broadcast of the latest state and world news on 16 July 1945 when he noticed men coming by in droves to the little office that housed the station. Porton had made a special agreement with a radio station in Albuquerque to broadcast their breaking news report at 12:45 P.M. daily. He remembers, "[On this day there was a] rumor around the post . . . [that] something big was going to happen. . . . Tom [Fike] and I were getting ready, and all of a sudden, scientists started coming in and crowding the studio, crowding the control room until there were about 40 or 45 of them—just jammed. Tom and I looked at each other and said, 'There's something.' . . . And the announcer opened his newscast by saying,

'The commanding officer of the Alamogordo base announced this morning that a huge ammunition dump had blown up on the base. There were no injuries, and everything is fine.' . . . And all of these guys' faces lit up in smiles. And they hugged each other and shook hands. They had not gone to Trinity site. That was their first knowledge that they had been successful because they didn't allow communications between Trinity site and Los Alamos. That announcement was prepared by a member of our legal staff as a fake to give to the Associated Press to put out."

The decision had been made early on that the uranium bomb would not need a prior test, but that both the theory and construction of the plutonium bomb were sufficiently uncertain that a test was necessary. Robert Oppenheimer had given the test the code name Trinity, and some years later General Groves wrote to ask how he chose the name. In good army fashion, Groves assumed that Oppenheimer had chosen it because there were rivers in that part of the country with the name, so that any mention of Trinity would arouse little suspicion. Oppenheimer replied that he did not recall exactly how he chose the name, but it was not because of nearby rivers. He thought it came from his reading of the poet John Donne, one of whose Holy Sonnets begins,

> Batter my heart, three person'd God; for you
> As yet but knocke, breathe, shine, and seeke to mend;
> That I may rise and stand, o'erthrow mee and bend
> Your force to breake, blowe, burn, and make me new.

The phrase "three person'd God" may have suggested to Oppenheimer the word *Trinity*, although he admitted he wasn't sure. The poem's theme of destruction and renewal seems appropriate for the thoughts going through the minds of the scientists as the test approached—tremendous concern about the force they were about to unleash, and ardent hope that it would bring an end to this and all wars.[4]

Shortly after the end of the war, Oppenheimer told an audience that when that first bomb exploded "we thought of Alfred Nobel, and his hope, his vain hope, that dynamite would put an end to wars. We thought of the legend of Prometheus, of that deep sense of guilt in man's new powers, that reflects his recognition of evil, and his long knowledge of it. We knew that it was a new world."[5]

At the moment the bomb went off, what struck several observers was the intense light. Enrico Fermi described it with a scientist's detachment and precision, in a recently declassified memorandum:

> My first impression of the explosion was the very intense flash of light, and
> a sensation of heat on the parts of my body that were exposed. Although I

did not look directly towards the object, I had the impression that suddenly the countryside became brighter than in full daylight. I subsequently looked in the direction of the explosion through the dark glass and could see something that looked like a conglomeration of flames that promptly started rising. After a few seconds the rising flames lost their brightness and appeared as a huge pillar of smoke with an expanded head like a gigantic mushroom that rose rapidly beyond the clouds.[6]

Brigadier General Thomas F. Farrell, a deputy to General Groves, recalled,

The effects could well be called unprecedented, magnificent, beautiful, stupendous, and terrifying. No man-made phenomenon of such tremendous power had ever occurred before. The lighting effects beggared description. The whole country was lighted by a searing light with the intensity many times that of the midday sun. It was golden, purple, violet, gray and blue. It lighted every peak, crevasse and ridge of the nearby mountain range with a clarity and beauty that cannot be described but must be seen to be imagined. Seconds after the explosion came . . . the strong, sustained awesome roar which warned of doomsday and made us feel we puny things were blasphemous to dare tamper with the forces heretofore reserved for the Almighty.[7]

William L. Lawrence, the *New York Times* science editor who was allowed to witness the test to record it for history, later wrote, "It was like the grand finale of a mighty symphony of the elements, fascinating and terrifying, uplifting and crushing, ominous, devastating, full of great promise and great foreboding."[8]

Fermi tried to estimate the strength of the explosion by dropping small pieces of paper from about six feet in the air, before, during, and after the blast: "Since at the time there was no wind, I could observe very distinctly and actually measure the displacement of the pieces of paper that were in the process of falling while the blast was passing."[9] He estimated a blast corresponding to that of 10,000 tons of dynamite. A few hours later he and another scientist, Herbert Anderson, drove to ground zero in a lead-lined tank to recover equipment. There they saw a "depressed area 400 yards in radius glazed with green, glass-like substance where the sand had melted and solidified again."[10]

At the time of the first detonation President Truman was at Potsdam for a summit meeting with Winston Churchill and Joseph Stalin, and awaiting word of the test. Groves sent him a coded message: "Doctor has just returned most enthusiastic and confident that the little boy is as husky as his big brother. The light in his eyes discernible from here to Highhold and I could hear his screams from here to my farm."[11]

In Los Alamos there was both relief and a sense of the magnitude of what had happened. Bill Jette, 12 at the time, remembers smiles: "I remember my dad getting on a bus and going off, and we didn't see him for a couple of days. He came back and he was all smiles. It was kind of a happy time. I remember hearing all the gossip. A lot of people had gone out to the south mesa that overlooks The Hill road. They had looked to the south and seen the flashing light." The experiment had been a success. Two and a half years of hard work had paid off. The "gadget" had worked.

But the initial elation that "the gadget worked" soon gave way to concern. For a number of the scientists, the enormity of what they had created hit home. Kenneth Bainbridge, the Harvard physicist in charge of the Trinity test, said succinctly after the test, "Now we're all sons of bitches." Oppenheimer later wrote that he thought of the words of the Bhagavad-Gita, "Now I am become death, the destroyer of worlds."[12] "It brought back memories of when I was a kid and read *The Arabian Nights*," recalls physicist Charles Critchfield. "It was like Aladdin and his wonderful lamp. Some people were terrified. Some were very ashamed, although generally that was not the case."

Eleanor Jette, observing the scientists as they returned home from the test site, recalled in her book *Inside Box 1663*, "After the first wild elation, the men were thoroughly chastened by the success of their work, and their depression was contagious. The gadget that vaporized a steel tower, melted desert sand, and was so "hot" humans had to enter the region in a lead-lined tank was to be used on other human beings. It was a somber thought."[13] She goes on to describe a party that the Oppenheimers gave "for the bomb makers and their wives" a few days after Trinity: "We decked ourselves in our best bibs and tuckers to dance and play a little before we faced the desperate reality of what was to come. There were a number of military people at the party whom we had never seen before, but who were present at Trinity. Their presence served as a grim reminder that not only we, but all humanity, had passed the point of no return at dawn on Monday."[14]

The world had passed the point of no return, but one would never know it from reading the bulletin delivered to project residents on Wednesday, 18 July: "Saturday night is dance night once again at Theatre 2. Music will be by the Keynotes featuring the Sad Sack Six. . . . Post Exchange requests customers to return Coca-Cola bottles immediately. Unless bottle shortage is corrected, there will be inadequate supply of Coca-Cola for sale. . . . Canning sugar applications must be filed by August 4. . . . The hospital requests that crutches and canes be returned."[15]

Realizing the tremendous power of destruction of the bomb, some scientists advocated a demonstration instead of—or before—its actual use. A report sent to the secretary of war in June by seven scientists at the Met Lab in Chicago suggested dropping the bomb over an unpopulated area of the desert or a barren island "before the eyes of representatives of all the United Nations."[16] The scientists strongly stated their view that the "best possible atmosphere for the achievement of an international agreement could be achieved if America could say to the world, 'You see what sort of weapon we had but did not use.' "[17] They said they felt an urgency to voice the concern because, while "in the past, scientists could disclaim direct responsibility for the use to which mankind had put their disinterested discoveries,"[18] an atomic bomb presented a whole new magnitude of danger.

The recommendations were dismissed as unrealistic. Most of the scientists at Los Alamos did not learn of the report—or of petitions written by Met Lab scientists urging that the bombs not be used—until after the bombs were dropped. "I was one of those people who wished we had done something in the way of a demonstration or negotiations with the Japanese before we dropped it," recalls Charles Critchfield. "My argument with Robert Oppenheimer was, 'This is not an ordinary bomb. This is a chance to do something imaginative, constructive.' It turned out I was not the only one [who thought that way], but I didn't know it because we were quite isolated. The people in Chicago were very active, but I didn't know about [their recommendations]."

Meanwhile, men were quietly disappearing from the mesa, headed for the Pacific—among them Peggy Parsons's father, Deak, who performed the final assembly for the bomb dropped on Hiroshima, and Paula Schreiber's father, Raemer, who carried the core for the Nagasaki drop to the island of Tinian. Peggy was 10 when her father left for Tinian and then flew over Hiroshima. She remembers, "When we were living at Los Alamos—and during World War II—there was this feeling that the Germans and particularly the Japanese were so horrible. I remember I had a poster above my bed that said, 'Wipe that Jap off the map.' They were taking it down in the post office and putting up some other poster, and I asked if I could have it. When I heard that my father had dropped the bomb, I mean, the Japanese guy on the poster looked subhuman. I thought, 'Oh, this is great. We've really wiped those Japs off the map.' . . .

"For my father to be the person who armed the bomb was really crazy because my father could not fix a leaky faucet. [But he practiced what he had to do carefully.] . . . He had seen planes loaded with heavy weights crash on takeoff, and if the plane crashed [with the bomb assembled], the whole island would blow up, so he asked General [Thomas F.] Farrell if he could do the final assembly after they had taken off. Farrell said, 'Have you ever done it?' My father said, 'No, but I have all night to practice.' He worked so long and hard that his hands got messed up, and I think he wore gloves when they took off."

After a pause Peggy adds softly, "Imagine taking the responsibility for doing the final twiddling of [the bomb's] parts. If you ask, 'Was it a good thing to drop the bomb?' I lean one way and then another. I know I'll never be able to answer for sure." Peggy is unsettled by the thought of the devastation wrought on Hiroshima by the bomb. She knows she "will never visit Hiroshima"—or even visit Japan. She was uneasy several years ago when she realized that her daughter Betsy, then working for the United Nations, was in Japan on 6 August. "I knew she wouldn't mention her family, but still I felt uncomfortable." She is uneasy whenever her husband, Nat, a stockbroker with a strong interest in Asian cultures, tells Japanese acquaintances about her father's role as head of the ordnance division at Los Alamos.

Still, Peggy is intensely proud of her father and believes he often doesn't get the credit he deserves. "It sometimes gets under my skin that [Paul] Tibbets [the pilot of the *Enola Gay*] got all the publicity, but he was only the bearer of the bomb," she says, pointing out that her father was not only the man who did the final assembly but also the official scientific recorder of the event.

Paula Schreiber Dransfield was just three when her father left for Tinian, but she has talked with him about the experience and incorporated it into her own frame of reference. "Dad tells the story about being on Tinian and waiting to find out whether or not they were going to load those bombs on the planes. And while they were there, a storm came up—and Tinian is a very low island. There was a hill, maybe 50 or 60 feet on this island. And one of the other scientists invited my dad to come up to the top of the hill and look at the lee side of the island. Which they did. And Dad said, 'All the way to the horizon were ships that had pulled into the lee of those islands to get out of the storm. Destroyers, aircraft carriers, landing craft, every kind of ship you could think of.' He said you literally could have walked from deck to deck to deck for miles. And that was the . . . invasion fleet for Japan. And he has said that 'if I ever have doubts about our use of the bomb, all I have to do is remember just the unbelievable number of ships and men that were waiting to find out whether or not they had to invade Japan. And so,' he said, 'You balance lives.'

"And so I think that's kind of where we are. . . . I think it's politically appropriate to be apologetic. And yet I cannot honestly be apologetic about it. . . . I think my own feeling . . . is that [my] father is one of the most ethical people one could ever hope to meet. And whatever part he played in the bomb that eventually destroyed Nagasaki and Hiroshima was not done out of malice and was not done out of hatred. It was done as a scientist being very excited about completing a project, an impossible project."

11

THE WAR ENDS

On 6 August 1945 the world's first atomic bomb was dropped on Hiroshima. The next day Undersecretary of War Robert P. Patterson sent a message to "The Men and Women of Manhattan District Project":

> Today the whole world knows the secret which you have helped us keep for many months. I am pleased to be able to add that the warlords of Japan now know its effects better even than we ourselves. The atomic bomb which you have helped to develop with high devotion to patriotic duty is the most devastating military weapon that any country has ever been able to turn against its enemy. . . . We are proud of every one of you.[1]

On 9 August President Truman sent a cable telling "the men and women of the Manhattan Project" that "a grateful nation, hopeful that this new weapon will result in the saving of thousands of American lives, feels a deep sense of appreciation for your accomplishment."[2]

On 9 August a second atomic bomb was dropped on Nagasaki. That same day a young medical student at Nagasaki Medical College started out to catch the tram to school but discovered that it had been derailed by an accident and turned back home. A few hours later he heard what sounded like a B-29 overhead, accompanied by a bright yellow flash and a blast of wind. Terrified, he went downstairs to hide. Later he realized that a hole had been blown in the roof and glass had shattered, cutting his shoulder. When he went outside he saw that the sky had turned black and a black rain was falling.

The student, Michito Ichimaru, decided to start out once again for his medical school but was deterred by fires all around him. The people walking toward him had shreds of skin hanging from their bodies. They looked "like ghosts with vacant stares."[3] The next day he succeeded in walking into Urakami, where the medical school was located, and found "all that I knew had disappeared. Only the concrete and iron skeletons of the buildings remained. There were dead bodies everywhere. On each street corner we had tubs of water used for putting out fires after the air raids. In one of these small tubs, scarcely large enough for one person, was the body of a desperate man who had sought cool water. There was foam coming from his mouth, but he was not alive."[4]

At the school Michito found that only the skeleton of the medical hospital remained. The school building, made of wood, had been destroyed. But the students, who had been attending a physiology class, were still there. Some were alive, but unable to move. "The strongest were so weak that they were slumped over on the ground. I talked with them and they thought they would be OK, but all of them would die within weeks. I cannot forget the way their eyes looked at me and their voices spoke to me, forever."[5]

On 14 August 1945, five days after the bombing of Nagasaki, Japan surrendered, and the war was over. When the war ended the people of Los Alamos did not know about the suffering of those in Hiroshima and Nagasaki, although some could imagine it. Some of the scientists felt heavy-hearted at the grim reality of the results of their work. The majority of the town, however, had not known the specifics of what they were working on. For them, the knowledge that their work had helped shorten the war was welcome, indeed. The scientists, too, could see cause for celebration. They had done what they set out to do, and believed that the "gadget" had saved the lives of countless young Americans. And with the war at an end, they could now focus on peaceful uses for energy they had learned to control.

As for the children, they celebrated just as children did elsewhere—with children's parades and pots and pans. Kim Manley was barely two, but still that day is etched in her memory: "At the end of the war, the kids in our area had a parade. We took pots and pans and spoons and lids and marched down the neighborhood banging them. That was our celebration." Martha Bacher, who was about 10, remembers that "Nick Metropolis [a young scientist the children particularly liked] came over and said that the Japanese had surrendered, and [the adults] had a drink then and we got to have pineapple juice."

Older children have more site-specific recollections. Bill Jette, who was 12, remembers, "When the war ended, that's probably the greatest town drunk in the history of the United States. [*Laughs*] There were a lot of explosives up there in the laboratories, testing areas and what not. . . . The day the war ended a bunch of folks . . . set off explosion after explosion after explosion . . . like fireworks. . . . The Fermis lived in the apartment [building] next to ours. To this day I remember Mr. Fermi sitting on the hood of a jeep driving up the street. They were just having a hell of a good time. It was quite a party. We were all glad the war was over, and everybody felt real good about playing a part in it."

Severo Gonzales, who had recently learned to drive, remembers that he was driving near the Tech Area, heading toward the center of town when he saw a woman "running by the Tech Area all excited. She said, 'Have you heard the big news?'" Bette Peters, about to start her senior year in high school, had a summer job at the Lab. She remembers that "people just poured out. . . . They evidently had this [news] flash [on the radio], and it just went like wildfire through the Lab. And I think it came across the PA system. . . . Everybody went on home, got their radios and brought them back, and everybody sat around just listening to the news all that day."

Bob Porton remembers, "There was a false rumor that [the war] was over a night or two before it really was, and there was a lot of celebrating [then]. When finally the war was really over, it was all night long. I think I went to 50 different houses and drank from 50 different bottles. . . . At six o'clock in the morning—people tell me this—they were having a dance, and I was playing the trombone—and I'm a drummer! Some guy took pity on me and took me to my barracks. . . . The next morning the colonel in charge decided we had to have a big celebration ball. . . . About four o'clock in the afternoon a couple guys from the band came [to my dorm]. I was still in bed. They said, 'You've got to get dressed. The colonel says we have to play a big dance.' All I wanted to do was die. I said I couldn't play. They said, 'You've got to play, man.' They picked me up and put me in a cold shower for about 30 minutes."

As the celebrations died down, thoughts turned to the future. The scientists realized that they now lived in a world where atomic weapons not only existed but had been used. What was to be the future of this science? Would it be shared internationally or remain a secret part of the military? What controls would be placed on its use? And how would responsibility for these controls be shared?

Along with thoughts about the future of the world came thoughts of their immediate professional futures—of returning to the teaching and research that had been put on hold "for the duration." Oppenheimer made one of the speediest exits, leaving for Berkeley in October. Others planned to return in time for the January term. Some planned to remain in Los Alamos awhile longer. As they tied up the loose ends of their work and wrote reports that fall of 1945, a cloud of uncertainty hung over the town. With its wartime mission fulfilled, would it continue to exist? And if it did, what would be its new mission? With the army pulling out, who would fund and administer it?

Just weeks after the bombing of Hiroshima and Nagasaki the Los Alamos community witnessed the horrors of a slow death by radiation. On 21 August, Harry Daghlian, a 26-year-old scientist from Purdue, set off a chain reaction for just a fraction of a second. His right hand received a large dose of radiation. Within days his hands swelled, he complained of strong internal pains and he became delirious. The agonizing death took 24 days.[6]

Daghlian had been working with colleague Louis Slotin, testing the interior mechanism of the bomb using two screwdrivers. They would watch the two hemispheres of the bomb slide toward each other on a rod. The goal was to allow them to get close enough to just reach the critical point—the first step in a chain reaction—and then to pull them apart with the screwdrivers. With each experiment he knew that if he was not quick enough in breaking contact, he could produce a nuclear explosion.

Perhaps to counter the seriousness of this critical assembly work, Slotin created whimsical names—he called the screwdriver tests "tickling the dragon's tail"; he dubbed individual assemblies Jezebel, Godiva, Honeycomb, and Topsy. A thin 33-year-old Canadian whose Russian parents had fled the pogroms, Slotin was a gifted scientist who had excelled at biophysics at King's College, London. He had volunteered for the Spanish Civil War, where he served as an anti-aircraft gunner. When World War II broke out he joined the Royal Air Force. Nearsightedness forced him to resign, and he was on his way home to Canada when a friend convinced him that he could serve the war effort as a scientist. He joined the Met Lab in Chicago and then came to Los Alamos.[7]

Following Daghlian's accident a colleague cautioned Slotin about the danger of the experiment, saying, "You won't last a year if you keep on doing that experiment."[8] On 21 May 1946 Slotin was working on Operation Crossroads, a series of tests supplying data on the effects of atomic weapons on naval ships at the Bikini atoll in the Marshall Islands, for which Los Alamos had taken on the technical direction. A screwdriver slipped, and the hemispheres came too close together. To save the lives of the other scientists in the room, he pulled the hemispheres apart with his hands, knowing as he did it, that radiation he received likely would prove fatal. One of those in the room with Slotin was fellow scientist Alvin Graves. Slotin calmly—and correctly—predicted that Graves would recover but that he, Slotin, would not. Louis Slotin died in pain nine days later.[9]

Both accidents were official secrets. Despite the efforts at secrecy, the people of Los Alamos knew—and the children remember the edgy, nervous, restiveness surrounding Slotin's death. "The only time I remember Mother being really upset," recalls Frances Smith Weiland, who was about 12, "was the time there had been an accident. Everything was hush-hush between the women neighbors. I never did know what all happened. They were talking about [people] being burned, near death. I remember they did say 'radiation.' "

Jane Flanders Ziff remembers realizing that something unusual was happening at Los Alamos when she saw Elizabeth "Diz" Graves worrying about her husband's fate. Al and Diz, both physicists, also shared a love of music and had become good friends of the musically inclined Flanders. "The first real puzzle was when Diz Graves, who played the viola—when her husband was exposed [to radiation] in an accident and she was terribly worried. I remember she looked pale, and my mother couldn't explain it to me, except that there had been some kind of accident. But there was so much discussion thereafter about the guy who was killed. This was a very mysterious issue that people didn't explain but was constantly talked over. I remember people saying, 'Well, he was a person who took chances. After all, he volunteered in the Spanish civil war.' "

Barbara Jean Hillhouse Wilson, who was about 10, remembers "how quiet the community was and how concerned." In retrospect, she looks back upon Slotin's death as a tragedy that brought the community together. A town with an average age of 24 did not experience death and grieving. She remembers the sadness of Slotin's death, but she believes that the shared sorrow and mourning "lent a normalcy to our community."

One of the bright spots of that fall of 1945 was the October day when the whole town turned out for the awarding of the army-navy E award. Eleanor Jette remembers that "the mountainsides were dressed in autumn patchwork of evergreen and shining aspen yellow. The faces of the people on the speakers' stand in front of Fuller Lodge were solemn. Our general was there with the visiting dignitaries. [Oppenheimer] was there to accept the award on behalf of the Laboratory and to turn its directorship over to Norris Bradbury. . . . The children rushed about collecting autographs. There was the unprecedented spectacle of a radio crew setting up microphones and equipment to broadcast the speech to the outer world. Bright colors intermingled with the drab. The bright shawls around the shoulders of the Indian women and gay plaid shirts worn by the scientists and their wives contrasted sharply with the Army's khaki, the Navy's blue. The scene was utterly typical of our contrasts and contradictions."[10]

What Paula Schreiber Dransfield, then three, remembers from that day is that her one-year-old sister got bored and leaned on the horn of the family Chevy, drowning out the speeches. One of the speeches that the horn drowned out for the two little girls were these words from Oppenheimer:

> It is with appreciation and gratitude that I accept from you this scroll for the Los Alamos Laboratory, for the men and women whose work and whose hearts have made it. It is our hope that in years to come we may look at this scroll, and all that it signifies, with pride.
>
> Today that pride must be tempered by a profound concern. If atomic bombs are to be added as new weapons to the arsenals of a warring world, or to the arsenals of nations preparing for war, then the time will come when mankind will curse the names of Los Alamos and of Hiroshima.[11]

In December a cold spell descended upon Los Alamos. Along with it came perhaps the lowest point of morale. Many of the pipes bringing in the precious water were above ground, and in the unusual cold they froze. The town found itself without any water at all.

Eleanor Jette vividly recalls the experience. Her husband, Eric, had decided to remain in Los Alamos—at least for a while—and the Jettes had been assigned the Bathtub Row house vacated by the Oppenheimers. After moving in their furniture, Eleanor looked forward to the luxury of a real bath and had started to fill the tub when a soldier rushed to their home to tell them that the town was without water—that she was at that moment draining off the last drops remaining in their pipes.[12] In February, the water lines froze once more, this time for weeks. The army hastened to send trucks to the Rio Grande, to haul water up to The Hill. Families were told to bring containers to get the brownish liquid. Somehow conditions that were bearable when all were working together to accomplish a mission of overriding importance now seemed overwhelming. A number of families who had been planning to leave decided the time had come, and an exodus began.[13]

AFTER THE WAR
AND LOOKING BACK

12

FROM SOLDIER TO CIVILIAN

By the beginning of 1947 the Atomic Energy Commission had come into being to administer the town of Los Alamos, and the University of California had signed a new contract to continue operating the Laboratory. There was now a renewed need for machinists and technical workers. And many of the soldiers were being offered civilian jobs as soon as they were discharged. Among them was Robert Y. Porton.

After being discharged, Porton returned to Los Alamos—to continue his work with the radio station as a civilian. In 1956 he left the radio station to become the Laboratory's first director of public relations. He orchestrated the Lab's popular "family days," started the Bradbury Science Museum, and planned logistics for such visiting dignitaries as John F. Kennedy, Ronald Reagan, and the queen of Greece. He continued to play with dance bands until a few years ago, when "the drums just kept getting heavier." Now in his late seventies and retired, Porton exudes strength and enthusiasm for the Lab, the town, and the role it has played in history.

"When it came time for me to be discharged," he recalls, "[the Lab was going to take over the radio station, and they were looking for a civilian to manage it]. . . . This special service officer came in to [my living quarters in the basement of Theater 2] . . . and said, 'How would you like to get out of the army?' Well, I didn't have enough points. I said, 'Who do I have to kill?' He said, 'They had a meeting today, and they decided they want to keep the radio station on even though the war is over. They were talking about hiring a civilian manager to manage the radio station. And when they were all through . . . the deputy director of the Lab said, 'Why do you want to go to Texas or California? We have a man who's been doing it.' . . . Fortunately . . . I [soon] . . . earned enough points to get a normal discharge. . . .

"I was discharged at Fort Sam Houston, San Antonio, Texas. The army sent me back to Tampa. Then the Lab hired me to come back and run the radio station. They paid my way back to Los Alamos. . . . But I was never really sure that Los Alamos would become permanent. . . . When I accepted the job with the radio station, I thought it would last about a year. . . . We moved to two different locations, and in 1948 we moved to a permanent, beautiful studio, but we were still operating only in Los Alamos. It wasn't until 1949 when we went commercial that they built a tower.

"We had these call letters KRS, Community Radio Station. The FCC assigned some terrible combination [of letters]. I had a friend in Washington who had a pretty [high up] position in the government and I called him and asked if he had any influence with the FCC. And he said, 'I've got a couple friends over there.' And I said, 'I'd like to keep the KRS and add any other letter of the alphabet.' I got a [response] from him that said, 'Is KRSN acceptable?' So we became KRSN, and it's been that way ever since.

"After the war was over, we brought in big bands. We had Duke Ellington, we had Count Basie. . . . I was in Hog Heaven because every time any of them came, we broadcast them live and I would say, 'Now, the music of Duke Ellington and his piano and his orchestra from Theater 2 in downtown Los Alamos, New Mexico.' After about 16 months the Laboratory decided that they really shouldn't be in the business of operating a radio station. By that time they had formed a contractor to take over the running of the town. So a decision was made that the Zia Co. would run the radio station, the library and the hospital. . . . I had beautiful equipment and a staff of 11. They were all [ex-GIs]. As they were discharged, one by one, I made arrangements for them to come back as civilians. . . . Everything was going real fine. . . .

"Then the AEC [Atomic Energy Commission] came into being [and took over from the Zia Co.]. The AEC decided they didn't want to operate a radio station, so they put it up for sale. It was offered to me and an associate of mine, but I didn't have any capital. . . . This guy bought it and hired me. . . . I did that for about 10 years, seven days a week."

In 1956 Porton decided that he "had had it" with the radio station and joined the Lab as the first director of public relations. "When I joined the Lab, . . . the high-level scientists, the old-timers, were opposed to public relations in any shape or form. It was undignified, unnecessary. . . . My first [challenge] . . . was convincing the director we should have a welcoming ceremony for the queen of Greece. They weren't going to do anything at all. . . . It was on a Saturday morning. I talked the high school band director into teaching the band to play the Greek national anthem. It's a difficult piece, and [the queen] was so impressed. Then we had the king of Belgium . . . so many worldwide figures, congressmen, military. . . . I was heavily involved in [the logistics for] the visit of John F. Kennedy when he came here a year before the assassination. I'm very proud. In my den I have a photograph that says, 'To Robert Y. Porton, with best wishes, John F. Kennedy.' . . .

"For 20 years, I was the civil defense director of Los Alamos County in addition to my other job. . . . We were the first community in the United

States to have fallout shelters and supplies in each fallout shelter paid for by the people themselves. . . .

"Once every five years . . . the Lab had something called Family Day where they opened up the Lab and the families come in and bring their relatives and the kids can see the place where Mommy and Daddy work. And I ran all of them. So in 1983 [after I had retired] they brought me back as a consultant to run Family Day and that took about six months. . . .

"The [Bradbury Science] Museum just kind of started by accident. There was opposition to taking school groups on tours [of the Lab]. I started out just getting on a bus and taking them around town and to the fringes of the Lab and telling them about Los Alamos. . . . When I opened the museum, I had, I think, three exhibits, a half a dozen pictures, and 25 folding chairs. The Laboratory had a classified museum, which they still have. The guy who was running it had a couple of dozen, I can't remember how many, unclassi-fied exhibits that he really wanted to get out of there. . . . So we got together, made a deal to have them sent over to my building. [I] hired a guy in the shops department who was a tremendous cabinetmaker to dress them all up. That's how we got started. At first it was just myself, an assistant and a secretary. People would come in, we'd have to drop what we were doing. . . .

"We used to have a lot of people coming in, pro and con [on the bomb]. During the 1960s when they were against everything because of Vietnam, we'd get a raucous group in there. I'd tell my staff, 'Let me handle this.' I'd say, 'Let me just leave one thought with you: many of your dads were poised for invasion. If we'd gone in there to invade the Japanese islands, many of them would have been killed, and if they had been, you wouldn't be sitting here.' "

13

ARRIVING AFTER THE WAR—AND AGAIN DECADES LATER

By the late 1940s Los Alamos was far from a normal community. The world now knew of its existence, but Los Alamos was still full of secrets. It remained a town where children did not talk about their parents' work and generally knew few details. Security investigations still preceded employment. The town remained fenced in—the gate and fence did not go down until 1957. For children, the fence and the physical isolation still created a sense of separateness from the rest of New Mexico and from the outside world. Los Alamos remained a town one entered only for Laboratory business (or occasionally to visit a resident).

As a civilian town, Los Alamos was in the process of defining itself. While wartime Los Alamos had drawn people coming for "the duration" to help win the war, the new town had an economic appeal. Jobs were plentiful and well-paying, especially when compared with the opportunities in small towns elsewhere. As new arrivals poured in, from 1946 onward, there was a hustle and bustle and noise of saws and hammers just as there had been earlier during the war. This time the contractors were tearing down the army-built apartments and putting up new, permanent houses. In 1947 the Atomic Energy Commission took over the administration of the town from the army, and the MPs, so prominent in children's memories from the war years, were replaced by a private security force. There were now fewer soldiers and fewer of the army vehicles that had fascinated those who arrived just a few years earlier.

The school system had grown with the town. In 1946 a new superintendent, Robert Wegner, had been brought in. According to a 1947 article in *Time* magazine, the first thing he did "was to repaint the drab classrooms green, blue, and yellow, because he said the soft pastels helped students to think better." In 1949 a brand-new high school opened. To continue to attract scientists to Los Alamos, the federal government was putting money into the schools—both the physical plants and the teaching staff. Teachers were offered a pay incentive. The new high school came equipped with state-of-the-art laboratories and a large gymnasium.

The adults still worked long hours, and often both parents were taking Laboratory jobs. All this left the children in a world of their own. Children arriving in the late 1940s look back with some surprise at how readily they were accepted. Anxiety at being a "new kid" vanished promptly. The "old-timers" who had come during the war had, after all, been on The Hill only a few years. And having watched many of their friends leave when the war ended, they were only too happy to welcome new playmates.

Verne Bell

In the summer of 1946 an 11-year-old boy peeked out from the home-made enclosure in the back of his father's pickup truck and looked in awe at the Jemez Mountains. The boy was from South Dakota, where his father had worked in the Homestead Gold Mine in a town where, the boy later recalled, "you are born, raised and die, knowing it's never going to be anything else." The family were on their way to Casper, Wyoming, in search of a better life when the father got word of the job as a warehouse chief at Los Alamos. Housing was not yet ready, so the family spent the first two months at the King's Rest Motel across from the Indian School in Santa Fe.

When they did finally roll up The Hill, Los Alamos was still, in the eyes of the 11-year-old, a military town. There was the guardhouse, a military tank, and soldiers. Gradually that began to change. Verne Bell went to junior and senior high school in Los Alamos and to college in Colorado, followed by jobs in defense department work in Colorado, which, after years in Los Alamos, seemed like the natural thing. Verne remembers the newness of the town and sense of acceptance.

"There were a lot of people arriving in 1946, and we quickly made friends. . . . To a boy from the Black Hills of South Dakota, Los Alamos was a whole new thing. I was always exploring, looking out toward the Jemez Mountains, fishing, camping, hunting. . . .

"When we first came you'd see this tank sitting there facing the [guardhouse at the] entrance. And there was a big, high-powered auto there ready for a chase. And when we first came, you couldn't leave at will. You had to schedule when you wanted to leave, and sometimes you were followed just to see what would happen. . . .

"Our first housing was temporary—plywood structures the army had put up. They were individual houses with two bedrooms, living room, and kitchen. There was lots of construction, and they kept moving us to newer houses. . . . We didn't want for anything. We had a new high school and the best gymnasium in the state. We probably had some of the best high school teachers in the whole country. They taught us how to grow up and accept responsibility."

Victor Heyman

To Victor Heyman, arriving in 1947, Los Alamos seemed full of possibilities. Before the United States entered World War II, Vic's father had worked in the patent office in Washington. He served in the navy during the war and then returned to the patent office. But somehow, after the intensity of his war work, the patent office no longer interested him. It didn't satisfy his craving for challenge and adventure. When he heard about the Atomic Energy Commission and the whole new field of patents involving atomic projects, he decided that was for him.

In 1947 the Heymans set off on the cross-country trip from Washington. Vic remembers that they were driving "a clunker of a car with a trailer hitched behind it." By the time they hit the Appalachian Mountains, just a few hours out of Washington, the car overheated and they began "throwing stuff out," a process by which they continued across the country. In Albuquerque they took a wrong turn in the hills and, in attempting to turn around, cracked the rim of a wheel of the trailer. Wheels were still hard to get, and this seemed like the last straw. They decided to leave the trailer there and come back for it later. They piled what they would need immediately into the car and chugged on into Los Alamos.

Vic was then "a pudgy 13-year-old" with city manners and speech that some of the Texans made fun of. Nevertheless, life in Los Alamos seemed pretty good. He remembers, "For a kid, Los Alamos was about as close as I think we'll ever get to a Utopia: a beautiful place, picnics, ice skating, a brand-new school, new housing, no poverty, no unemployment, and people doing work they found interesting. None of us knew what our parents did, let alone who outranked whom. . . . They were involved in their world, we in ours, and they were very separate worlds."

He recalls a town where kids readily accepted differences. "Personality and accomplishments had more to do with acceptance than who you were or where you came from. What was really amazing was that the kids who lived in White Rock [then a trailer camp for construction workers] were not looked down upon at all. I think that was because this was a town where the kids raised themselves. . . . We hadn't been 'carefully taught.' . . . I never felt any prejudice at being Jewish. Religion never got into the act. . . .

"One of the biggest problems of the town was the damn construction. The town was growing, and there was construction everywhere. I still remember the smell of the tar on the roofs of the new houses, and I remember walking home one night and falling into a ditch. They had dug a ditch right across the middle of the road as part of this construction, and in the dark I didn't see it. . . . Because the town was geographically compact, a bicycle got you around pretty well, and it was easy to visit back and forth. And being a closed community made hitchhiking a lot easier. People didn't have to worry about who they were picking up. . . .

"Los Alamos was still federal property, and the federal driving age was 14. So I had a motor bike at 14. That wasn't possible elsewhere in New Mexico. One of the kids had a father who worked at the motor pool. He showed us how the gas pump was controlled by a fuse which was sitting over the pump. You could screw in the fuse, fill up your tank and unscrew it again. So for a while we had free gas."

Jim Wearin

Jobs were scarce in Griswold, Iowa, in 1948, so when Jim Wearin's father saw a poster in the post office that said that the AEC was looking for security guards, he applied. He was sent to Kirkland Air Base in Albuquerque for training, then up to Los Alamos, where he soon brought his family. Jim remembers the newness of the town, the sense of specialness, and the security that the gate offered, especially when one was being chased by a carload of youths from Santa Fe. "We had a brand new high school our sophomore year," he recalls, "and money to support extracurricular activities that other schools simply didn't have. . . . The school system was federally supported, and they paid good money for some of the best instructors I've ever seen. . . .

"We used to go to drive-in movies in Espanola or Santa Fe. Sometimes one of our dates wasn't allowed to go off The Hill, and her parents had taken her pass away. So that individual would be in the trunk of the car going through the gate and coming back through. When we were in high school, we realized that the purpose of the town was unique, but I don't think we thought of ourselves as unique. Only in retrospect do I realize how unique it is that anyone who came here from wherever was so readily accepted."

Polly Richardson Boyles

Polly Richardson Boyles came to Los Alamos from Wisconsin by way of Santa Fe for the same reason that people had come to New Mexico in the early part of the century—for the healing qualities of the climate. Polly's sister had been diagnosed with a lung abscess, and the doctors back in Wisconsin did not think she would live. Polly's mother had read the Willa Cather novel *Death Comes to the Archbishop,* set in Lamy, New Mexico, and decided the climate might cure her daughter. While Polly's father stayed in Wisconsin, where he worked as an accountant for the state, the females set off for New Mexico, where Polly's mother got a job teaching high school in Santa Fe during the war.

The family moved to Los Alamos in 1948 when Polly's father got a job with the AEC doing accounting for the Lab: "My mother, sister, grandmother and I came to Santa Fe in 1943. Our first trip to Los Alamos, at least part of the way, was that year. We were on an excursion [from Santa Fe] to Bandelier. . . . We wound up on the wrong road—on the narrow winding road to Los Alamos. Guards with machine guns met us and made us turn around in the middle of the steep part, with no guard rails. I remember my mother was not thrilled about that.

"I don't think anybody spent any time inside to speak of. I lived on horseback and roamed every square foot of the mountains. One game we liked was to ride out [of the fence] avoiding the gate, then ride up to the gate and say, 'I can't get in. I don't have my pass.' Horses, camping out, fishing in the river—that was our life. I'd be away all day, and nobody panicked. It wasn't that they didn't care: they figured you had enough sense to know what you were doing. You hitchhiked everywhere and never gave it a thought. It was very secure.

"We were all nonconformists—each going our own way and not feeling we had to do what everyone else was doing. We didn't divide people into groups [but saw each other as individuals]. . . . We were taught to think for ourselves."

Bob Martin

Bob Martin arrived in Los Alamos in 1949 when his father took a job as a senior budget analyst for the AEC. Bob was 14 years old and apprehensive about how a new kid from an Irish/Italian working-class neighborhood in

Denver would be received by his Spanish-American classmates. That worry was put to rest immediately when he went out for sports teams. "I played all kinds of sports in high school," he recalls, "and on the bus going to games I would sit with the Spanish guys. They would teach us to sing Spanish songs and teach us how to swear in Spanish. . . .

"We had a brand-new gymnasium and a swimming pool, and I think other towns resented it. We played small schools at first—in Pojoaque, El Rito, Española. It seems that the poorer the school community, the worse the resentments toward us were. Sometimes there were fights after games because of a feeling that we were rich and snobby. With my blond hair and blue eyes, I stood out. But my Spanish-American friends were there for me—they never let me down.

"In high school we used to go to Santa Fe occasionally to chase girls, and to play pool. I remember walking into a pool hall and seeing a friend who thought he was an expert at pool. He borrowed my food money to 'make lots.' When he lost that, he played 'double or nothing'—without the money to back it up if he lost. After he lost several games, his opponents insisted on payment after the next game. When my friend agreed, he whispered to me that, if he lost, we'd run like hell to the car, which is exactly what happened. There were a few minor skirmishes on the way to the car. Then several cars chased us at top speed all the way to Los Alamos. When we were safely inside the gate, we got out of the car and shouted at our pursuers. I never went back to that pool hall!"

On the last weekend in July 1992, the Los Alamos High School class of 1952 converged on The Hill for their first official reunion. From a class of 80, 30 showed up, many bringing spouses and coming from all over the country. Some talked about the incidence of cancer among their parents and their classmates and wondered whether there could be any connection between the cancers and reports of contamination in one of the canyons. They joined together in a song dedicated to a classmate who had died young of cancer. In a lighter vein, they looked back on the senior class trip to Red River and upon long-ago crushes and romances. While they reminisced and crooned the popular tune of their high school years, "Good Night, Irene," they remembered their teachers' high expectations that the class would go on to college and to professional success. As they recollected, they wondered aloud, "What makes us so close? And what keeps pulling us back to Los Alamos?"

Verne Bell, a retired defense contractor, has been thinking all weekend about the bonding of the class. The day after the banquet he stands in the lobby of the Los Alamos Inn, gripping a piece of paper on which he has written two words: "fission" and "fusion." By "fission" he alludes to the force that powered the first atomic bomb. But with the word "fusion," he's thinking

114

not of the powering of the hydrogen bomb but of the "bonding of the Los Alamos children."

"The Lab was working on the fission, and we kids in town were doing the fusion," Verne explains. "We came from all over, and we hit it off extremely well. What happened was a fusion of people from all over, from different backgrounds, different ethnic origins. It was really an amazing thing. . . . I feel a real bond to these people, and I always will. . . . We learned from the beginning that you formed friendships and worked together. Secundino and I started out as crossing guards together. I don't think any of us has ever lost these friendships." Part of the reason for the bonding may be the isolation; part may be the mission of the town, the involvement of the parents in the same endeavor. Part may be the times. "The era itself was different. The 1940s and 1950s were a friendlier atmosphere, not as competitive as what I see now and not as ethnically splintering."

"Los Alamos was like an extended family," remembers Jo Redman, who lives in Cyprus, California, and teaches physical education at a state university. "We visited back and forth in each other's homes and learned different styles of life. My best friends' parents had gone to college and encouraged me. . . . My father being a construction worker we moved a lot. When we got to Los Alamos, I told my parents 'I want to stay here.' And I did even though they moved to Albuquerque while I was still in high school. I live in California in a house that is Spanish on the outside but New Mexican on the inside— I collect Indian pottery and Navaho rugs. That's as close as I can get to home now but when I retire, I'm coming back. [Los Alamos] is my home."

Bob Martin, general manager and vice president of a cable company in Texas (from which he is partially retired), has lived all over the country and currently lives in Lewisville, Texas. Martin confides the ambivalence he feels about Los Alamos. He loved living there as a boy, likes to come back for visits and admits to "getting teary-eyed" at seeing old friends. But he would not want to live in Los Alamos as an adult. In 1964 he returned to manage Fuller Lodge, then the town's only hotel. He left after a year, disappointed and hurt, convinced that this was not where he wanted to raise his three sons.

From his own teenage years in Los Alamos, Martin remembered "the closeness of friends—and their absolute reliability." "In Denver, where we lived until I was 13, there was a rich side of town and a poor side of town," he explains. "Here there weren't social classes. I remember that having lived in an Italian/Irish neighborhood, I was worried about getting along with Spanish Americans. I grew to love the Spanish language and culture."

While cultures blended, so did children from different academic backgrounds. The son of the Laboratory director, Jim Bradbury was "one of the guys." But in 1964 Martin saw the town differently. It seemed more stratified and snobbish. His son could not go to nursery school with his neighbors because the school was sponsored by the American Association of University Women (AAUW) and to be eligible the child's mother must be a college graduate. (Jean Martin had not completed college at that time.)

The positive side of the return to Los Alamos, Martin remembers, was dealing with a variety of cultures. "We had Spanish-American waitresses and bartenders, and scientists coming from all over the world to be catered to. Imagine a Russian scientist trying to order an American breakfast in broken English with a Spanish-American waiter with broken English. That was a challenge!"

Years later, as he approaches retirement, Martin thinks more and more about his appreciation of Spanish-American culture, and he worries about the Mexicans coming over the border into Texas, "sitting on the backs of trucks, waiting for someone to hire them for something like shoveling, to work them like hell and pay them a few dollars an hour. What do they have to look forward to? What do they have to call their own? And how will they ever be assimilated?" Martin contemplates starting an organization that will help these Mexicans learn English, fill out applications, and buy homes. Just as assimilation was something that happened in the 1940s to families who moved to Los Alamos from all over the country, Bob Martin would like to help foster another kind of assimilation in the twenty-first century.

Vic Heyman was a high school junior and "sort of bored" when he decided to take second-semester physics—without having had the first semester. This gave him the extra credit he needed to graduate a year early. "Instead of being salutatorian of the class of 1952—behind Jim Bradbury—I became valedictorian of the class of 1951." A young man in a hurry, Vic set out for Washington University in St. Louis at age 16. Six years later, at 22, he had a Ph.D. in political science.

He credits his fast-paced achievement to the sense of unlimited possibilities ingrained into the children of Los Alamos. "It was a freewheeling place with the attitude, 'If you can, then do. There's nothing standing in your way.'" Los Alamos, he believes, "provided opportunities that would not have been possible in a more staid place. The sense that there are no limits doesn't exist in a more settled environment. The school system was very responsive to the needs of the individual."

He also credits his "mentor"—English teacher Shirley Frieze—remembered by many of her former students as the inspiration (and the task master) behind their achievements. A graduate of Cornell University, Frieze expected of her motley crew of students the decorum and polish of an East Coast prep school as she propelled them toward prestigious colleges and universities. Following in his mentor's path, Vic began his career as a teacher—a political science professor at Marshall University in West Virginia. Seeking some practical experience in government, he came to Washington. The year that John F. Kennedy became president Vic joined the Pentagon staff as one of

Secretary of Defense Robert S. McNamara's "whiz kids." Today he operates a thriving mailing service, just north of Washington in Rockville, Maryland. What he has carried away from Los Alamos, he says, is "the mindset of the possible."

Jim Wearin, who had come to Los Alamos from Griswold, Iowa, as a high school freshman in 1948, now lives in Fresno, California. "At the time we were in high school," he recalled in a note to his classmates, "the United States was at once recently victorious in war, naive, arrogant, and completely ignorant as to what to do with the worldwide role it had assumed. The place, Los Alamos, had a singular reason for being and collected a most diverse group of people and their children. It just happened to exist in the midst of what is still the most intriguing place in my world. . . . The people, parents and children, came from all places for all reasons. . . . So varied were we that castes and strata simply had no chance to develop; we were alike. After 40 years of living numerous other places, I still think of Los Alamos and New Mexico as home."

14

THREE FRIENDS

Secundino Sandoval, Jim Bradbury, and Brant Calkin have been friends since their arrivals in Los Alamos in 1943 and 1944. They went to school together from grade school through high school, where they formed an intertwined triumvirate in the class of 1952. All three have gone on to careers in which they have gained national recognition—careers that had their impetus in Los Alamos.

Jim, growing up as the son of a respected physicist and Laboratory director, was impelled toward physics both because he thought it a filial duty and because of the excitement of discovery he vicariously experienced as a child. Secundino learned early that his artistic talent could compensate for his lack of fluency in English and the sense of inadequacy he often felt among his friends from more intellectual, worldly backgrounds. Brant spent much of his childhood roaming the land, sometimes for days at a time. His work as an environmentalist, including presidency of the Sierra Club, is a natural outcome.

Jim liked to visit Secundino's home, finding there the roots, traditions, and extended family that he lacked in his own home far from grandparents. Brant, on his own from a young age, found that same stability in the Bradbury home. When his parents divorced, and his father had left Los Alamos, Brant moved in with the Bradburys. In their senior year, Jim was valedictorian, Secundino co-captain of the football team and senior class president. In college Secundino and Brant roomed together.

As adults all three worked at the Lab for a number of years—Brant and Secundino soon after graduation. Jim returned later, after his father retired as Laboratory director. Jim still works there, as director of the Meson Physics facility, from which he is in the process of retiring.

Jim Bradbury

When he was a child, Jim Bradbury had the impression that boys grew up to become physicists. Shortly before he turned 12, Jim's life changed dramatically when, in October 1945, Robert Oppenheimer asked Norris Bradbury to take over the directorship of the Laboratory. Originally the appointment was a temporary one, but Bradbury remained Laboratory director for a quarter of a century. It was Norris Bradbury who rebuilt the Lab after the war, found new missions for it, oversaw its expansion (including a whole new campus), and hobnobbed with politicians, both national and international, on its behalf. His quiet, older son was suddenly thrust into the limelight. While his friends still lived in Sundt apartments, Jim moved to a brand-new house with a living room large enough for all the necessary entertaining. Most of the great names in physics visited the Bradbury home, conveying to the teenager the excitement of scientific discovery.

Soft-spoken, articulate, and analytical, Jim steers away from personal questions such as how it felt to grow up the son of the Laboratory director. Friends say he always seemed to be a bit apart, somehow sensing that his father's position required him to be a good student and model citizen. He views growing up in Los Alamos as a kind of scientific experiment and is interested in statistics, hypotheses, and theories. How, he wonders, did the urgent concern of the parents during the war get transmitted to the children and what are its consequences? He wonders how often his classmates have moved, changed jobs, or experienced such upheavals as alcoholism or divorce.

While he enjoys physics, Jim gradually has come to realize that he is "more of a people person" and is also fascinated by medicine. He finds his job as director of the Lab facility working on medical applications a good fit. With the end of the cold war and the collapse of the Soviet Union, the Lab is collaborating more with the Russians, resulting in frequent business trips to Moscow.

Divorced, and the father of two grown children, Jim Bradbury lives in a contemporary adobe on a hillside overlooking Santa Fe. He recalls, almost wistfully, his yearnings as a child for the sense of tradition, place and connection to an extended family that he found among his Spanish American friends, especially Secundino. "There were plenty of times—it might hurt my parents to hear this, but probably not—there were things that I derived from being in the household of the very stable family relationships extending through several generations, as they do in the Spanish-American families. Some sort of sense of knowing who you were and where you were. They belonged here. There were things I encountered in being parts of those families that I did not get in my own family. They might say the other thing: how nice it was to come and visit Jim. Then I thought it was special, and I still do."

He recalls, too, his decision to become a physicist and later to return to Los Alamos. "I went into science largely as what I perceived as parental pressures. . . . I knew it would make my dad happy. . . . I [was also attracted by the] excitement and accomplishment [of the early days at Los Alamos]. . . . I don't know that I've ever encountered the sense of urgency in terms of something being really crucial [as it was during the war], but I have a number of times encountered that sense of excitement on the verge of discovery. That's what physics is all about. When you see something you believe as a hypothesis confirmed by counters clicking away, that's a beautiful feeling. . . . That I have encountered both at Stanford, where I went to graduate school, and back here. I've been happy as a physicist. I enjoy that kind of stuff. I'm sort of an ex-physicist [more an administrator now]. I was never in the first ranks of physics. I really think I've got more of the caregiver in me. I think medicine or something would have appealed to me more. . . .

"There was something so different and probably unique about Los Alamos that it's important to get [away to gain] some perspective. . . . This was not our parents' home, but it was our home. Somehow that stuck, and New Mexico was home. It seemed as if there were some sort of magnetic attraction back to this area. The desert-mountain combination, the colors [pull us back]. I commute to Los Alamos [from Santa Fe] every day, and every day I love that drive—still.

"I was away for 20 years [from high school graduation in 1952 to 1972] and then came back because northern New Mexico offered to me things that I found missing in the other places I lived. The sense of connection to the land. The space, the confluence of these cultures. . . . The things that stand out in my mind are these relationships with the Indians. They were much more than maids. They were surrogate parents in our case. And I still visit Isabel [Atencio, the Bradbury's housekeeper]. She's in her nineties now. That family is still very special. . . .

"There were stratifications. It was very much like a university town in some ways. There were these social layers. . . . [But] the kids experienced none of this. I never even thought about differences—ethnic, racial, whose father did what. Now I find that beautiful but I also find it peculiar. I don't know if it was the setting that made that possible, but there were absolutely no barriers. I'm not saying there weren't the usual kinds of groups that develop in a high school or junior high school setting. But they seem to have been populated by mixtures of all these different kinds of people.

"It's hard to know if the separateness of Los Alamos from the surrounding communities is what created that kind of a bond. . . . The son of the barber, the son of the janitor, the son of Enrico Fermi—we all did things together, and there was never any thought about that. In retrospect I love that about that growing up experience."

Brant Calkin

One who visited Jim often—and eventually stayed for a year—was Brant Calkin. The only child of mathematician Jack Calkin, who had come out from the East in 1943, Brant spent much of his childhood playing in the canyons and wandering through the hills and woods. He came to think of the outdoors as his real home. It was a lot more beckoning than the apartment he shared with his father, who was totally preoccupied with his work, and his mother, who, he says, felt so isolated that she increasingly turned to drink. Later she left Los Alamos and divorced his father.

Brant remembers Los Alamos as "a hard-drinking town" but thinks the drinking was "symptomatic of other things. . . . What you had basically were nonparticipatory families where one member, usually the male, was totally absorbed. The isolation for some people was pretty complete. They could not visit where their husband worked. The husband appeared at the house at the end of a very long day and left again the next morning." For a number of women, including Brant's mother, the physical and mental isolation were unbearable.

By his teenage years, Brant was on his own. "My family situation gave me enough independence that I could be gone. A lot of other kids had a more conventional arrangement whereby they're supposed to be home for supper. But especially [as a teenager] I often didn't have that pressure." He spent time in the Jemez Mountains and in the canyons just yards from the family's apartment: "The neat thing for me was that the land was available—I had it in my back yard." He would visit his favorite haunts over and over again. "It's kind of good, I think," he says, "to learn something on a small scale pretty well because it gives you an appreciation of the grander scheme of things. . . . I remember I went to one canyon over in Bandelier National Monument, called Capulin, several times a year over about 17 years and never met somebody there whom I hadn't brought myself. . . . You get to know a place pretty well, and you begin to see things changing. . . . I did a little calculation and calculated that I have spent six months at Capulin spread out over years. If you spend that time someplace, you begin to develop an appreciation for what's going on there."

A biologist by training, who spent his first several years out of college working for the Los Alamos National Laboratory, Brant has, over time, become a seasoned and effective environmental activist. As a volunteer for the Sierra Club, he held just about every job there was from membership to newsletter editor, went on the board of directors, and, in the mid-1970s, was elected national president. He later worked for the Sierra Club as regional representative for the Southwest. He has also worked in state government in New Mexico as secretary of the Department of Natural Resources.

In the late 1980s Brant ran for state land commissioner. After the election, which he lost, he treated himself to a long-anticipated "extravagance": a 10-week canoe trip along the length of Baja California. A week after returning to Santa Fe, broke and unemployed, he landed the job of executive director for the Southern Utah Wilderness Alliance, for which he has worked for the past eight years. Today he has expanded the territory he calls home.

"I no longer have a specific hometown," he explains. "What I have is a neighborhood—a half-million-square-mile neighborhood in which I feel perfectly at home." That neighborhood, which embraces the Colorado Plateau, includes much of the four states of Colorado, Utah, New Mexico, and Arizona. "Whether it's the western slope of Colorado, or Red Rock Canyon in Utah, or the Grand Canyon, in which I've hiked 1,800 miles, or the Jemez Mountains, that's all my neighborhood, and I'm as at home in almost any place in that neighborhood as I was in . . . Los Alamos."

From his childhood, Brant retains a fondness for canyons. "They shaped the things we did. . . . They defined where we lived, [and] how we got to and from [our homes] and they defined where we couldn't go. . . . Every other street practically backs up on a canyon. . . . You could see neighbors whose air distance is half a mile, but it's seven miles to drive around. . . . In almost any place in Los Alamos, you can walk a matter of yards and be on a canyon rim. . . . If you want to get away, you can literally drop out of the world. It's very quiet; it's peaceful. There's antiquity [Indian artifacts], there's water, there's wildlife. If you feel a little stress, you just go into a canyon."

Another special destination was the Valle Grande, a seemingly endless, 18,000-acre mountain meadow. Sketching a circle on a paper, Brant says, "Imagine an almost perfectly circular [mountain] ridge, and a series of inner mountains: This one goes to 11,200 feet; this one is a little bit smaller. In between these are the most beautiful lush high mountain meadows you can imagine including the Valle Grande. It was only a day's walk from Los Alamos."

After college, Brant took a job at the Lab, first in electrochemistry and then in high-temperature chemistry. He found the Lab "a good place to work with interesting people around. The work was challenging even for a technician. It was a place where you could do a lot of problem solving by being clever." Now that he had a car, he could explore areas further from Los Alamos. Weekends he generally set out on solo hikes. "I would go home for lunch on Friday, get my backpack, put it in the car, and at five o'clock I'd leave to go hiking somewhere. I'd write on the bulletin board at the Lab where I was going. The idea was that if I wasn't back by Monday, no big deal. If I wasn't back Tuesday, somebody ought to look around and see where I was. If I wasn't back Wednesday, it was probably too late anyway: I was high-protein litter somewhere.

"The one time when I had real occasion to wonder about the system was the time that I wrote 'Ross's Creek,' took off, went across the valley up in the Pecos, got to the other side of the valley about dark, put my pack on, walked down this trail that goes up along a stream. It was still light enough, nice country. About 10 P.M. it was too dark to walk, a good time to make camp. There was a little clearing right next to the stream. There was a tree that had fallen down across part of it. I took my pack off and leaned it up against the trunk of this tree, spread my sleeping bag out, and I thought, 'In the morning I'm just going to reach over, get out my camp stove and make tea right here in my sleeping bag.'

"Then I went to sleep. Sometime in the middle of the night, on the other side of the log, I heard this snuffling and gruffling. I thought, 'Here you are with all this food right next to your head; that bear is going to come over here; you have no place to go.' All this is going through my mind pretty quickly. 'I can either try to rip out of my sleeping bag and and get across this clearing and try to climb that tree before the bear gets here or do I have the courage to lie here and get mauled before it thinks I'm dead and goes away? By the time the guys read the bulletin board at work it's going to be too late.'

"I was lying there thinking about this, and the stars over my head disappeared and this giant God-damned head came over the tree and dropped down to me and I was looking up there, and it opened its mouth and went, 'Moo.' "

Brant was 10 years old when the bomb was dropped on Hiroshima. He never talked with his father about his role in the development of the bomb. "World War II was no sooner over than we were on to the H-bomb. There wasn't a break when you would say, 'Now I will ask about that.' . . . And until the day my dad died, he was always doing classified work, so you never were quite sure what you might pick the scab on." Brant himself "made my peace with [the dropping of the atomic bomb] some time ago. Using the bomb at the end of World War II, I think was a rational decision at the time. There weren't many people around urging otherwise and we were losing people every day." Since then, however, he thinks that nuclear weaponry has been "pursued with a vigor that was beyond a rational evaluation of need."

Secundino Sandoval

After a rocky start—feeling as if he had been set on a different planet, feeling insecure in his new life on The Hill—Secundino Sandoval became a high school "hotshot." Today he is a nationally known artist. His large, light-filled studio on the second floor of his home on Los Alamos's Trinity Drive is crammed with canvases and a few choice pieces of Indian pottery. Holding up a postcard-size reproduction of his well-received painting of the famous potter Maria Martinez, he explains, "I met Maria in 1945—in the fifth or sixth grade—when she came to one of our classes and she formed a piece of pottery. I became fascinated with her back then. I became fascinated by the Indian culture, the pottery. In 1978 I had the privilege and honor of having a show with her in the state capital. She died while I was still working on the portrait of her—she never saw the finished product."

Another artist he met as a child was Georgia O'Keeffe. After the war, Secundino's father, Sam, a skilled carpenter, moonlighted in the small towns surrounding Los Alamos, sanding floors and laying down linoleum. Georgia O'Keeffe learned of his work and hired him. "She and my father became friends. They argued quite a bit because they were both stubborn. She was very demanding. I was always fascinated by what she had to say because she was a very outspoken woman. I was too timid to ask anything or say anything, but I was fascinated by her art because in my early days as a child I was also painting skulls and large flowers. That's before I even knew who Georgia O'Keeffe was!

"My father was not versed in art, but my father was a very smart man. She would invite [him] in and say, 'Mr. Sandoval, what do you think of this painting?' I remember she was working on a large canvas. It was inside her house, and it was going to a museum or show in New York City. It was a huge canvas with a great big circle. My father said, 'To me, it looks just like a great big circle.' [He] said it just like he felt it. It was an inspiration that I had known about Georgia O'Keeffe, that I had known about Maria Martinez."

Although there were many playground skirmishes in the early years and calling of names by the various ethnic and cultural groups within Los Alamos, Secundino remembers that it wasn't until he left the community that he realized the forms that discrimination could take. And he was shocked. "As a sophomore my father sent me to help an uncle bale hay in Colorado. We went to a small town in Lamar, Colorado [for haircuts]. My cousin, who had blue eyes and red hair, had no problem. He got on the barber's chair, got a haircut. They said, 'We'll give you a haircut, but not your Mexican friend.' I was appalled. I had never been rejected. I said, 'Maybe this is the real world.'"

Secundino drew and painted all through grade school and high school, garnering high praise throughout the community. When he got to college, however, he wanted to become a musician. He played the guitar, the trumpet, and the clarinet, and his ambition was to have his own big band. His love of music had been fostered by Bob Porton, by the classical music Porton broadcast on the radio, by Porton's combo, and by the big bands that performed in Los Alamos. In the early 1950s big bands were on their way out, and as Secundino recalls, everybody was studying engineering. So he "took up architectural engineering." Architecture had fascinated him from the early days of watching buildings and other structures go up on the mesa. He had been fascinated by the building of the new high school, which opened in 1949, and by the building of a bridge across one of the canyons, allowing the relocation of the Lab on the other side of the canyon.

After college, Secundino returned to Los Alamos, where he has lived ever since. He worked for many years as a mechanical design draftsman at the Lab until he decided to try to make it on his own as an artist. He likes to paint landscapes—views he loved as a child and loves today. A favorite inspiration is Camp May, part of the old Ranch School property where Secundino and his friends often hiked.

"Time and time I go to Camp May. I go to the bottom of the canyon and hike up to the reservoir. I get a lot of my ideas from there. I've painted the bridge [leading to the Lab] over and over again. Even though it's a structure, a contemporary sort of thing, it's still beautiful if it's done in the right light. I've done paintings of the old lodge. There are a lot of areas of the town that are inspiring."

Sometimes Secundino "carves" messages on the trunks of the trees he paints. "When I portray my messages in my paintings, it's not Catholic and it's not Presbyterian; it's just a message of goodwill: 'Peace.' 'Have a nice day.' If there's something pleasant in the painting that attracts you to it, and it makes you feel at ease and peace the way I felt, so much the better."

Back in 1945 a very different scene caught his eye—the mushroom cloud formed by the bomb dropped on Hiroshima. "There was a picture that came out in the newspaper. And I saw this mushroom cloud, and I said, 'This is fascinating. This is different.' I sat down and I did a painting of it in oils. I gave it to my teacher. I often wonder why a kid in sixth or seventh grade would do a painting of a mushroom cloud. [In] 1945 when the bombs were exploded, it was all very, very exciting to me. I said, 'My goodness the bomb that ended the war was made right here.' We had to be proud of that sort of thing. When I went to college [in 1952] I was almost bragging about it. Like I wanted to bring some of the children from the college and tell them, 'This is the road we [drove] into Los Alamos. This is where the Lab used to be,' to tell them, 'We really did it!' Now, 50 years later, it's almost like, 'I don't want to know about it.' I'm not that proud of it. Even though I had nothing to do with the bomb, I don't want to talk about it."

When the Los Alamos Kiwanas Club asked him to design a medal to commemorate the town's fiftieth anniversary, Secundino quickly dismissed the obvious idea of a mushroom cloud. Instead he sketched the head of Robert Oppenheimer with a dove.

15

"ATOMIC BOMB, ATOMIC BOMB"

In December 1951 Marge Agnew, an elementary school music teacher new to the mesa, introduced her young students to the Christmas carol "O Tannenbaum" ("O Christmas Tree"). The students picked it up quickly and were singing merrily when she suddenly stopped them and asked the class to tell her the words they were singing. They said in unison, "Atomic bomb, atomic bomb." The children in the class were born about the same time as the atom bomb and had heard the words said with a certain pride. Singing a song to an atomic bomb seemed perfectly natural.

For these children, life in the early 1950s had an overlay of innocence, security, and trust. It was partly the innocence of the times—and of pretelevision, small-town America. In many ways Los Alamos resembled other single-industry towns, where the parents worked together and the children played together. In Los Alamos, however, the children's sense of safety and independence were heightened. Ironically the work of the town, the development of bombs, created for the children a cocoon of security. The fence surrounding the town kept out anyone who wasn't part of their carefully screened world. Everyone within the fence had been invited to live in the town and had been investigated. Everyone had a job and a house or apartment. No one could wander in from the outside. There were no traveling salespeople, no strangers. Everyone had been carefully vetted. Everyone belonged.

Because no one locked doors, one child recalls, "You were on your honor not to wander through others' houses, even though you knew you could." Another recalls that the delivery person from the dry cleaner would "walk in and hang your laundry in the closet if you weren't home." The children remember a total absence of the idea that there could be "bad people" or people who would harm children. Like young children elsewhere, the schoolchildren of Los Alamos were taught that an atomic bomb had hastened the end of the war, but few knew the role that their parents had played.

One of the landmarks for the children was the guardhouse. Leaving the guardhouse meant leaving the town for a trip; approaching it on your return drive up The Hill meant "welcome home." One child remembers that when her family returned from trips in the early 1950s, it was often dark and she would be asleep in the car. She would awaken to the sight of a guard shining a flashlight into the car as he examined passes. This is a soothing, friendly memory, she says: "Like—oh, we're home."

Two brothers, Louis and Bob Critchfield, who lived in Los Alamos as babies during the war and returned with their parents for the year 1952-53, remember "playing guard gate" in their cul de sac. "We would set up cardboard boxes, crates, and stuff and make ourselves a gate," recalls Bob. "Each of the kids would have a pass, and we would tricycle around and check in and out of the gate, imitating the actions of the adults."

Like children anywhere, the children of Los Alamos accepted their environment as normal. It was only after they had left Los Alamos that many realized it was unusual. "Because it's natural, normal to you, I think it's extremely hard to step back and say, 'This is extremely unusual,' " muses Paula Schreiber Dransfield. "You have to keep recognizing that your point of view is very definitely colored by what you believe is normal but to everybody else in the world is very strange."

Paula remembers "two incidents [that] . . . made me start thinking . . . maybe I was living in something other than a normal town. . . . The first was when they took the gate down when I was something like a sophomore in high school and there were people whose families had worked here . . . and those children had never even seen the town . . . where their parents worked. So there were lots of people coming in and just driving around town to see what it was like. . . . And it began to occur to me that this was not a normal situation. People didn't normally live behind locked gates.

"And then when I got to college, one of the first assignments that we had in creative-writing class was to write a description of one's hometown. . . . And [I had] a young . . . professor who was very liberal—we're talking the early 1960s. He was absolutely horrified at the regimentation of the town I grew up in because I talked about the point system and how you lived in a certain part of town depending on where your father was in the Laboratory and this kind of thing. It began to dawn on me that I had grown up in something abnormal and that this was not the way that most people grew up."

As she looks back on life in the early to mid-1950s, Paula portrays both the "wonderful small town, tight community" and some peculiarities. She remembers the way the town pulled together to find a lost child—and the chill that went up her spine when someone blew the air raid whistle as a signal that the child was found. "I remember a little girl about three got lost, and they could not find her. The call went out on the radio . . . that there was a lost child in the Western Area. There was a tremendous fear that she she may have fallen into a canyon, and they needed volunteers. . . . Every able-bodied man went to help find her, enough so that they could walk almost touching hands for . . . [a] great distance. . . . They eventually found [her] sleeping under a tree. By this time it was probably 8:30 or 9 o'clock. . . . When the little girl was found, they blew all of the air raid whistles so that all of the men would know she was found. I remember being in bed and hearing the whistle blow and our hair stood up because we were trained— this is another aspect of living here—that when those whistles blew, that was serious stuff. You got out of town. We had practices. We would literally empty the town. . . .

[Our family was] building a house down by Black Mesa on the road toward Española from the time I was eight or nine until we finally moved in when I was about 12 or 13. . . . My parents had both grown up on farms, and my dad particularly was very uncomfortable with the fact that this town was all government-owned so you could not own your own land or house. . . . He found property 11 to 12 miles out of town, and we built a traditional adobe house. . . . We would go down and spend our weekends there building. So when the air raids would go off in Los Alamos, all of our friends would come down and a lot of times they would bring pot-luck and we would end up having dinner because everybody had to exit out of the town. . . .

"It was kind of fun and kind of scary at the same time. As a young person, all of us living here knew that we could be killed by a bomb. And I think we also realized that we wouldn't be able to get out of town. Because we knew what the traffic jams were like. . . . We got the other side of what's it's like to have introduced the atomic age."

In 1949 and 1950 Paul Teller and Elizabeth (Yibi) Mark were tromping off to school together as first graders. They lived down the street from each other on 49th Street in Los Alamos's newly opened Western area. Both had come as very young children during the war—Paul from Chicago at about three months in 1943 and Yibi from Canada at age two in 1945. When the war ended Yibi's father, Carson Mark, decided to stay at the Lab as manager of theoretical physics, while Paul's father, Edward Teller, took a teaching job at the University of Chicago. Christmas and summer vacations the Tellers would hustle out to Los Alamos, and in 1949 they were back for good (at least for a couple of years). Then, in 1952, Paul and his younger sister Wendy were whisked off to California, where, at the Lawrence Livermore Laboratory, their father developed the hydrogen bomb. But it's the years 1949 to 1952 that Paul thinks of when he thinks of his childhood, and it's Los Alamos that he thinks of as home.

For Yibi, Los Alamos has always been home. She grew up there in a house overflowing with six boisterous children and their friends. Paul and Yibi remember playing together up and down 49th Street along with the children of Rose and Hans Bethe, the children of L. D. P. and Edie King, and the youngest son of Norris and Lois Bradbury. Yibi likens their relationship to an extended family, while Paul describes it as "a gang in the sense of 'Our

Gang' in the old comic strips." Paul majored in mathematics at Stanford University and earned a Ph.D. in the philosophy of science from MIT. After years of teaching philosophy of science in the Chicago area, he moved to Davis, California, where he now teaches at the University of California. Yibi Mark Smith also lives in Davis, where she teaches high school chemistry.

"In a real way, we were all family," Yibi recalls. "The whole neighborhood [was our family] because nobody had [an] extended family. . . . [Relatives lived far away, often in another country]. At Christmas time we'd get together and have big parties and all sing Christmas carols together and all make cookies. . . . We had a lot in common. Our parents were spending time together and we spent time together. . . . I think my mother tended to be around more, because we tended to be worse. . . . If there was a fun thing to do, we'd usually do it. . . . [At Paul's birthday parties] . . . we played 'Go fish.' . . . [Paul's] mother hid behind this curtain, and we'd take this fishing pole and hang it over [the curtain], and she hooks this little present on, and we pull it back and have a little present. . . . And [Paul] had a birthday cake that had dimes in it. We knew they were going to be there, so we were looking for them. . . . I'm trying to remember whether [Paul's] father was there. Fathers weren't really very present in most of our lives."

"I don't remember much of either of my parents being very present," recalls Paul. "My memory is being darn near an independent entity, especially during the summer—just go out the door in the morning and come back for refueling, go back outside. . . . There was another regular feature that I was involved in as a kid. The parents, a lot of them, were fairly energetic hikers and during the summer. . . . I remember a fair amount of [overnight] expeditions. . . . I remember being carried on my father's shoulders. I must have been quite small. I think that probably also contributed to the feeling of extended family . . . [that] we had this big happy extended family. . . . I remember not having any friends other than kids who lived on 49th Street. . . . First and second grades we walked half a mile maybe [to school], but for a kid that age it seemed like a long walk. We went down, not on the street, but down the middle of that part of town and there were big discussions about which was quickest. There was the short cut and there was the super short cut. . . . I can't believe there's any place today in the United States where you push a first grader out the door and tell him to walk half a mile to school."

"It was so safe," says Yibi, "that it never entered my head to think about it. It wasn't that I felt safe and secure. It was that it never had occurred to me that there was any other way to be. . . . I remember it was quite a revelation to me when I realized . . . that Los Alamos was different from other places. . . . I just started thinking about it . . . well, what I first noticed was kind of inconsequential but I noticed that our curbs were round. In Santa Fe they were square [*laughter*] . . . and then I started thinking that there were some other differences between Los Alamos and Santa Fe and one of them was that you didn't have to have a pass to get into Santa Fe. . . . That, at that time, was kind of a revelation. I was probably about seven. . . . I was really miffed that I never got to have a pass. They kept raising the age level and I was never old enough."

"With me," says Paul, "there was this feeling, at least on my mother's part, that we were in a very insecure environment in Chicago. So that was part of Los Alamos being paradise, the place you did feel safe and secure. You could go out and play. You couldn't do that in Hyde Park [the Chicago neighborhood]. . . . And basically my mother wouldn't let me out of the yard. And because I was never let out of the yard, I had no playmates. . . . I do have a sense that [Los Alamos] was the place I grew up, very much so. . . . [It was at Los Alamos that] I probably developed a sense of what it's like to have friends, what it's like to have fun with people, what it's like to have buddies and playmates."

For Paul, the idyll came to an end just after third grade. He had begun the school year in Los Alamos, then moved back to Chicago, where he remembers only that he put together "this big notebook on trains. But that's the only thing I remember doing all year. Then the last one or two months we were back in Los Alamos and . . . I was just lost. I had this terrible sensation that the whole class had learned all kinds of stuff that I didn't know. . . . Then we moved to California."

Paul's sister Wendy was six when the Tellers moved to California. She had spent most of her life shuttling back and forth between Chicago and Los Alamos, where she was born in 1946. "From the point of view of having a secure, caring society for little kids, I don't think you could get any better," she recalls. "[There were] tons and tons of kids to play with. . . . Everybody knew everybody else. There were a bunch of extremely bright people who, you could guess, cared a great deal about raising happy, intelligent children. . . .

"There's a story told about the time during the war when my mother went to the grocery store and got some cartons for my brother and put my brother outside in the backyard with the cartons. There was a new fence in the back yard. My mom was real happy because she could put Paul out in the yard and forget about him for a little while. Well, of course, the first thing the little guy did was to stack the cartons and climb over the fence. He was off into Los Alamos. In another place this might be considered dangerous. But in Los Alamos, it's sort of like, 'Well, that didn't work. Call the neighbors. Look around. Oh, there he is.' . . . I remember being upset when we left Los Alamos and begging my parents to go back. . . . Somewhere there are records of my father telling fairy tales and singing songs on the radio [there]. . . . I would dearly love to get my hands on them."

Henry Bethe, David Bradbury, and Lidian King have similar memories of the innocence and fun of swinging open your front door and joining a flock of children roughly your age in imaginative adventures. Lidian and David grew up in Los Alamos; it wasn't until she landed at Wellesley College outside of Boston in the early 1960s that Lidian realized how sheltered her environment had been. David started thinking about the independence and security of his childhood when his own children were growing up—very differently. For Henry, some of the specialness of Los Alamos was manifest to him as a child. Henry, like Paul and Wendy Teller, moved away at the end of the war but made frequent returns, usually for the summer. In 1951 he was back for a full year.

"In a lot of ways," he recalls, "I look at Los Alamos as where I come from. . . . I feel it's home when I go there. The area looks like home, tastes like home, feels like home. . . . I spent most of my summers from the time I was five to 15. I remember [those summers] with enormous fondness. . . . When we were back in 1951 I was seven years old. We lived on 49th Street. The house next door was the Tellers. The house across the street was the Kings. The house at the end of the street was the Marks. There were kids my age at all of the households. . . . When we weren't in school, some group of [us] . . . were together somewhere. . . . I remember the guardhouse. And I remember being very frustrated in 1957. I was finally old enough to need a pass and they had taken the guardhouse away. . . .

"[Back then in the early 1950s] the idea that there were bad people out there who might want to hurt you was not part of my lexicon . . . but I think the whole basic theory of this country was, 'If you saw somebody in trouble, you helped them.' There wasn't a fear of getting involved. If a kid was lost, you all went and looked for the kid and usually found them. . . . . One reads about the era of Charlemagne where a virgin could walk down the road carrying gold and not be molested. . . . I think that could have happened in Los Alamos and maybe still could."

It was when he had children of his own and was living in Tucson that David Bradbury began to think that maybe his childhood had been unusual. "You'd run out the back door and to . . . the Marks, and off into the forest and play Indians, set up a teepee and do all these things. . . . We played army and Indian scout and making forts out in the woods. A lot of 'kick the can.' The Indian [games] had no conflict. Sort of a tribe. One guy was the chief. He had his teepee. There were the squaws. And I'd always be a scout because I thought that was the macho thing to be. . . . The camaraderie we had as neighborhood kids and the exposure to the environment—the outdoors always right there, right at your back door. . . .

"It's just incredible to me [that] as little kids, 10, 11, 12, [and] 15 years old, we used to hike, go down to Bandelier and stay overnight by ourselves and walk all the way up to the Upper Crossings, which is a seven [or] eight mile hike, to be picked up the next day, fishing on the way up, catching snakes. . . . Now, you know, you're afraid to do that."

Lidian King recalls that "when I went to Wellesley College and traveled to Boston and New York at the age of 18, it hit me strongly what an unusual community I had grown up in—almost ideal, but on the other hand, unrealistic in many respects. So it took more adjusting to get in touch with some of the realities of life. . . . There are certain codes you have to follow that I was not aware of [like distrust of strangers]. I was somewhat naive. . . . I was never exposed to materialism, people trying to get ahead, make a lot of money in business, real estate, things like that. We were a community of brain power. The Mark family were our close friends next door. We kids created a little Indian camp and actually went down in [the canyon] and lived there. . . . In some ways, we were quite spoiled. It gave me a solid foundation. . . . The security came from the fact that there was so little to fear.

"I just missed getting a pass. My brother had to have one. That was always one of the fun things—coming back to Los Alamos, stopping at the guard gate, and showing our pass. Also I remember—probably a very early memory—driving to Los Alamos and [past] the guard gate and seeing tanks lined up. For me it was a sense of excitement. I never had any fears about a war there, but it made our life there a little more exciting. I thought of it from a very positive viewpoint. I have these wonderful memories of the community, the personalities and the people, the scientists that we knew. My father was close to Fermi, Oppenheimer, Stan Ulam, Hans Bethe. These people were humanitarians at heart. My contacts with these people were going on hikes and going on picnics and parties. So I developed my views of these people separate from their work.

"That was another thing: as a child, I never really knew what my father did. I knew my father went to the Lab to work. But what he did was not known. I think I began to learn somewhat when we went to Geneva to the Atoms for Peace conferences in 1955 and 1958. [The conferences] mostly focused on the peaceful aspects. That's what I focused on—that my father was a nuclear physicist and he was doing all kinds of neat things that I didn't understand, but that were connected with peaceful uses of atomic energy. So the actual war work was never focused in my mind until I left home and began to read about the war. We felt proud of our community. It was only later when I found out what the war [work of the Lab] was all about—it didn't change any of that for me, but it smashed the idealized image that I had built up."

16

THE SPY, THE H-BOMB, AND THE HEARING

On 29 August 1949—during the lazy end of summer—the Soviet Union surprised the world with the explosion of its first atomic bomb. Suddenly the balance of power had shifted. The United States was not the only country with an atomic bomb. The cold war had become a nuclear reality. Although such a development had been anticipated, no one had expected it would be so soon. The *New York Times* editorialized, "We are prepared for the event intellectually, but not emotionally."[1]

A few months later the world got a hint of how the Soviets had caught up so quickly. On 27 January 1950 a pale man, about five feet eight, with receding brown hair and wire-rimmed glasses, got off a train at London's Paddington Station and walked to the War Office.[2] There he dictated a statement that would reverberate from London to Washington and Los Alamos. The man was Emil Julius Klaus Fuchs. He was 38, one of Britain's top atomic physicists, head of physics research at the atomic energy research center, Harwell. What he told Scotland Yard investigators was that from 1942 to 1949 he had regularly and deliberately passed atomic secrets to the Soviets.

Klaus Fuchs had a lot of secrets to share. He had been at the center of the development of nuclear weapons both in England and the United States. In the early part of the war he worked in Birmingham, England, with Rudolf Peierls. He worked in Los Alamos from 1944 to 1946, when he returned to England and came to Harwell. Fuchs had given the Soviets a virtual blueprint of the uranium bomb, the plutonium implosion bomb, and the early work on the hydrogen bomb. As one of his biographers, Norman Moss, states, "It is given to few scientists to have so direct an influence on the course of international relations as Fuchs had."[3]

Many of the children of Los Alamos remember Fuchs. They also remember a preoccupation with spies. Why else the fences, guard gate, censored mail, bodyguards and pseudonyms? Klaus Fuchs, however, did not at all fit the children's image of what a spy would be like. Nella Fermi Weiner recalls, "There were jokes all the time about Japanese spies infiltrating the place. But Los Alamos was too class conscious and race conscious [for this to happen]. There was a story told about a strapping young man—a big blond—on the bus to Santa Fe. A woman asked him, 'Why aren't you in the service?' and he replied, 'Lady, I'm a Japanese spy.'

"We thought of a spy as someone who would come in, sneak through the fence, grab the secrets and run—at least that's what we kids thought. Of course, the real spy was in our midst. He was as improbable a spy as you could pick. He was sort of a protégé of the Peierls [family]. We used to take Sunday excursions with the Peierls [family], and Klaus Fuchs would come along. He just struck one as a very shy young man. [His confession] came as a big surprise."

Gaby Peierls remembers, "He would come to our house every Sunday, and we would go hiking or do something. He was very nice to us, perhaps one of the few grownups who didn't talk down to us. He always gave very appropriate presents. Just before he was apprehended he had given us a Christmas present of records for dancing. I was sort of mystified [when I learned that he had been a spy]."

Martha Bacher Eaton is one of the few to remember a negative reaction. She did not know Fuchs well, just saw him in passing. She remembers "saying something to my mother about this man that I didn't like. 'Oh,' [my mother] replied, 'He's a very nice man.' Turns out, he was Klaus Fuchs. He was stiff. He was very unfriendly. He never spoke to us. He just went into the place [where] he lived and closed the door. The word I would use now would be 'elusive.' "

Like Martha's mother, Jean, the adults remember Fuchs as being "a nice man," congenial if reticent and aloof. He had a reputation in the Lab of being eager, industrious, and very bright. He was especially popular with the mothers, to whom he made himself available as a babysitter, something much in demand on The Hill. Peggy Parsons Bowditch remembers her mother telling her that Fuchs used to sit for her—and that he had said he would come on the condition he could play the piano.

The young teacher Jeannie Parks Nereson recalls Fuchs's shyness and gift-giving. She and Fuchs had arrived in Los Alamos at the same time. Her vivaciousness attracted him, and he invited her to a dance. But his shyness made her nervous. As she chatted and asked questions, he said nothing. She made a point of dancing with as many others as she could. So she was surprised when some days later, as she was walking to school, she saw him standing by a tree, waiting for her. Close to 50 years later, she remembers how he "pops out, gives me this pin, and takes off. I couldn't believe this. I thought, 'Gee, he hardly even talked to me.' "

Fuchs also struck up an acquaintance with Richard Feynman, the brilliant, iconoclastic physicist just out of graduate school whose wife, Arlene, was dying of tuberculosis in a sanitarium in Albuquerque. Fuchs, who had a car, occasionally lent it to Feynman to make weekend visits to Arlene. (In between visits, Feynman and Arlene corresponded in codes. While the codes gave Arlene a mental challenge and amusement, they did not amuse the censors at Los Alamos.) Feynman and Fuchs became friends and once jokingly talked about spies. Anyone looking for a spy among them, Fuchs said, was likely to think of Feynman, because of his codes and his regular trips off The Hill.[4]

The real spy was also making excursions off The Hill. On a Saturday in June 1945, Fuchs drove his blue Buick to the Castillo Street bridge in Santa Fe, paused, opened the car door wide enough for his contact to jump in, and continued to drive around. After a while he pulled an envelope from his coat pocket and handed it over. The envelope contained information about the upcoming Trinity test and detailed descriptions, including dimensions and detonating systems, of the workings of the plutonium and uranium bombs.[5]

Klaus Fuchs was born in Germany in 1911. His unusual childhood experiences—and what he wrote of them in his confession—help shed light on his motives. His father, Emil, was a Lutheran pastor. He was a strong individual who believed in personal conscience. In his confession, Klaus Fuchs wrote, "I think that the one thing that mostly stands out is that my father always told us that we had to go our own way, even if he disagreed. He himself had many fights because he did what his conscience decreed, even if these were at variance with accepted convention. For example, he was the first parson to join the Social Democratic Party."[6]

Fuchs grew up in a time of political turbulence. As a teenager, he joined the Social Democratic Party and later the Communists. After the burning of the Reichstag, he went underground. "I was lucky," he writes in the confession, "because on the morning after the burning of the Reichstag I left my home very early to catch a train to Berlin for a conference of our student organization, and that is the only reason why I escaped arrest."[7] He also experienced turbulence within his family. His mother committed suicide when he was a boy (as one of his sisters would later). Fleeing Germany, Fuchs went to France and then to England, where he earned a doctorate in physics and began research. He was interned briefly in Canada along with other enemy aliens, became a British citizen, and went to work with physicist Rudolph Peierls on a project known as Tube Alloys at Birmingham. This was the British equivalent of the American Manhattan Project. The Peierlses rented a large house, and Fuchs lived with them, treated almost like a member of the family.

In his confession, Fuchs says that when he learned the nature of the work at Birmingham he decided to re-establish contact with Communists with whom he had had little or no contact for some time. When the Tube Alloys project went to New York and then to Los Alamos, Fuchs told his party contacts of the change in location. For a while he gave information only about the work with which he was directly involved. Then he began giving information about the work of others. At Los Alamos, access to this information was surprisingly easy to obtain. The scientists met in weekly colloquia, usually in Theater 2, to tell of their progress and to hash out problems and possible solutions. Oppenheimer had fought hard for this regular sharing of information. Groves had given in, recognizing the value of the gatherings "to maintain morale and a feeling of common purpose and responsibility."[8]

Seeking to understand Fuchs's motives, biographer Norman Moss theorizes,

> Most of us have ties that might inhibit us from acting on strict political or even moral logic; ties created by background, environment, and family and other personal loyalties. We obey the law as a matter of habit. Setting out to give information to a foreign power would mean breaking out of the framework of laws and customs in which we live our lives.
>
> But Fuchs had none of these ties, and there was no framework to break through. He had grown up in a German society in which the outlines were fluid, one that did not command the natural loyalty of all its citizens. Although he had applied for British citizenship, he did not seem to consider himself to be a part of British society. The flag of his native land was now the swastika, which he had every reason to hate. His only national commitment was to a Germany that did not yet exist, the post-Nazi Germany for which he had been told to prepare himself when he left Berlin. His only tie of loyalty was the one he had worked out in his own mind, to the abstraction of Communism; and because of this to a country that was, for him, hardly less abstract, the Soviet Union.[9]

Fuchs's confession reverberated within the now widely dispersed Los Alamos community. For Gaby Peierls's younger brother Ron, the day the story appeared in the papers is etched in his memory. He and Gaby were walking down the street in Birmingham and saw the headlines. Not too long before, the Peierlses had been skiing in Switzerland, along with Fuchs. Ron had fallen behind, his parents had spoken sharply, urging him to hurry along. Fuchs had quietly stayed with him. Upon seeing the headlines, Gaby and Ron ran home to ask their parents if the accusations could possibly be true. "No," said their stunned mother, Genia, firmly. "They could not be true."

When the story hit the American papers the American Physics Society was meeting in New York, and several wives of physicists who had been at Los Alamos were enjoying a mini-reunion luncheon. As they talked about Fuchs's confession, they realized how little any of them knew about Fuchs the man. The confession was politically delicate for the British government, for the work Fuchs was doing at Harwell was secret. Parts of his confession were deemed too sensitive to read aloud in court. Because he had given the secrets to an ally, he was not charged with treason but was, instead, tried under the Official Secrets Act.[10] He was found guilty and sentenced to 14 years in prison. After nine years he was released and went to live in East Germany.

In the United States the Fuchs case hit the newspapers just as the anticommunism movement that would escalate to a hysteria of loyalty oaths, blacklists, and spy fever was gaining momentum. The shock of the Soviet nuclear explosion and of the victory of the Communists in the Chinese civil war had intensified the fear of Communists.[11] Less than a month after Fuchs made his confession, Senator Joseph McCarthy grabbed the headlines with his now-famous speech in Wheeling, West Virginia, claiming a list of 200 Communists in the State Department.[12]

Just days before Fuchs's confession, President Truman had given a go-ahead for the development of the hydrogen bomb, and a month later he would strengthen the commitment to it. Edward Teller had been pushing for the hydrogen bomb for years. It had been on his mind, even before the details of the early atomic bomb were worked out. With the successful test at Trinity and the end of the war, he was ready to go to work in earnest on the new bomb that would release energy through nuclear fusion.[13]

Other scientists were not so enthusiastic. Some wanted nothing to do with it. Many simply wanted to return to their universities, to the teaching and research that they had dropped to come to Los Alamos. A number, Oppenheimer among them, hoped to see international control of atomic energy and the sharing of information and applications, which could benefit other nations in their biological and medical research.

After the war Oppenheimer, who had left teaching to direct the Institute for Advanced Studies at Princeton, was highly sought after and deeply involved in government consultation on atomic energy. By the early 1950s, according to one estimate, he served on as many as 35 important panels and committees on atomic energy concerns.

In 1947 control of atomic weapons had become the realm of the newly created Atomic Energy Commission and its advisory council, the General Advisory Committee (GAC). Oppenheimer was elected chairman of the GAC. The committee had wrestled with the issue of developing a hydrogen bomb and had come out against it, as had the AEC.[14] The decision pitted the AEC against the powerful State and Defense departments, which wanted to go ahead with the fusion bomb.

Even after President Truman had made a commitment to the bomb's development, some felt that Oppenheimer still was using his influence to dissuade scientists from working on it and perhaps even attempting to slow down the effort. As the cold war intensified in the early 1950s such behavior appeared, to those concerned about Communist sympathizers, increasingly suspect. Back at Los Alamos, Oppenheimer's colleagues had revered his leadership abilities in unifying the scientists and his capacities to grasp the specifics of the various scientific problems and suggest workable solutions. Now, however, colleagues were beginning to notice what seemed like an arrogance and an intolerance for government bureaucrats who did not immediately grasp scientific concepts. Oppenheimer's sometimes cryptic comments and what appeared to some as undue sarcasm had made him enemies.[15]

During his four and half years as the executive director of the Joint Congressional Committee on Atomic Energy, William L. Borden had become increasingly concerned about Oppenheimer's viewpoints and his influence. Shortly after resigning his post, Borden sent a letter to FBI director J. Edgar Hoover listing his concerns about Oppenheimer and concluding that "more probably than not he has . . . been functioning as an espionage agent" and "more probably than not, he has . . . acted under a Soviet directive in influencing United States military, atomic energy, intelligence and diplomatic policy."[16]

Borden's main concerns were Oppenheimer's associations with Communists in the late 1930s and early 1940s, coupled with his lack of enthusiasm for the hydrogen bomb. There was plenty of evidence linking Oppenheimer to Communists up until 1942. His wife, brother, and sister-in-law, and a former girlfriend had been party members, along with several of his students.[17] General Groves had known this when he chose Oppenheimer to head the Lab at Los Alamos. In 1942 these Communist associations had not seemed menacing. In the 1930s many academics had had some association with the party. As Groves himself later wrote, "Almost all our original scientific workers came from academic surroundings. Most of them had been in universities as students or young teachers during the depression years, when there was more than the usual amount of sympathy for Communist and similar doctrines. Almost all of them at one time or another had been exposed to Communist propaganda and had had friends who were secret or even semi-open Communists. I realized what the temper of the times had been."[18]

By the early 1950s the temper of the times had changed drastically. By then such associations, especially by a person so involved in the national security, so influential in both scientific and government circles, and so steadfastly opposed to developing a new bomb, could be interpreted in a more sinister light. Was a man with these associations, and these views, the best person to be making decisions affecting the security of the country? Borden thought not.

Hoover consulted President Eisenhower, who decided as a precaution to revoke temporarily Oppenheimer's clearance while the AEC looked into the matter. Oppenheimer was offered the option of a hearing—ostensibly a simple hearing on whether or not to continue his clearance. Just before the hearing was to start, in the spring of 1954, Senator McCarthy, who was rapidly losing credibility, made a last-ditch effort to revive his cause. In a televised speech, he demanded, "If there were no Communists in our government, why did we delay for eighteen months, delay our research on the hydrogen bomb, even though our intelligence agencies were reporting day after day that the Russians were feverishly pushing their development of the H-bomb? And may I say to America tonight that our nation may well die, our nation may well die because of that eighteen-month deliberate delay. And I ask you, who caused it? Was it loyal Americans or was it traitors in our government?"[19]

Before the Oppenheimer hearing had even started, it had grown from a quiet hearing on a security clearance to what many came to regard as a trial of loyalty. During the hearing Los Alamos scientists flocked to Washington to testify in Oppenheimer's behalf. Among them were Hans Bethe, Norris Bradbury, and Enrico Fermi. Edward Teller also testified, but with a different viewpoint—one that shocked and angered many of his Los Alamos colleagues. "In a great many cases," he said, "I have seen Dr. Oppenheimer act . . . in a way which for me was exceedingly hard to understand. I thoroughly disagreed with him in numerous issues and his actions frankly appeared to me confused and complicated. To this extent I feel that I would like to see the vital interests of this country in hands which I understand better, and therefore trust more."[20]

Asked at the hearing if he felt that Oppenheimer was a security risk, Teller replied, "To the extent that your question is directed toward intent. . . . I would say I do not see any reason to deny clearance. If it is a question of wisdom and judgment, as demonstrated by actions since 1945, then I would say one would be wiser not to grant clearance."[21] Teller's testimony was but a small part of the hearing, but it was a part that his colleagues in Los Alamos would not soon forget.

In June the hearing board declared Oppenheimer a security risk and revoked his clearance. Reactions among his old colleagues at Los Alamos were strong. The children of Los Alamos remember their parents' emotions. "The Oppenheimer case made my father so goddamn mad I couldn't believe it," recalls Bill Jette. "I think it just crushed him," says Bette Peters Brousseau. "If you look at pictures from before and after that time, I think it just took him." People at Los Alamos, she recalls, "couldn't imagine anybody ever accusing Oppenheimer of being unpatriotic. Most of the talk was . . . the feeling I got was . . . that most people were just very mad at Teller."

Martha Bacher Eaton, a college student at the time, remembers "feeling very surprised and very sad about it. . . . He was such a gentle person and very bright. I guess I got the feeling that someone must have been afraid of him. When the hearings were published I remember reading parts of it. I remember thinking what a thoughtful person he was: He never answered a question unless you knew he had considered it. I guess I thought if he had explored communism back then, there was probably a good reason for doing it." Catherine Allison Marshall, also in college, recalls, "My parents were completely on Oppenheimer's side—totally opposed to Teller and appalled at the whole thing. I absorbed that view and continue to be astonished at the way Edward Teller has manipulated our defense policy."

Peggy Parsons Bowditch will never forget the day her father heard of the initial revocation of Oppenheimer's clearance. Her father, Admiral "Deak" Parsons, who had formed a close friendship with Oppenheimer when they lived next door to each other on Bathtub Row, died the next day. He was 52. Peggy believes that the news caused his fatal heart attack. "The night before he died he heard that Oppie had lost his Q clearance. He was so agitated, thinking about how he could prevent this from happening," recalls Peggy. Feeling a sharp pain in his chest, he consulted the encyclopedia and decided he was not having a heart attack. He died of a heart attack the next day in the doctor's office. A political science major at Vassar at the time, Peggy "became militantly anti-McCarthy tactics." "I think I felt that more strongly because of [the cause of] my father's death," she says simply.

Paula Schreiber Dransfield, daughter of physicist Raemer Schreiber, was about 12 during the hearings. She says that the scientists who worked under Oppenheimer were "never able to forgive Teller for what they believe he did to Oppenheimer. . . . It's a little bit disconcerting now for the modern scientific laboratory to be impressed by Teller. Here in Los Alamos! When 10 or 15 years ago none of the scientists here would want anything to do with the man. So that's a deep prejudice that I grew up with: 'If anyone was traitor, Teller was the traitor.' You say that now to a group of scientists, and they are horrified that anybody would have thought that. Yet the scientists who are now my father's age, in their seventies and eighties, really believed it. And I grew up with [the thought that] Teller is probably one of the worst things that could have ever happened to science."

Dorothy McKibbin, the personnel director who welcomed scientists and civilian personnel in Santa Fe, was particularly upset by the Oppenheimer hearings. In an interview with an Albuquerque television station a few years before her death, she spoke of her admiration for Oppenheimer. Asked to compare the characters of Oppenheimer and Teller, Dorothy spoke with passion. The one, she said, is like an orchid, a hothouse flower that is fine and subtle; the other, like a dandelion, "that you kick with your heel."

Henry Bethe, who was about 10 at the time of the hearings, remembers, "My memories are most importantly of the pain that my parents felt at being split from the Tellers. The Tellers were very, very close friends of my parents. My father and Teller had been friends, good friends both scientifically and personally since their student days in the late 1920s in Munich, and the friendship continued after they both came here. In the summer of 1938,

I think, the Tellers and my parents took a car and drove around the American West. . . . They were very close friends. And my father felt an enormous sense of betrayal when Teller testified as he did in the Oppenheimer hearing.

"My father felt his first betrayal at Los Alamos when Teller said there is nothing to work on for the atomic bomb anymore: 'We know how to do that. I want to work on the super bomb.' And my father said, 'No, we don't know how to make the atomic bomb yet. We need you.' Teller apparently was furious that my father was appointed head of the theoretical physics division and not he. But the two of them were fond of each other. Teller's behavior at Los Alamos and his subsequent eagerness to build the super were strains, but it was nothing compared with the enormous and never-healed breach of his testimony at the Oppenheimer hearings. I remember how strained it was in 1957 [a few years after the Oppenheimer hearings] when we were all in La Jolla at the same time. It was very hard."

Paul Teller, who was about 11 during the hearings, remembers that for a long time his father was not welcome in Los Alamos: "My impression is that he felt very unwelcome there for a long time. I didn't have a clue what was going on. Remember that when my parents chose not to involve the kids, they spoke Hungarian. My sister and I spoke no Hungarian at all. It was the official secret language. Those matters were not discussed with people outside the family in my hearing. And when it was discussed between my parents, it was done in Hungarian. . . .

"In retrospect I can see how he seemed weighted down by concern with what was happening in the world and a responsibility for doing what he could. It's probably been that way my whole life, maybe a little less so the very first year of my life, but it's certainly been that way ever since I can remember."

For many years Edward Teller felt uncomfortable in Los Alamos. On a trip there shortly after the Oppenheimer hearing, he saw a colleague from the early days, and walked up to him hand outstretched. The colleague looked at the outstretched hand and turned away. Teller felt ostracized from much of the scientific community, at Los Alamos and elsewhere throughout the country. On the effects of the ostracisim he later said, "If a person leaves his country, leaves his continent, leaves his relatives, leaves his friends, the only people he knows are his professional colleagues. If more than ninety percent of these then come around to consider him an enemy, an outcast, it is bound to have an effect. The truth is it had profound effect."[22]

Peter Oppenheimer was about 13 during the hearings to decide whether Oppenheimer's clearance should be renewed or revoked. At the time he wrote on a blackboard in his room:

> The American Government is unfair to Accuse Certain People that I know
> of being unfair to them. Since this is true, I think Certain People, and may
> I say, only Certain People in the U.S. government, should go to HELL.
> Yours truly,
> Certain People[23]

Some nine years later, when the anticommunism fervor had died down and a new administration had come to power, announcement was made that Oppenheimer would receive the 1963 Fermi award. The prestigious award is presented annually by the AEC in honor of Enrico Fermi, who died of cancer not long after the Oppenheimer hearings.

The award was viewed by many as a reinstatement, an acknowledgment of Oppenheimer's contributions. Still, there was discussion about the political fallout that might result if the president himself were to present the award to the controversial scientist. Then, on 22 November, the White House announced that President Kennedy would personally bestow the honor on Oppenheimer later that month. That afternoon Kennedy was shot in Dallas.

17

A HAT TO REMEMBER

Paula Schreiber Dransfield, daughter of Raemer Schreiber, a young physicist whose Ph.D. project at Purdue University had consisted of building a cyclotron, wasn't yet school age when the war ended. Among her strong early memories of Los Alamos was the gentleness of Robert Oppenheimer. Once, when her father took her to dine at one of the long tables at Fuller Lodge, Paula saw "down the table a little ways . . . a hat and a kind of gangly, elbowy man trying to coax this little boy into eating something. . . . I was very impressed because we were not allowed to misbehave when we went out somewhere, and this little boy was carrying on something terrible, and his father was letting him get away with it and urging him to eat something. . . . We joined them for dinner. It was Oppenheimer and his son Peter.

"At the time I was more in awe of the fact that this little boy was able to behave like that and not get pounded on than I was that that was Oppenheimer who could not discipline his child. That was a memory that was floating around until sometime when the [Los Alamos] historical museum opened. There was quite a to-do about Oppenheimer's hat. And that was his trademark, and when I saw either a picture or the hat, there was a trigger, and I thought, 'Gosh, I've seen that somewhere before,' and I kind of had to go through the memory bank . . . and remember where it was because at my height, at two and a half, the only thing I could see was the hat. . . . Just the little memory that I have of him—of this gentle man totally inept at trying to help his child eat dinner. But you had a sense of that gentleness and that thoughtfulness."

Robert Oppenheimer had exhibited both the depth and breadth of his formidable intellect as a young child. While still a boy, he developed a passion for mineralogy, becoming so knowledgeable that he delivered a paper before the New York Mineralogical Club at the age of 12.[1] In his youth he was voracious for knowledge and was able to grasp ideas quickly. His wide-ranging interests eventually led him to learn eight languages, including Sanskrit; to learn Italian in order to read Dante in the original; and to write poetry, while keeping up with the revolution occurring in physics in the early twentieth century.

The summer after he graduated from the Ethical Culture school in New York, the family took a trip to Germany where Oppenheimer became ill. To build him up before he went off to college, his parents asked one of his high school teachers to take him west to the mountains.[2] The teacher took him to Colorado and New Mexico where he experienced the exhilaration of riding a horse through the wild and desolate countryside.

Oppenheimer entered Harvard University in 1922, graduating just three years later, summa cum laude. After considering such diverse professions as architect, classics scholar, and painter,[3] he had settled on a major in chemistry. In his senior year he became interested in physics through a course in thermo-dynamics. He followed this interest in physics to Europe, where he studied with the world's greatest physicists at the Cavendish Laboratory in Cambridge, at Göttingen in Germany, at the University of Leiden, at the University of Utrecht and at Einstein's alma mater, the Federal Institute of Technology in Zurich.[4]

Oppenheimer returned to northern New Mexico in the summer of 1928 to recuperate from tuberculosis. This time he rented a cabin looking out on the Sangre de Cristo mountains.[5] Once more he took long horseback rides, regaining his health while developing a deep connection with the land. He soon got a job teaching and doing research at the California Institute of Technology in Pasadena and later jointly at the University of California at Berkeley and CIT. By the beginning of World War II, Oppenheimer and experimental physicist Ernest Lawrence had turned Berkeley into a center of physics scholarship in the United States, a bubbling cauldron of ideas, excitement, and eager graduate students, some of whom even followed Oppenheimer back and forth from Pasadena to Berkeley.

It was some time in early 1943 that Dorothy McKibbin, who'd also come to New Mexico to recuperate from tuberculosis, met Robert Oppenheimer. She knew at once that there was something special about this thin man with very blue eyes who walked on the balls of his feet as if he never touched the ground. Whatever this secret project he was heading up might turn out to be—she decided then and there that she would sign on. Dimas Chavez, who graduated from Los Alamos High School in 1955, vividly remembers Oppenheimer "smoking that pipe and his famous hat. I used to sell him the Santa Fe New Mexican newspaper. He was a handsome man. I remember his blue eyes more than anything else. A very gentle man. He had a great smile that would melt me."

Paula Schreiber Dransfield says she grew up with a reverence for Oppenheimer: he "was worshiped up here by the scientists who worked under him during the war." And to the physicists he recruited for the secret project, Oppenheimer conveyed his love of the land. "[Oppenheimer] loved the place, and he gathered about him a bunch of people who also loved it, and I think that kind of spread," recalls Catherine Allison Marshall, who came to Los Alamos in 1943 with her parents Samuel and Helen Allison.

Still, despite the intensity, excitement, and sense of discovery and accomplishment of the early days of the Laboratory when his father was in charge, Peter Oppenheimer says matter-of-factly but forcefully, "In my parents' family there was no romanticizing of Los Alamos. None." He furthermore dismisses the idea of his father as ahead of his time and as seeker of world peace. "My father was a science student and teacher and a creative force in a new field of physics," he says. "In World War II, he became deeply involved in the project at Los Alamos, an effort which seemed worthwhile during the actual war years. But what did he have to do with war and peace? He could be realistic and hard-boiled. He enjoyed being part of the real world. I'm sure it was discouraging to see how crazy the world remained."

The woman who worked briefly as a housekeeper for the Oppenheimers at Los Alamos, now a potter known as Blue Corn, remembers a sense of worry in the Oppenheimer household. "Dr. Oppenheimer was quiet. He kept in his office by himself. I didn't go into his office. That was a sacred place. He was tall and nice-looking. I can picture him yet—with his hat and the pipe he always had in his mouth. [He] was worried. You could tell it by his face; it was down. Even his wife was worried. I didn't know what they were worried about. I sensed a lot of tension. I was wondering why it was. I didn't feel right, so I quit. . . . Later on I realized why I felt that tension. . . . I heard about the bomb from the newspaper and radio [and] . . . I felt bad."

Ellen Wilder, the young girl who had decided that the secret of Los Alamos was the ducks, met Robert Oppenheimer at Los Alamos in 1955. Ellen's father, Ed, an explosives expert, had stayed on at the Lab after the war. While Ellen had stopped playing spy by the time she was six, she remained sensitive to the peculiarities of the town, including the regular explosions. Playing on the playground at school she would listen for these explosions, noting if one were particularly loud and often thinking, "Oh, that was a good one."

In high school, she gained a new perspective on the town when her classmate Butch, a projectionist for the school Radio Club, suggested that she come watch some film clips that he had been asked to show for a gathering of scientists. Ellen recalls, "I had second or third period free, so I went up to see Butch. The film he was projecting was unedited films of Hiroshima and Nagasaki that the Japanese had taken and, I guess, that the army had taken. I think it was the first conference on the effects of radioactive weapons. Of course, no kids were supposed to be there.

"Now, who knows why they hired a kid to show the films, but they did. There was no narration, just all this footage of people walking around with their skin falling off and those reverse kimono burns where the flowers burned onto their skins. We watched . . . and I was appalled. I thought at first,

'Maybe the people at Los Alamos didn't know this was what happened.' It did not seem possible to me that they would have known that it was going to be like this. I thought about it a lot. . . . Those pictures are still in my mind. . . . It made real to me something that I had probably never really thought about. Then I went around and tried to figure out what had happened. . . . At some point, someone told me, 'I think Oppie was worried about this more than any of the rest of us.' "

One of Ellen's close friends in high school was Jim Bradbury's younger brother, John. On one of Oppenheimer's visits to The Hill, the Bradburys were hosting a reception for him. Ellen decided to tell Oppenheimer that she shared his worries about the effects of the bombs. She remembers, "I was at the Bradburys' for a cocktail party, and Oppenheimer was there. He was always surrounded by a lot of people because he was really a hero at Los Alamos. I was passing hors d'oeuvres. I was in awe of him. I was probably 16 or 17. I went up to him with this tray of whatever I was passing, and I said, 'Oh, I think you're a saint.' He was really taken aback, and he said, 'Why did you ever say a thing like that to me?' And I said, 'Well, because you had second thoughts.'

"He was just stricken. I could see his face change. It was like he was going to cry or something terrible was going to happen. He turned away and went over to the piano. He had put his hat on the piano. He put his hat on and went outside for a minute . . . Lois [Bradbury] came up to me and said, 'What did you say to Oppie?' I was sort of stricken, too. . . . The idea that anything I said to Oppie would have affected him had never occurred to me. . . . I think he was really taken unaware that the question was recognized that widely, that there was no place he was safe anymore, that he had opened the Pandora's box and it was never going to close anymore. . . .

"I hadn't intended any of that. . . . He was the only person I could think of who had tried to figure how complicated this was. . . . I [had] thought, 'Well, here's the man who really worried about this.' I thought maybe he and I were the only people who were worried, so I was going to tell him I thought he was a kindred soul. . . . The idea that I had touched him really scared me."

18

THE LURE OF THE LAND

As the site of the development of the atomic bomb, the Pajarito Plateau has a singularly appropriate geological history. It was formed more than a million years ago by a huge explosion—the eruption of the Jemez volcano.

The volcano spewed forth ash that formed a soft rock called tuff, which is in some places 1,000 feet thick. Then the unsupported top of the volcano collapsed, making a huge caldera or depression, 15 miles across and 50 miles around. Observing this caldera today from a lookout at Bandelier National Monument, one sees a vast hole lined with rocky cliffs—in shades of pink, salmon, and gray. The rocks have a hollow sound and bits of mustard-yellow or grayish-green moss clinging to them. Along with the rocks are tiny shrubs, prickly cactus, small yellow flowers, and gnarled gray branches with shapes eerily reminiscent of reindeer antlers. Within the caldera are peaks and valleys. The best known of the valleys—etched in the memory of the children of Los Alamos—is Valle Grande. It looked like a gigantic sea of undulating grass—in some seasons full of wildflowers.

There has always been something magical about this land. Those who have lived there say it has the bluest skies anywhere. The air is crisp and dry. The sun almost always shines, yet even in summer the nights are cool and rejuvenating. A hail storm can pelt the earth with clattering ice balls, then end as abruptly as it began, leaving the colors brighter, the air fresher, and a pungent smell of wet earth and trees that those who breathe as children never forget. "One of the greatest delights of the New Mexican climate is the magical quality of the atmosphere," Martha Bacher's mother, Jean, would later write. "The clarity of the light is a shimmering and tangible thing."[1]

In the early 1900s the area's dry air and sunshine attracted those seeking to improve their health. Several people who would influence the direction of Los Alamos originally came to northern New Mexico to regain their strength. The first of these arrived at the turn of the century. He had enlisted with the Rough Riders in the Spanish-American War, but a bout of typhoid nearly finished him before he saw any action. His name was Ashley Pond, and he came to northern New Mexico to recover. He would die before the

Manhattan Project was even envisioned, but his dream would provide Robert Oppenheimer and General Groves with a suitable site for their top-secret project.

Taking long horseback rides over the rocky scrub land, cooking over a campfire and sleeping under the stars, Pond felt invigorated. During these rides he thought about his childhood as a frail child spending long, lonely days in boarding-school infirmaries. As his daughter, Peggy Pond Church later wrote, "He began to dream of a school where city boys from wealthy families like his own could regain their heritage of outdoor wisdom at the same time that they were being prepared for college and the responsibilities which their position in life demanded. He was convinced that hours spent on the trail with a knowledgeable cow pony would teach a boy more that he needed to know as a man, than he could ever learn from textbooks."[2]

In 1917 Pond bought an 800-acre homestead on an isolated spot high on Pajarito Plateau and began his school with one pupil. In its 25 years of existence, the Los Alamos Ranch School never grew big (its largest enrollment was 46 boys ages 12 to 18), but its graduates are an impressive lot. They include writers William S. Burroughs and Gore Vidal and businessmen Arthur Wood, former president of Sears Roebuck, Inc., and Bill Veeck, former owner of the Chicago White Sox.

The school was largely a self-contained community. It had its own stables, machine shops, electrical plant, ice house, and extensive vegetable and flower gardens presided over by Adolfo Montoya, a man who loved the earth and all that grew on it. Montoya could coax from desert soil prize-winning flowers along with every kind of vegetable.

"My dad had on both sides of the road rows of flowers—with smaller ones in front, then taller," recalls his daughter Margaret Montoya Caperton, who grew up on the ranch. "There were some flowers blooming at all times. My dad took the flowers to flower shows. He won ribbons and trophies for [them]. Anything he took in—he'd get a prize. . . . Then we had rows of berries—raspberries. He had just about every vegetable imaginable. . . . He loved working with the earth. He read widely, had all kinds of books and tried all kinds of things."

When the army arrived, Margaret remembers, "They tore up everything. They drove in with these big trucks. Trees went down that you'd watched grow. . . . It was devastating, really devastating, to know that such change was taking place. We didn't know what they were going to do. All these beautiful lawns [the school] had, they'd drive right over them as if they weren't there—something we had taken care of so carefully. . . . I cannot believe how much has happened in such a few years." The Manhattan Project would bring vast and permanent changes to the Pajarito Plateau. Peggy Pond Church, who spent her early years discovering the wonders of the mesa, devoted her later years to chronicling the changes. In poems and stories she wrote of her sadness at the transformation of the land from an open wilderness of timeless beauty to a closed, bomb-producing government city "with its fierce and guarded laboratories . . . and the forbidding metal fence bearing in enormous red letters the warning DANGER! PELIGROSO!"[3]

As a child in the years preceding the founding of the Ranch School, Peggy had spent long, solitary hours riding bareback, feeling connected both with her surroundings and with those who had explored the same land hundreds of years earlier. Once she rode to the ancient village of Tsirege and whiled away hours "wondering about the vanished people who had chosen to build their homes in situations of such extraordinary beauty."[4]

Many years later she revisited the same spot to spend a night out-of-doors. "As I slept and woke and looked up at the turning patterns of the stars, I could hear through the earth the hum of great dynamos that I knew had to do with modern man's purpose of destruction. . . . I never drove past the forbidding fences without tears in my eyes, and my hatred of the new city of Los Alamos was still sore," Peggy would later write.[5]

Despite the changes wrought by the Manhattan Project, children arriving at Los Alamos in the 1940s found magic and enchantment in the land and responded to it. "There was something about it—being up there that high—that made you feel close to God," remembers Frances Smith Weiland, who arrived in Los Alamos as a child in 1945. "As a teenager sometimes I'd drive up to the mountains and just go sit on a rock and look out," adds Frances's classmate Robert Martin. "There's a real spiritual quality to the land here, a real grabbing quality. It's automatic and instinctive," observes another classmate, Laurie Archer. "In spite of the harsh visual quality, there's something very nurturing about this land. Here you see the bare bones of the earth without the superficiality of greenery and pretty flowers."

The children also responded to the sense of exhilaration, of wildness, discovery, and oneness with nature. Bill Jette remembers his "experiences with seeing that part of the world and being able to ride a horse through it in places that very few people have ever gotten to see, of catching trout in a mountain stream that nobody has ever fished before. That's the kind of experience that you're just damned lucky to have."

Joe Smith, who lived in Los Alamos from the summer of 1945 until he left for college in 1953, recalls "a lot of great fishing trips, fishing the Rio Grande, sleeping on the rim of the Rio Grande, then hiking down and catching fish for breakfast and bringing it back up to cook on an outdoor fire. That's heady stuff, even today it's heady stuff."

"As a child I took long walks [in Bandelier]," recalls Martin Kellogg, who arrived in Los Alamos in 1946 at the age of seven. "I remember camping by a creek and listening to it gurgle all night." Kellogg, who works at the Lab, as his father did before him, has never seriously considered leaving Los

Alamos. His sense of connection to the land—and the views—is too strong: "It's important to be able to see the mountains from where I live."

When the children of Los Alamos talk about their childhoods they invariably describe a favorite view. Views were important for their parents, too, especially the mothers, for whom isolation, lack of amenities and army red tape varied from frustrating to unbearable.

"Whenever things went wrong at Los Alamos—and there was never a day when they didn't—we had this one consolation: we had a view," writes Ruth Marshak, who taught third grade at the Los Alamos school during the war.[6]

"I love this country—the mesas, the valleys, the hills, the quietness, the solitude," says Paula Schreiber Dransfield, who grew up in Los Alamos, left for many years when she went to college, then found the land pulling her back. "This house is on a canyon. . . . You can climb down over the side here and be in the canyon and relatively away from everybody within five minutes."

Dimas Chavez, who grew up in Los Alamos and later worked at the Lab, remembers the joy he felt as a grown man, going for a noontime walk. "Fifteen minutes and you're off in a canyon. There's no one around you. You sit there on a rock looking down a canyon, watching deer . . . watching birds. There's such a . . . quietness."

The children also remember the special quality of the horizon. "Something that's absolutely clear is my heightened sense of horizons," says Joan Bainbridge Safford. "If you come from the East you don't see these expanses."

"The sky's enormous. The horizons are much further. You feel like the world's a bigger place," says Henry Bethe, who was born in Los Alamos during the war and spent most of his childhood summers there. "You get used to seeing the horizon," says Lew Agnew, a physicist who has lived in Los Alamos since 1950. Seeing the horizon, he says, "seems to lend something to understanding. . . . It is the need to . . . look forward . . . to the next decade, to the next turning point in human affairs." "I think the landscape gets into your blood," adds Joan Mark Neary, who arrived in Los Alamos at age six, left to go to college, and later brought her husband to a rural area outside Santa Fe to raise their three sons in the land she loves. "I really enjoy the brightness and the sunshine. I would have a terrible time moving into a place that was dark and cloudy. . . . I've taken a lot of pictures of landscape. I like to go outside and look at it. . . . It's an important way to get away from chaos."

19

COMING OF AGE IN THE 1960s: VIETNAM, THE ENVIRONMENT, AND CIVIL RIGHTS

As the social ferment of the late 1960s swirled around them, Graham Mark, David Bradbury, and Clayborne Carson, Jr., were in their mid-twenties. All three had grown up in Los Alamos, leaving for college in the early 1960s. By the time they graduated, the sit-ins, protests, and marches for peace and civil rights were at their height. All three reacted to this new world of activism based on their individual experiences at Los Alamos. Graham and Clayborne jumped in wholeheartedly—Graham into the Vietnam resistance, Clayborne into the civil rights movement. David thought back to the sense of harmony with nature that he had assimilated from his many visits to the pueblo and to the peace he had felt as a boy sitting quietly alone on a rock. He remained aloof from the frenzy of the times. But he did develop strong views about a cause that would become another legacy of the 1960s: environmental protection.

David, Graham, and Clayborne all arrived in Los Alamos in the 1940s. David was born there in 1944; Graham arrived as an infant in the early summer of 1945, when his father, mathematician Carson Mark, brought his family from Canada. After the war Carson Mark stayed on to head the Lab's theoretical physics division. In 1948, when Clayborne was four, his father, Clayborne Carson, took a job as a security guard with the Atomic Energy Commission, becoming one of a very few African Americans employed there.

All went on to academic achievement, eventually earning Ph.D.s—Clayborne in African-American history, Graham in evolutionary biology, and David in biogeography. Both David and Graham now work at the Lab. Clayborne is a professor at Stanford University and director of the Martin Luther King, Jr., Papers Project.

Graham Mark

Graham Mark was just a few weeks old when he came to Los Alamos from Montreal in the early summer of 1945. He arrived by train with his mother and his older brother and two older sisters. Graham left for college in 1962, returned for a year in 1968 to work at the Lab, left again in 1969 for graduate school, and returned to work at the Lab once more in 1984.

During his tenure in 1968–69, Graham became something of a cause célèbre. Like many other young men across the country he was opposed to the war in Vietnam and active in protests. His mother remembers his saying he would not eat the food in her house because it was the "fruits of war." Graham simply recalls that he was "thinking things out."

He recalls, "[I] went away to college in 1962, came back here and worked for a year in 1968. That's when my Vietnam opposition was really strong. I [worked at the Lab] in basically a peon job because I didn't know what I wanted to do. [I] figured eventually I'd go back to school. . . . [I] worked on a project that was described to me as being completely not related to weapons. Turns out it was weapons-related. When I took that job, I thought it was pretty ironic that I was working at the Lab while opposing much of what it was doing and I enjoyed the irony. . . . I organized high school kids. We had a few marches against the war. I started a free school. I got hauled in eventually by the FBI. They were questioning my clearance [to work at the Lab]. We had a big fight basically, and I told these guys off. At that time, I really thought if there were something I could do to stop the war that required breaking security I'd do it. . . .

"I believed that the war was really an undemocratic situation. I don't know where those ideas came from. My mother was pretty sympathetic. My dad— I remember once we were watching some TV news, and there was a story about some demonstrators getting dragged out of a building, and these guys were limp, and they were getting dragged out. And my dad was really— shall we say emphatic?—with the idea that these guys ought to be dragged down with their heads knocked on the stairs. . . .

"But they were basically pretty supportive. I was prepared to go to jail [instead of be drafted]. They never tried to talk me out of it. I still don't know how my father felt about it. He never said he thought it was the wrong thing to do, but he never really supported it explicitly either. [The] draft board up here wanted me in jail because I had given them a lot of trouble. The state Selective Service also wanted me in jail as an example, so they set it up that I would be the only guy inducted this particular day except for some guys they knew wouldn't give any trouble. There were about 15 of us, I guess. The Resistance group in Albuquerque organized a big demonstration at the induction center. . . .

"People at the induction center were real upset because of the demonstration. We all went in for physicals, and the doctor detected a heart murmur, so he sent me off to a public health doctor to get a test. And the public health doctor said I couldn't go in. I became 4-F. It turned out later—I talked with a guy who worked at the induction center—that the public health doctor shouldn't have done that. There was no medical basis for their letting me off. But this doctor was angry at the draft. He was using me to give them a hard time. I actually saw a doctor [still later] who said there was a heart murmur there, but it was not significant. There was a judgment call there, basically, I guess. They could have inducted me, I think, and they should have really."

In 1969 Graham and his wife, Carol, moved to Albuquerque, where he started graduate school, initially in history. "I thought to protest the war I needed to learn something about U.S. history. I got burned out with that after a while, started law school, was in law school for a year, dropped out of school, worked with guys building a house, and finally decided to go back to school in biology. I got a masters and a Ph.D. We were gone from Los Alamos from 1969 to 1984."

Part of the reason Graham returned to the Lab in 1984 was to give his three sons—Zachary, Jesse, and Jacob—the opportunity to live close to nature and to get to know the land as he had as a child. He also wanted them to live near their grandparents—an experience he had not had. "One of the things I remember about growing up here was being far removed from my relatives other than my immediate family. So for my kids, I wanted to have them close to relatives if possible. Another thing I remember a lot from growing up here was the country. The rocky country, the dryness, the mountains, the fact there's still a lot of wilderness around here. Being able to go skiing and hiking; the small-town part of it.

"In 1984 I had finished a postdoctorate in biology, and I didn't have any job prospects. I still had friends who worked here. This guy offered me a job in computers. So I stopped being a biologist and became a computer guy. [My work is] not directly related to the weapons program. [But] I write programs that could be used by people who use the computers to design bombs, and I get paid basically because of the big computer facility here to design weapons . . . so I can't pretend I don't help with the effort.

"It was a big conflict and still is in my mind—less now, I guess, than it was for a while. I'm not comfortable working on weapons projects. But at this point in my life I feel like I just have to put up with some stuff I'm not real comfortable with in order to give my kids a good home. If I had perfect freedom of choice I wouldn't do it, but I don't feel that I have. I have to sacrifice some of my conscience for some other benefits.

"Growing up here, there was the Lab over there. [It] was totally mysterious. My dad worked there all the time. I hardly ever saw him. I didn't know what he did. I still don't. . . . It was not discussed. Every once in a while there were open houses. I got to see really neat stuff. I never really understood what was going on. Well, that's not true. . . . You knew nuclear weapons was part of the work. You could hear explosions . . . stuff like that. It was always in the air, but not something I ever talked about with my folks, at least when I was little. Part of it was that my dad was always working. . . .

"I was influenced by the scientific culture. My dad was a big shot in the Lab. We used to have a lot of Nobel Laureates coming around. I grew up with the idea that that's how everybody was—that everyone was at that level of intellect and achievement. . . . [It was stimulating] in a way. It was also kind of intimidating once I realized I probably would never make it. [The scientific culture at Los Alamos] certainly influenced my going into science. I still kind of think that scientific work is the only really important kind of stuff you can do. . . .

"As a little kid, I thought a lot about nuclear war—fallout, stuff like that. I didn't actually appreciate what my father did until we moved back here in 1984. By then I had gotten interested in Los Alamos as a sort of historical phenomenon. The difference between Vietnam and World War II is something that interested me and that I've done some reading on. It seems to me that during World War II there really wasn't much choice about developing the bomb. There were enough reasonable grounds to believe that the Germans could get atomic weapons before the United States could. That's up to about 1945, before Hiroshima probably. At that point it was not clear that the weapons had to be used. So that gets a lot harder. By then, the people here didn't have any control over it. After that, it gets even more confusing—the work that happened after 1945, all the way up to now. . . . If nuclear weapons had been used in Iraq I would have left [the Lab]. That was a case I really thought about."

David Bradbury

Just when or where the idea came to him David Bradbury doesn't know, but gradually he came to think of the natural world as having greater value than the world of people—and of people as intruders into that world. "People are not my favorite thing," he says simply. Natural history, on the other hand, has fascinated him since childhood. He honed this interest in college and graduate school, delving into the relationship of plants to soils, rocks, and man—and "man's impact on the earth's ecosystem."

After completing his doctorate at UCLA, David taught at the University of Arizona, then returned to northern New Mexico as he had always known he would. First he worked for the New Mexico State Land Office in Santa Fe. Then, in some ways coming full circle, he took a job in environmental restoration at the Los Alamos National Laboratory.

Not yet two when his father was named Laboratory director, David grew up in a one-industry town, with his father head of that industry. One effect of his father's new job was his mother's growing involvement in official entertaining and the additional role for the Indian woman, Isabel Atencio, who worked for the family as David's nanny. David's brothers were eight and ten years older, and while they were in school, he followed Isabel about. He recalls with fondness his closeness to Isabel and the traditions of the pueblo. "The Indian lady that worked for my mom, Isabel Atencio, was like a nanny to me, more than a maid really. She would direct me around as I grew up. [Isabel] used to teach us the words here and there. I know a few words in Tewa. I used to stay [at the pueblo] in the summer sometimes when the folks would travel. I have two—no, three—memories of [when I was little] at the pueblo. One is peeing in the little can under the bed at night. Another is going out early in the morning one time—I'm not sure if this was part of a ceremonial thing—and having Isabel tell me about yucca, using it to wash your hair. And the other [memory] was as mundane as Isabel's daughter playing with me on the bed, [showing me] how to hook a key chain. To me that was magical. I didn't see how she did that.

"I was very, very close to Isabel and that family. [After I'd grown up] I would visit about once every year, for a feast day or something. One Christmas they were doing special dances in their home, and only one at a time could come out of this room to talk to me, then go back into the room. When I brought my first born to visit in San Ildefonso, Isabel was curing some older person there in the house. You do not go into the houses at this time. It's a sacred business. They sort of said she was busy doing something. No one will tell you. We're not supposed to know. But they said that it was fine for the child to visit because a child is pure. So her son took the child to see her. To me that's beautiful because they have their integrity."

During the social and political activism of the 1960s David remained detached. "The 1960s era was not difficult for me," he says. "I was mostly apolitical." He adds that he would have no problem working with weapons. "I don't have big feelings about that. I would classify myself as pro-peace, but then I'm also very much anti-growth. I think the world is going all the wrong way. We're beyond the resource space right now. One nest can support so many birds. Maybe weapons are the only way man can reduce population. Weapons are a last resort, but the fact is, the world's population needs to be pared down, and conflict may be the only way we're going to do it. But I am not pro-war, not at all.

"I'm most strongly pro-nature, pro-earth, pro-tree. It's hard to say where my reverence for the natural world comes from—from just being in it, I guess. It's the serenity [that I remember]. [As a child], I used to sit sometimes on a rock, just go sit. Just watching an ant, not thinking, 'What's its place in evolution?' but just watching, [experiencing] tranquility, peacefulness, quiet.

"I went to graduate school at UCLA. Los Angeles must have been beautiful in the 1930s, but now—people, people, people, people. Too many people. I was always going to come back. I never felt that I was going to live anywhere else for very long. It was all temporary. I always was going to come back to northern New Mexico, not necessarily Los Alamos [he lives in Santa Fe]. It's curious to me—the whole New Mexico environment that draws people, [the reasons] artists came here. There is something different. You can be in Tucson—it's not the same when you see the clouds, the rain, the blue sky, the harmony of the mountains. . . .

"I don't have any problem with what [our parents] did—made the bomb or whatever. What people are lacking when they think in these terms is the urgency that was there at that time. Something needed to be done. Then you take it out of context and say, 'Hey, that was the wrong thing to do— you killed many thousands of people.' But at that time, in that context, it wasn't the wrong thing to do. There was another part of it. They were scientists, [facing the question], 'Does this science work?' A lot of them were just into that. And Trinity. Boom: it worked. It doesn't bother me enough to have to justify it. I don't dwell on it.

"I can argue that man doesn't have good foresight. He's very, very good at working in crises but doesn't look ahead much. Some may have. For instance, Oppenheimer's Hindu quote at Trinity, 'I am become death, the destroyer of worlds,' may have expressed his concern with the magnitude of the deed. I don't know. That man was very, very bright and may well have been thinking way ahead of his time."

Clayborne Carson

"If you think growing up in Los Alamos was special for white kids, that was many times truer for me. My upbringing made me totally exceptional as a black person. It set me apart from just about everyone." Clayborne Carson is a professor of history at Stanford University, specializing in recent African-American history. He is also the director of the Martin Luther King, Jr., Papers Project, whose goal is to publish 14 volumes of King's papers. He figures it will keep him busy until he retires.

A scholar who weighs his words, Clayborne came to the study of the civil rights movement through his own involvement in the mid-1960s. In 1963, after his freshman year at the University of New Mexico, he traveled to Washington, D.C., to attend that summer's civil rights march. There he heard Martin Luther King, Jr., give his famous "I Have a Dream" speech. By 1964 Clayborne was in Los Angeles, "a small-town kid thrown in the midst of an urban, sophisticated life."

He remembers: "My parents were pioneers . . . and I think it took a lot of nerve to be pioneers like that . . . to take their kids to an all-white town. . . . For my dad and, I guess, a lot of blacks of his generation, life during the depression had been hard. The military and federal employment were their way out. My dad was in the military during World War II. I was born in 1944 while he was overseas. He joined us in 1946. That's my first memory of him. He got a job as a security guard in Los Alamos, working for the AEC, and we came to New Mexico in 1948. First we lived in Santa Fe and in Espanola. Then, in 1949, we finally moved to Los Alamos when the houses in the north community were built. Our house was a duplex on the outskirts of town. We had a spacious three-bedroom house—something we would not have been able to afford elsewhere.

"I could walk out my front door and be in a canyon or go climb a mountain. They were our playgrounds. . . . The canyon and mountain shape my memory. I spent a lot of time hiking, increasingly by myself as I got older. I think those times by myself were important.

"Was Los Alamos unusual? Sure. First there was the notion of a fence around the town that sticks in my mind. My dad was a security inspector. He wore a gun. So I kind of grew up with the notion that this was a protected place and that there was a strong distinction between those on the inside and those on the outside. My dad was not a scientist. He had not gone to college, and we didn't have a lot of books around . . . and here I was going to school with all these kids of scientists. . . . The school had well-motivated students, bright, disciplined. . . . I remember school as a positive experience. . . . I knew I was pretty bright, but it took a lot to stand out, particularly since I was interested in math and science. I had a fascination with that area, and there were some precocious kids.

"There was a sense of security in the town. You could let your kids go. That developed in the kids a sense of having control, especially as we got older. I don't recall any fear of crime. The only thing that could [hurt you physically] was an accident.

"There was [also] a strong sense that we were privileged middle-class kids. When we would play other schools in sports, they would try hard to beat us [because of this]. . . . I recall a sense of resentment [that they held against us for all we had]. I encountered more racism in sports than in other areas. I played a lot of baseball. I remember the first day of practice of the Babe

Ruth league, the coach said, 'I don't care if you're nigger or white.' And I had a basketball coach who watched me jump, and said, 'You colored boys all jump well.'

"It's almost worse when somebody doesn't realize they're prejudiced. I remember going to the ice-skating rink about the time of Little Rock [when Arkansas Governor Orval Faubus called in the National Guard to keep black students from attending classes at Central High School]. Some older kids blocked my way saying kiddingly, 'We're not going to let you pass.' There again was that insensitivity. I think the anti-black feeling was stronger among the Spanish. . . . There was also a lot of anti-Spanish prejudice [from the whites]. That was more upfront. There were two other black families at Los Alamos then, the Stones and the Johnsons. We were closer as a family to the Johnsons. I remember a lot of get-togethers with them. Patty Johnson was in my class.

"When I came to dating, it was hard. . . . I dated white girls. But I knew there was some pressure from their parents not to. . . . So I never knew, when a relationship ended, if it was just ending [naturally] or if they were being pressured to end it. . . . For black girls, I think it was harder. I don't think my sister had a date in high school. And I don't think Patty Johnson did either, other than me. . . .

"I had this identity of being black but not being exposed to black culture. . . . I had a fascination about the black community. . . . I remember I went with my dad to Denver and I went to my grandad's funeral in Detroit. In both those incidents we stayed in black communities. I remember with fascination that I could walk outside and see all these black people. . . . And I remember when our cousins came to visit, they were dancing differently and talking in a different way. There was something going on there that I felt I was missing. . . . I had a strong sense of the civil rights movement back in high school. I remember that my [white] friends had no empathy for it. Most couldn't conceive of why I would be interested.

"After my freshman year at the University of New Mexico, I was restless. I wanted out. I applied to Harvard and to the Peace Corps. I was accepted into training for the Peace Corps and sent to Arizona State. I was one of two blacks there. I did well in the training, but in the end I was not accepted. I still don't understand why. . . . I had a sister living in Los Angeles so I enrolled at UCLA. . . . Los Angeles was nirvana. I found excitement and new opportunities. . . . I just kind of went wild over it. . . . It was some of the best times of my life.

"My first job was working at a doughnut shop at 5th and Hill [in the heart of the hustling district]. I worked 11 P.M. to 7 A.M. I was this wide-eyed kid who didn't even know what hustling was. My second job was with Columbia Pictures at Sunset and Gower. I lived first in West Los Angeles, where I got to know people in the civil rights movement. . . . I became increasingly active and started working for the LA *Free Press*. I had a car, a motorcycle, and an apartment in the hills above Hollywood. For someone 20 years old, [I felt I had arrived].

"I worked for Columbia Pictures in advertising research. . . . Every hour I wanted to work I could work. I was also trying to be a student and got decent grades. And I was being an activist and beginning to write. What I did was to cut out sleeping. . . . It was the absolute opposite of Los Alamos. I was doing things I could never do in Los Alamos. It was my antidote to Los Alamos. And my politics moved very rapidly to the left.

"I majored in Latin American history because that's what I had the most classes in. . . . In June 1967 I graduated from UCLA, with the draft hot after me. My wife and I decided to leave the country. We bummed around Europe for six months. Then she got sick in Spain. It turned out that she had diabetes. I was trying to get landed-immigrant status in Canada, [but that didn't work out]. We came back in the spring of 1968, about the time Martin Luther King was assassinated.

"I had tried to file for conscientious-objector status, but the Los Alamos draft board wouldn't give it to me . . . partly, I think because I had been a nominee to the Air Force Academy and West Point . . . and partly because my dad was a career military person and here I was claiming to be a CO [conscientious objector]. . . . Basically I was an antiwar protester. My own sense is I was not opposed to war in principle, but it has taken me a long time to come to this view. . . . I kept appealing everything. My father had high security clearance. He got called in and asked about my political activities. We got to the point—he and I—that we just did not discuss politics. We'd only talk about sports. . . . My mother and one brother got called in [too]. None of them ever asked me not to do it, but I know they all paid a price. . . .

"I never got conscientious-objector status, but after I fought [the draft board] for many years, they gave it to my brother. Eventually I think they kind of gave in on that point. . . . Of my four brothers, two went into the navy—one died there. One went CO, and the other was too young. I would not have gone to fight in Vietnam. I would have gone to jail or to Canada first. . . .

"Even now I have reservations about pacifism. I'm close to it, but my arguments are more pragmatic. . . . Is it moral to be personally so morally pure that you're against evil but you won't fight it? Or is it better to compromise your personal purity and fight the evil? The argument that one should maintain personal morality at all costs is troublesome to me. . . .

"I saw the fact that I had grown up in that community and once worked on weapons [myself] as an irony. . . . I had worked at the Lab summers [during high school and before college]. I saw how much waste and extravagance goes into weapons. . . . One summer that I worked at the Lab I was doing physical testing, pouring a solution into capsules. I would dispose of the excess solution. One time [a scientist] watched me do this and started laughing. I didn't know why. Then he told me, 'That solution costs $3,000 an ounce.' Here I had been discarding it because no one told me not to. . . . That was part of this sense of extravagance, that with the government paying, you could do a lot of things. . . . When I became aware of poverty and found that money was not available for other social purposes, it gave me a special anger."

20

YOU *CAN* GO HOME AGAIN, BUT ...

Dimas Chavez

One day in 1966 Bob Porton answered the telephone in his office in the public relations department of the Lab and said to a co-worker, "Dimas, you're not going to believe this, but this joker here claims he's Sargent Shriver and wants to talk to you." Dimas picked up the phone to hear a "guy with this Eastern, Bostonian accent" ask, "Is this Dimas Chavez?" As Dimas recalls the conversation, Sargent Shriver went on to say, "I'd like you to fly out to Washington. I've got a job for you."

The trip to Washington was a milestone in the career of Dimas Chavez. It was also a heady experience for a man not yet 30, who had arrived in Los Alamos speaking no English and gone through school convinced that he could not compete academically with the children of scientists and other professionals. Dimas's father had come to Los Alamos as a heavy-machine operator and laborer; his mother was a homemaker with five children. The family lived in a small cabin that had once housed a grounds-keeper of the ranch school. Graduating from Los Alamos High School in 1955, Dimas had taken a course to become a telegraph operator, worked at a gas station, operated a forklift at the Lab, and eventually worked his way through college. Returning to the Lab after college, he worked in the personnel and the public relations departments where, among other things, he headed up efforts to hire people with disabilities.

Because the Lab's work in hiring people with disabilities had won national attention, Shriver sought out the person responsible for the Los Alamos success when he was looking for a new head for the Joseph P. Kennedy Foundation. Dimas did not take that job, but, with Shriver's assistance, he did take another. This job took him away from both Los Alamos and a sense of inferiority that had dogged him since his grade-school days. As a child he had often felt frustrated by his humble beginnings. Away from Los Alamos, Dimas climbed quickly through the ranks of government service. He returned to the Lab at a higher level, then came back to Washington. Today he works for the State Department in technical security for embassies, and he lives in a posh Washington suburb with his Brazilian-Japanese wife and two young daughters.

As Dimas advanced in Washington, he earned what, to him, is the badge of status in Los Alamos—knowledge of science and a highly classified technical security clearance. In his early days at the Lab in personnel and public relations he had felt second-rate. He might be a college graduate, adept at working with people, but he did not feel respected. "In Los Alamos, to work in the Compartmentalized Program, one needed to have a special, highly sought-after clearance. So when I accepted this position at the State Department, the undersecretary said, 'You're going to need a Compartmentalized Clearance.' I said, 'Wow, I've heard that before. Gee, it's here too!'"

The moment of triumph came when the State Department asked him to make a technical presentation at Los Alamos. "I arrived in Los Alamos to make a technical security presentation," he recalls. "And here are all these guys sitting there, and I'm sure they're wondering to themselves, 'What the hell is this guy going to talk about? . . . Here's a guy who, five years ago left here wet behind his ears. All he knew was EEO [Equal Employment Opportunity] and affirmative action and how to get the handicapped on the payroll. He began as a truck driver/forklift operator. What the heck's he going to talk about?' Well, I'll tell you, it was my moment of glory. . . .

"My birthplace was in a farming and ranching village behind the Sandia Mountains, a little town by the name of Torreon. My father was a farmer, rancher. . . . Then in the early 1940s there was quite a drought. A lot of the crops withered. Dad went to Santa Fe looking for employment as a laborer. My father was an uneducated man. He finished the tenth grade. My mother finished the sixth grade. I was the oldest of five. We moved to Los Alamos in August of 1943. I was six.

"My father was offered employment as a heavy-duty operator. He was involved with leveling the land so that they could build the various temporary technical areas. Later he advanced and became involved with the water and sewage treatment part of Los Alamos. My father was able to get one of the original [Ranch School] log cabins for our residence, which was about a rock's throw from Bathtub Row. During the era when Los Alamos was a boys' [school], that particular building belonged to one of the grounds-keepers. My father paid a whopping $12 or $15 a month's rent. He even sweet-talked one of the construction army captains to add a wing to the house, which in essence became the bedroom.

"When we moved to Los Alamos my dad had an old '39 Chevy coupe, so it was Mom and Dad and Dolores, who is the second oldest of my sisters—she was born with Down's syndrome—and Lenora, who was about 12 weeks old—we all drove to Los Alamos. It was a frightening experience. We had never been in that area. And as we wound our way along the side of this cliff on a dirt road, we didn't know where in the world my dad was taking us. There was a tremendous amount of security and secrecy involved during the trip.

"Now, for me, it was somewhat unique because I went to Los Alamos not speaking English. . . . For some reason in the early years, there were few Spanish-speaking students or residents. There were numerous Spanish-speaking personnel who worked there, but they all commuted from down in the Rio Grande valley. One thing that is very vivid in my mind is that my mother with a sixth-grade education did things that are just overwhelming. My mother is a tremendous cook. Our house was centrally located in the small community and there was always a wonderful aroma coming from my mother's kitchen. A lot of the wives of scientists who lived nearby were very bored. They had just come from city life, and they thought this was the last stop. My mother, unknown to me for several years, made an agreement with some of the ladies of leading scientists who were hungry to learn about the culture of northern New Mexico and the culinary aspects—that if you show us how to make this and that, we will tutor your son in English. So I had the pleasure of these ladies spending time with me after school and teaching me how to speak English. In return, my mother would show them how to make a variety of northern New Mexico dishes. . . .

"We were protected. I mean, we had a chained-off city where no outsiders could come in and bother us. Everybody had to have a special pass. Back then many times the mothers and fathers would punish their kids by taking away the pass; they couldn't leave The Hill. We used to do no-no's by sticking them in the trunk and sneaking them off The Hill. Friendship was very strong at that time because you relied on each other heavily. We played in the old Sundt apartments. In each of these buildings the vent for the central heating system was right by the outside stairwell, so in the wintertime, we would all sit by the vent where this nice heat would come out. We would sit there and tell stories. . . .

"Los Alamos to me was a Camelot all of its own. It had lots of money, lots of academia. That was a problem I had as a young boy just breaking into English language. And if you're grading by the curve, I was way behind the curve because of the fact that all of my peers came from very well-educated families. My goodness, to teach you mathematics, who better to have than your father, Enrico Fermi? I didn't have that luxury. I always had to do double time. I always had to be in overdrive in order to keep up. Los Alamos was—and continues to be in my opinion—an area you either like or dislike. There is no in-between. . . . And there's been a lot of great families raised and a lot of broken families just because of that—people not being able to adjust to that kind of confinement and regimentation. Los Alamos was a very regimented community. Everybody marched to the beat of whatever drum was being beaten on. The army was there in full force—I can recall vividly looking out the window and watching the troops parade by. . . .

"The Lab was very good to me. I graduated from high school in 1955. I was not any academic giant by any means. I graduated in the lower fourth of the class. Again, it was this thing about academia. I had this stigma. I just had to work too hard. I accepted a position to go to a trade school in Pueblo, Colorado, to become a telegrapher. That's like becoming a stage coach driver! It was a rip-off: $375 my dad paid for it. . . . I became capable of receiving and sending in Morse Code all the requirements for employment. I was interviewed in Washington State. When they recognized I was of Mexican descent, they refused to even talk to me.

I returned to Los Alamos in August of 1955 and took a job at Metzger's gas station [at] $1.08 an hour, I remember. There was a gentleman who I always liked named Jack Sweeney. He worked in W-division at the Lab. He said, 'Dimas, why don't you go to college?' I was afraid of college. I was scared to death that I would flunk. It comes back to this academia thing, this pressure with all these outstanding students, where everybody was super smart.

"I remember in August of 1956 . . . [I was at Mr. Reed's Burger Buggy and] I heard people talking about the excitement of going back to college. I was working at the Laboratory at the warehouse as a truck driver and forklift operator. I had left the gas station by this time, and I knew my life was going nowhere. I heard someone talking about Eastern New Mexico University in Portales, New Mexico. They said, 'It's such a nice town.' So I said, 'The heck with it—I'm going to try it.' I went home that night, looked up Eastern New Mexico University, wrote a letter, said, 'I'd like to come to your school. I'm not the brightest student, but I'm willing to try.' Two weeks later, they wrote me, said, 'We'll give you a try.' I had saved enough money, and I had given myself six years to do a full four-year thing.

"I got away from Los Alamos and the mentality I had in relation to academia. My first year was very tough. It was basically learning how to be a student. But once I got to do my own thing, and I didn't have that stigma right in front of me, I said to myself, 'Hey, I can do some of these things.' So C's and D's became B's and A's. I finished in four years, and I worked part time in the cafeteria, at a body shop, on ranches, and milking cows. . . . I look back, and I say to myself, 'What has driven my success?' I think of what I had as a model. There were milestones in front of you. There were examples. There were exhibits. There were things that you wanted to do. . . .

"I finished college in June of 1960, went into active duty with the Naval Reserves. When I was honorably discharged, I was offered a job at the Laboratory as a purchasing agent. I was there for six, eight months. Then two gentlemen by the names of J. V. Young and Bob Porton came to me and said, 'Dimas, how would you like to work in public relations? You know the community since you grew up here.' Because of my sister's handicap, Down's syndrome, I developed the first program at Los Alamos Laboratory for the handicapped. I obtained the first security clearance for a mentally handicapped person at the Laboratory, and through those efforts and Special Olympics, the Laboratory was awarded the Employer of the Year from the Association of Retarded Citizens, and I accepted the award for the Laboratory director. One of our first Down's syndrome employees at the Lab is still working there. . . .

"When I got that phone call from Sargent Shriver, I was flabbergasted. . . . Sargent Shriver at the time was director of the Peace Corps. He also was in charge of the Joseph P. Kennedy Foundation for mental retardation and was just starting a brand new program called Office of Economic Opportunity, the War on Poverty. I disqualified myself for the Joseph Kennedy Foundation job. I didn't have sufficient experience and background to deal with media and so forth. He said, 'Would you be interested in coming to work for me with the Peace Corps?' I said, 'Gee, I don't know.'

"So I'm sitting in Sargent Shriver's office, getting ready to head back to New Mexico and he says, 'Wait a minute. What about OEO?' I said, 'What about it? What is it?' We started talking about the War on Poverty. Sargent Shriver said, 'Before you go home, let me make a call.' He picked up the phone and he called Bill Crook, a personal friend of Lyndon Johnson, and his regional director of OEO in Austin. He said, 'Bill, I've got a young man here. I'd like to fly him to Austin and see if you might be able to use him down there.' So they routed me through Austin. . . .

"Shortly after I began working in Austin, I was assigned to work and travel with a young attorney, Bruce Babbitt, who is now the secretary of interior. I just had a ball. And climbed very rapidly. . . . I was working in Washington, enjoying myself, when I received a call from Dr. Harold Agnew, then director of the Los Alamos National Laboratory. He said, 'Dimas, I'm starting a new program up here called Employee Relations Office, and you came to mind. Would you be interested in talking about it?' The call could not have been more timely because I wanted to go home again. I returned to New Mexico in December of 1972. And I vowed at that time that I would never leave Los Alamos again."

But Dimas did leave Los Alamos again when President Ronald Reagan named Los Alamos scientist Dr. Ed Knapp to head the National Science Foundation in Washington, and Dr. Knapp asked Dimas to come with him as an administrative assistant. Much as he liked Los Alamos, Dimas was ever aware that he was not a scientist, that he did not have a Ph.D. and the status that went with it. "I came to the National Science Foundation and I was basically going to be an administrative assistant to Dr. Knapp, and Ed really gave me the push that I needed and the guidance. He said, 'Dimas, why don't you go work in the international field for me for a while, see what's going on? You're fluent in Spanish and Portuguese.' So I started doing a little of this, doing a little of that. I got hands-on experience with science and technology.

"The National Science Foundation was in the process of developing scientific, bilateral cooperative programs in Latin America, where they match U.S. scientists with someone in Argentina, Chile, or Brazil. When Dr. Knapp left after two years to return to Los Alamos, I was offered an extension in the NSF International Division. It was there that I started blossoming in the field of science. I was now dealing directly with scientists. My job was to develop cooperative science programs between the United States and Brazil, Argentina, and Chile. . . .

"After I finished my stint with the National Science Foundation, I really felt good about myself because I had made so many good inroads with the scientific community. . . . I was getting ready to go home to Los Alamos. I received a call from the Department of State, the undersecretary for diplomatic security. Ambassador Robert Lamb . . . said, 'I have a little project that I'd like to talk to you about. I've got this special program in the field of countermeasures in diplomatic security.' Now I travel all over the world. . . .

"As Mr. Thomas Wolfe tells us—you can't go back where you came from. But there is a peacefulness that I've never in my life experienced anywhere else. Sitting on a point overlooking Los Alamos and feeling at peace. There are smells in Los Alamos that to this day haunt me in a very positive way. There's that smell that comes from the mountains and the dirt—that would come right before a rain storm and afterwards. . . . The rumbling thunder. It's exciting. It's erotic. It's sensual. . . . There's an element of comfortness like returning to the womb. I want my children to experience that. I want them to be telling a [future interviewer], 'There's this special smell in Los Alamos.' "

Lucia Ortiz y Garcia

Back in grade school, Dimas sat behind a girl whose long dark braids he sometimes could not resist pulling. The girl was Lucy Garcia. She had arrived in Los Alamos during the war when her father, Walter Garcia, became a carpenter with the Army Corps of Engineers. A self-described tomboy, Lucy hung out with her five brothers and their friends, bicycling fast around Los Alamos, playing Red Rover and pickup baseball, and, in the evenings, visiting to trade comic books. Like Dimas, Lucy Garcia, now known as Lucia Ortiz y Garcia, has left Los Alamos—and returned—several times.

Graduating the same year as Dimas—1955—Lucy attended a Catholic women's college in Kansas. Between then and her first return in 1971, she acknowledges, she had changed radically—as had Los Alamos and society at large. By 1971 she had a very different view of the bomb from her idyllic childhood memories that "we were all working together for a common goal." Graduating from college in 1959—and filled with idealism—Lucy joined an international community of nuns, becoming Sister Lucia. As part of this community, she taught around the world, including teaching English in Micronesia in the late 1960s. There she saw and heard firsthand the effects of bomb tests—among them, cancers in the people she came to know well.

At the same time she became disillusioned with changes in the Catholic church, eventually leaving the order. She came back to Kansas City, then returned to Los Alamos to work as a counselor at a program for teenagers dealing with drug and alcohol problems. She married a midwesterner of Norwegian heritage, and in the mid-1970s she and her husband moved to his native Wisconsin. There Lucia earned a masters degree in counselling, for which she had discovered she had a flair. Her last return to Los Alamos was in August of 1991, when she took a job as coordinator of cooperative education for the University of New Mexico at Los Alamos. She is glad to be back in northern New Mexico but readily admits she would prefer to work in one of the Spanish towns and villages surrounding Los Alamos.

"By the time I came back in August 1991 I had become radicalized, and Los Alamos had changed. At one time the janitors and the scientists were working together for an ideal. Today that has disappeared. We went from an era of striving for an ideal, however cockeyed that was, into an era where individual success and achievement and monetary success is more important. I'm not comfortable with the rarefied environment here today where people are well-educated but less tolerant of—less able to empathize with—other segments of society. And I consider myself an 'other.'

"People have recommended that I could get a much higher salary at the Lab, and I suppose I could. But I will not. . . . There's still a lot of weaponry. Unless the Lab changes radically, I could never agree to work there. I saw so directly what happened in the islands as a result of the bomb. . . . The impact it had on the people I dealt with intimately in the islands is just beyond measure. . . . And Los Alamos's reason for being was the creation and building of the bomb. I'm also very much aware of toxic contamination. . . . That my daddy did develop cancer. That could have been an indirect result of his being present and working in and around the Laboratory. My dad . . . went to White Sands to help build the scaffolding for the bomb and was present at the first detonation [Trinity test]. My father is an incredibly honest man. He never even spoke to his wife about all this. Of course, we children were totally oblivious. We didn't know what was going on. We just knew Daddy went away for a couple weeks. I was hardly aware of the war, except that several of my uncles were in the war, and there was a lot of concern and worry. . . .

"I was born in Colorado, where my father had inherited the family ranch. He began to suffer asthma badly, and we moved to New Mexico. Then we moved to Southern California, where my father and my mother both worked in an airplane munitions factory and I attended kindergarten and first grade. Then my daddy got really, really sick with asthma and we decided to move back. That was 1943 or 1944. So my dad got a job here in Los Alamos as a carpenter.

"I went to second grade in Espanola. We moved to Los Alamos in 1945, when I was in the third grade. I remember very distinctly playing jacks with my girlfriends. We used to play jacks every recess. We became very expert at it. . . . We had excellent teachers. They used to encourage imagination. I recall an assignment in third grade in which we etched out a picture on a piece of paper covered with Crayola, and then we were to write a story about that. I wrote about how a tiger got its stripes or something. This may sound real old fashioned, but one of the wonderful things I recall about fifth and sixth grades is that our teacher used to read us a story. We used to have story hour. It was wonderful!

"School was enjoyable. It was an adventure, and it was a very comforting place to be because it was so secure. At the time, I was not aware how secure Los Alamos was, but I felt it. I sensed it. At the beginning, there were military with machine guns at the gate and there were MPs. Later on, they became security guards. There was a feeling of camaraderie among all the people at that time. I think there was very little racism. There were Spanish people coming in from the valley and there was an Indian population, coming in from the pueblos and working as maids. There was a sense of unity . . . although most of the jobs the Hispanic people were in were kind of like service jobs. There was just this wonderful sense of equality: We were all people working toward a single ideal. . . .

"When we moved to Los Alamos, we lived in what were called expandable trailers. It was just one large room with two little wings on either side and a little kitchen down the middle. We lived in something like a camp. Instead of sidewalks, we had boards. We had a central rest room or bathroom facility because we had no bathroom in the trailers. That was not a hardship at all. It might have been for my mother in terms of washing clothing for five children and a husband, but I never viewed it as a hardship. Then we moved to Manhattan Loop. . . . These were two-bedroom duplex units. Then from there we moved to the Sundt apartments. . . .

"Going to the grocery store for my parents on a bicycle with a basket strapped to the front—that was fun. And we had a wonderful library. I also recall that there was a PX exchange, I remember walking in as a child and falling in love with a book. It was *Hansel and Gretel*. I lusted after that book for so long. I remember saving my pennies and going back there and buying that book. The military provided for all of our needs. They had to because it was too problematic to get off The Hill and go down to shop in Santa Fe.

"One of the significant things for me—and it helped to form a lot of my character—is that I never felt afraid. I recall walking late at night by myself as a child—[age] 10, 11, 12—without a concern. I'd go to the movies with my girlfriends. They lived in different parts of town. We'd leave the theater about 10 P.M., and I would walk all by myself. There were always security guards. There was a canyon right behind our house. When I would fight with my brothers, or when I felt I had been unjustly treated, I would walk away and go into the canyon and walk and walk and walk. Then I would return feeling very peaceful, self-confident and feeling good about me. . . .

"I babysat a lot for very educated people. After putting the kids to bed, I would listen to music and look at their books and magazines. . . . My parents read and my grandmother had a library, but it wasn't that conscious environment where books meant something very important. In the evenings, the radio had classical music. I used to listen to it and daydream. My five brothers were very rambunctious. Both parents worked—my mother was a matron in a dormitory—and I was expected, as a good Spanish young lady, to do all the housework and to take care of my younger brothers. [Classical music and books] were my way of escaping from the chaos.

"I remember we'd get on the bus and spend Saturdays in Santa Fe. That was our great adventure. My brother and I would go with [Secundino Sandoval] and his sister Clara. We'd go to the drugstore. I remember looking at [storybook dolls] and wishing I could get one. We'd walk around the Plaza, go visit the Cathedral, shop for clothing, mainly hang out. One of the great things was to get comic books and trade them. . . . Comic book trading was a big pastime—Donald Duck, Captain Marvel, romances. We'd go out on our bicycles after the dishes were done to trade comic books. There was such innocence.

"I think there was a little bit of snobbery—that we began to believe that we were better than anyone else. . . . I remember very distinctly that I took on that attitude for a while. When we would go to visit friends and relatives in the valley, it was like we were special. When the new high school was built, it was considered the best high school in the state in terms of physical plant and teachers. We were aware of this. By that time there was a lot of resentment building up that the people on The Hill had the best of everything. . . .

"I was one of very few [women] in my graduating class who went on to college. I received a scholarship from a small Catholic women's college in Kansas. I completed my degree in English literature in 1959. I had an aunt who was a Franciscan nun, and there were other nuns in my family. I had become friends with a community of missionary nuns who were European. The mother house was in Spain. The women were astounding, very strong and very noble. In those days there were all kinds of ideals—this was just prior to the Kennedy era. We had a Novitiate House in Kansas City. I was the first American to enter that community [to become a nun] after many, many years. That was the beginning of a new era of my life. It really formed me into who I am today: The ideal of service, sacrifice, life of prayer and contemplation—and action. There was this desire to go out and save the world. . . .

"I taught in Micronesia, in Saipan, which had a connection to Los Alamos. Because Saipan was the last Japanese stronghold in the Pacific, Micronesia was a trust territory of the United States after the war. . . . To kind of round things off, the bomb that was dropped on Hiroshima had actually been kept on an island just three miles from Saipan, Tinian. It was flown from Tinian and dropped on Hiroshima. I was very much aware that there was this connection. By that time, my perception of the world had changed considerably. I felt the United States was an intrusion on the lives of these people. And the bomb and all the events that followed the bomb had an incredibly negative impact. The people of Enewetak were suffering cancer because there had been a lot of testing there. The United States had promised that the island had been cleaned out and was fit for human habitation, but it hadn't been. . . .

"I began to feel a lot of resentment and disillusionment. That was one of the reasons why I left the islands. . . . Eventually I left the religious community because the religious community was supporting U.S. policy [in Micronesia]. I . . . came back here, got a job as a counselor at a boys' ranch in the valley, worked there for a year, then got a job at Casa Mesita, a house for young women who were considered incorrigible [here in Los Alamos]. It was a very interesting return. Having lived what I had lived, I realized that I could never live here again. I could not reside in Los Alamos.

"My maturity [had given me] a different perspective on nuclear warfare, weaponry, and what the Laboratory stood for and what a lot of the lives here stood for. Then I was also very much aware of how the economy in northern New Mexico was so dependent on the work that was being done at the Los Alamos National Laboratory. And how it had impacted the lives of the Spanish community and the Indian community. And how things were changing radically. Values were beginning to change very, very rapidly. People were becoming more affluent. Their values were becoming more focused on money and materialism, and that was sad to see. . . . You sometimes forget struggles when you become affluent. There's still a lot of struggle in the world."

Epilogue

On a bright, crisp December day in 1962, President John F. Kennedy came to Los Alamos. It was just two months after the Cuban missile crisis, 21 years to the day after the invasion of Pearl Harbor, and exactly 20 years after the day that the head of the Los Alamos Ranch School had called the boys together to tell them that the school would be closing. In 1962 Los Alamos was a thriving town of 13,000, known throughout the world. The cold war had given the hastily constructed military camp a permanence and a continuing mission—research into the production of nuclear weapons to keep the world safe for democracy.

As Kennedy arrived in town, the thought of the arms race was high on everyone's mind. The very recent difficulties in Cuba had brought the superpowers face to face and raised the possibility of the use of nuclear weapons. The town turned out to hear the president speak at the high school football field. Stores closed, as did the schools, and the Lab dismissed employees at noon. More than 10,000 people jammed the bleachers and field. "There is no group of people in this country whose record over the last twenty years has been more preeminent in the service of their country than all of you here in this small community in New Mexico," Kennedy told them. "You here in this mountain town made a direct contribution not only to the freedom of this country but to those thousands of miles away. Therefore I am proud as president of the United States, to come here today and express our thanks to you, and to also tell you how much I have admired, from reading an article some years ago, the kind of schools that you run here and the kind of boys and girls that you are bringing up. We hope from them the same kind of service that you have rendered."[1]

That day is enshrined in the memories of those present. It was a day of rejoicing, celebration, and hope. The town glowed in the national spotlight (more than 100 journalists and broadcasters recorded the event). Kennedy had proposed a manned voyage to the moon by the end of the decade, and the Lab was playing a part. During the president's visit, Laboratory director

Norris Bradbury and assistant director Raemer Schreiber briefed him on the Lab's progress in developing nuclear reactors for rocket propulsion. A smiling Kennedy even tried his hand at the remote-control manipulators used to handle radioactive objects behind lead glass windows in the "hot cell" area of the chemical and metallurgical building.[2]

Kennedy's mention of the children of Los Alamos struck a responsive chord. What people remember—and talk about decades later—is not his exact words but the fact that he singled out the children of Los Alamos. "It served as a charge to us," recalls Dimas Chavez, who at the time was starting his career climb at the Laboratory. The optimism of Kennedy's visit would fade all too soon. Eleven months later Kennedy was killed in Dallas, and soon an unpopular war was raging in Vietnam, bringing a re-evaluation of war-related industries and protesters to the town. The honor, respect, and veneration that had been bestowed upon Los Alamos by a grateful nation in 1945 and again by Kennedy in 1962 soon was replaced by criticism. Physicist Lew Agnew remembers the time in the late 1960s when a group of physicists proposed boycotting meetings where Los Alamos scientists would be present. "We'd gone from the top of the pyramid to its depths," he recalls. "It didn't last very long, but it hurt."

In the late 1960s Los Alamos "children" who were away at college or working outside the area recall efforts to avoid telling people where they were from. They wanted to forestall the discussions, and often diatribes, that they knew would follow. The initial hope on the part of many that the release—and the control—of the vast new energy source might make future wars unthinkable had given way to the realities of the nuclear age.

This, then, is a legacy of the Manhattan Project, and for the children of Los Alamos there is a singular inheritance: the knowledge that in the strange, bustling yet beautiful town where they innocently played, events were unfolding that would change the world. Some of the "children" view their Los Alamos experience matter-of-factly: "Hey," they say, "there was a job to be done and our parents did it. What's the big deal?" Many, especially those who have lived in the town most of their lives, view the Lab primarily as an employer and believe they were lucky to live in a town with such steady employment. Some would rather not be working on weapons; others take pride in their role in keeping the nation militarily strong. Still others— especially those who returned to university towns soon after the war ended— speak of having "purged" themselves through participation in the peace movement or antinuclear demonstrations. Some say their parents' work intensified their own reverence for life. A number note the irony in the fact that the jobs created by the Lab have provided economic security to the Indian pueblos and Spanish-American villages. The work of building nuclear weapons offers a future to young people of the villages and pueblos, enabling them to remain at home and in touch with their heritage, and their traditions of living in harmony with the earth.

For many of the children of the scientists at Los Alamos during the war, there is another legacy. They glimpsed, however fleetingly and indirectly, a collective community of brilliant people working together with a mission, an intensity, an excitement and a cooperative spirit that seldom occurs in human affairs. They summon forth memories of Renaissance men and women who were intelligent, clever and quick-witted, brimming with curiosity and zest. Some have been seeking in vain for such a community ever since.

Fifty years after Los Alamos completed its mission, it is still a one-industry town. The Lab remains its predominant business, with weapons research its main job. After more than half a century, the Lab still operates under contract to the University of California, making the University of California the town's major employer. But today's bustling metropolis of 18,000 bears little resemblance to its wartime beginnings. The wartime apartments and small houses—the Sundts and Morgans—were demolished soon after the war. The original Lab structures were torn down, and new facilities were built on the other side of Los Alamos canyon when a bridge was constructed across the canyon.

A McDonald's restaurant now stands where part of the Lab used to be. Theater 2 has also succumbed to progress. The United Church that met there now has a building of its own. Denominations have split off and built their own churches over the years. Today there are 34 churches in Los Alamos, and a visitor's first view of the town, upon rounding the final hill, is not of a guard gate but of two church spires.

Mary Jeanne Nilsson, the teacher who in 1945 led her fourth graders on make-believe trips "across the Lincoln Highway," still attends the United Church. As she looks out of the church windows, she gazes upon the open ground which, in the early years, formed the playground for the old Central School. In her mind's eye, she can see the children of her earliest classes playing there. Los Alamos residents still enjoy walking, climbing the nearby mountains, and skiing. And several of the wartime toddlers are among the stalwarts who kick up their heels at the weekly square dances in Fuller Lodge.

The town's civic-mindedness and concern with schools, music, and governance has continued. Los Alamos boasts more than 220 civic and recreational organizations. The musical groups, founded within weeks of the start of the town, still present regular concerts. And educational issues still get long and heated debating. The average age of the residents has grown with the town. Where once it was 24, today there are a large number of retirees—and senior citizen fellowships are some of the most active organizations.

The Atomic Energy Commission, the governmental organization that took over administration of the town and Lab in 1947, was abolished by Congress in 1974. The Department of Energy now oversees the Lab. The federal government began selling the houses it had built in Los Alamos to the residents in the mid-1960s, and the town of Los Alamos now manages its own schools, police, and other municipal functions. People still dress casually. The story is told that one can tell the year a man arrived in Los Alamos by the cut of his suit—because he hasn't bought one since. The story seems to have a strong grounding in reality.

Crime remains virtually nonexistent, but people have gotten in the habit of locking doors. There do not appear to be any unemployed or poor. The local Chamber of Commerce reports that Los Alamos has the lowest unemployment and the highest household income of any town in New Mexico. In 1995, it reports, 49 percent of Los Alamos households have incomes of $50,000 (compared to 15 percent of households nationally). Despite its high income, The Hill boasts few major stores. One can buy groceries, shoes, and simple electronics, but for serious shopping most residents continue to travel to Santa Fe or Albuquerque (90 miles away).

Los Alamos has been an open town since the guard gate was taken down in 1957, yet it remains isolated from the rest of the state. As one wartime "child" of Los Alamos observes, "In some ways, it's as if the gate were still there." People on The Hill remain a well-educated, well-traveled, well-to-do but somewhat insulated anomaly. While Los Alamos's neighbors appreciate the jobs that the Lab has brought to the area, many worry about the ramifications of the jobs, particularly health hazards. They worry about contamination of the land and the consequences of radiation.

Sometimes their neighbors' fears strike Los Alamos residents as farfetched. They realize, though, that whether or not the fears are grounded in provable, scientific reality, they are still very real to those who hold them. One Los Alamos "child" who commuted to the Lab from Santa Fe for several years, decided, some time ago, to sell the car in which she had commuted. The sale was about to go through when the prospective buyer discovered that the car had been driven regularly to Los Alamos. "No way," said the buyer. "I don't want to get contaminated with radiation."

A concern raised a couple of years ago brought these worries home. Tyler Mercier, a sculptor who lived in Los Alamos, had volunteered for an environmental project placing radiation monitors around the town. During the course of the project he learned from a Lab scientist that there had been seven cases of brain cancer within one neighborhood. Mercier brought this up at a public meeting, stating the names. Soon more people were telling him about cancers in their families.[3]

"Tyler publicly raised concerns that maybe had been simmering," says the editor of the Los Alamos Monitor, Evelyn Vigil.

The Department of Energy agreed to fund a study of the incidence of brain cancer in Los Alamos and to monitor the canyon where radioactive waste had been dumped in earlier years (which a number of residents were now calling "Acid Canyon"). The studies concluded that today there is no danger from radioactivity in the canyon and that there is no statistically significant increase in the incidence of brain cancers in Los Alamos. The town breathed a collective sigh of relief, although private worries persist.

By the early spring of 1995 the town faced another controversy—one originating with schoolchildren at the end of the 1980s. Contemplating the dismantling of the Berlin Wall and the end of the cold war, an elementary school class in Albuquerque had thought about ways that they might help promote world peace. They knew about the Hiroshima Peace Park and the statue there commemorating the young girl, Sasaki Sadako. In 1957, suffering from leukemia caused by radiation from the atomic bomb, Sasaki had tried to fold 1,000 origami cranes, hoping, in accordance with Japanese tradition, that it would bring recovery. She died after folding 644, and her classmates completed the remaining 356 cranes and raised money for the famous statue in Hiroshima. The Albuquerque students decided to raise money for a sister statue to be placed in Los Alamos. In 1990 they started sending letters to students across the country, and by 1994 they had pledges of support from all 50 states and 53 countries. A national design contest—open only to children—drew more than 6,000 submissions from which a panel of judges chose "The Peace Garden," an abstract globe of Earth surrounded by trees and shrubs. The project ran into a snag when presented to the Los Alamos County Council, whose approval was needed for the site. Council members, sensitive to the criticism the town has taken over the years for ushering in the nuclear age, suggested that the statue and garden could be viewed as "anti-nuke, anti-Los Alamos." After several tempestuous meetings, the council turned down the proposal.[4]

The end of the cold war has affected Los Alamos in far-reaching ways. The Lab now confronts a crisis similar to that at the end of World War II: What is its mission? Today's emphasis on reduction of nuclear weapons (rather than the design of new types) calls into question the very existence of the Lab. As in the past, the Lab's fate will be decided outside the community—by the federal government—and it is less certain today than it has been any time in the past half century.

Los Alamos's climate remains crisp and dry. The sun still shines. The wet earth continues to give off a distinctive pungent aroma, and the sky is still blue, although the old-timers say it's not quite as blue as it used to be.

No one is sure just why.

Methodology

More than 70 interviews were conducted in 1992 and 1993 for *Children of Los Alamos*, all of them in-person: most were tape-recorded, and many were several hours long, on a wide range of subjects. The edited transcripts were sent to the interviewees to be read for accuracy. Some interviewees made changes to elaborate a point or to state it slightly differently. Some of the 70 interviews do not appear in the book but were helpful for background and direction.

Interviewees were not asked a set list of questions, but the topics explored were generally the same. These included first impressions of the town and recollections of daily life, such as school and the interplay of people with different backgrounds and cultures. The subjects were also asked about how their childhood experience at Los Alamos affected their choice of career and feelings about national security, and about the significance in their lives of "having been in a place at a time that changed the world." Responses varied according to the questions people felt most comfortable discussing and elaborating on.

In grouping the stories I have tried to cluster like experiences—that is, people who are recalling the same years from a similar vantage point. In some instances stories are clustered around a specific event, such as a child's first sight of Los Alamos or memories of the end of the war. I have ordered the stories so that the book develops chronologically, from the formation of the Manhattan Project though the war years to the end of the war. The book's second half deals with the end of 1945 to about 1952 (when work on the hydrogen bomb began in earnest). This part also deals more with the significance in the interviewees' lives of their Los Alamos childhoods.

Appendix: Biographical Notes on Interviewees

The interviewees are listed by the chapter in which their comments first appear.

1. The Secret Project

Jeannie Parks Nereson
When Jeannie Parks Nereson started teaching elementary school in Los Alamos in 1944, she could not imagine living there permanently. But she remained—marrying, having children, and continuing to teach. At the time of her recent retirement she was teaching the grandchildren of some of her wartime students.

2. Arriving at P.O. Box 1663

Secundino Sandoval
Secundino Sandoval is the son of Sam Sandoval, who was a carpenter at the Lab and in the late 1940s an active member of the School Board. Secundino worked for some years as an architectural draftsman at the Lab before embarking on a career as a professional artist. Now nationally recognized, he lives in Los Alamos's Western Area.

Martha Bacher Eaton
Martha Bacher Eaton is the daughter of Robert Bacher, who was head of the bomb physics division. She spent much of her childhood in California, where her father was on the faculty of California Institute of Technology. She is a psychologist in Santa Barbara.

Nella Fermi Weiner

Nella Fermi Weiner, daughter of Nobel laureate Enrico Fermi, returned to Chicago after the war and spent most of her adulthood there. She worked as an artist, taught art to high school students, returned to academia for a Ph.D. in sociology, and finally embarked upon a career in financial planning. She was starting to write a recollection of her life with her famous father when she died of lung cancer at the end of February 1995.

Joan Mark Neary

Joan Mark Neary is the eldest child of mathematician Carson Mark, who came to Los Alamos in 1945 from Montreal as part of the British delegation of scientists. Joan left Los Alamos to attend Radcliffe College, remaining in the East for some years. In the 1970s she and her husband, John, were living on Long Island when they decided to to move to New Mexico to bring up their their three sons in a less pressured environment, closer to nature. They live in a rural area near the Indian village of Tesuque outside Santa Fe. Joan worked at the Lab as a writer and editor from 1983 to 1986, finding that the experience "solidified my negative feelings about Los Alamos" in terms of stratification and bureaucracy.

3. Three Naval Officers and a Child's Secret

Peggy Parsons Bowditch

Peggy Parsons Bowditch is the daughter of Admiral William "Deak" Parsons, who headed the ordnance division and did the final assembly of the bomb that was dropped on Hiroshima, as well as serving as the mission's scientific observer. A botanist, Peggy lives in a plant-filled home outside Philadelphia with her husband, Nat.

Jim Bradbury

Jim Bradbury is the eldest son of Norris Bradbury, who headed the Los Alamos National Laboratory for 25 years. Jim lives in a contemporary adobe home on a hillside outside Santa Fe and is in the processing of retiring from the Lab, where, for many years he directed the Meson Physics Facility.

Ellen Wilder Bradbury

Ellen Wilder Bradbury is the daughter of Ed Wilder, who worked in the explosives division. She also lives in Santa Fe, where she heads up Recursos, a nonprofit organization that sponsors seminars on topics relating to New Mexico history and culture.

4. Diversions and Safe Havens

Robert Y. Porton
Robert Y. Porton, sometimes called "Mr. Los Alamos," still lives there in a house full of photographs and other memorabilia from his band and radio careers and his many years of public relations with the Lab.

Dorothy McKibbin
Dorothy McKibbin worked out her office at 109 Palace Avenue until the mid-1960s. After the war, scientists returning to Los Alamos for a few days or a year invariably made a trip to her home. Several of their children, including Peter Oppenheimer, became close to her, remembering her warmth.

Kevin McKibbin
Kevin McKibbin, Dorothy's son, worked at the Lab for several years, then joined the National Park Service, ending his tenure at Bandelier National Monument. His house just outside Los Alamos opens to a view of the Jemez Mountains.

Lidian King
Lidian King, daughter of physicist E. D. P. King, graduated from Wellesley College with a major in art history. She earned a master's degree in music and worked in that field for a number of years; when interviewed, she was studying for a second master's degree—this one in counseling and psychotherapy.

Catherine Allison Marshall
Catherine Allison Marshall, daughter of physicist Sam Allison, moved to Chicago after the war, growing up amidst many of the friends she had known in Los Alamos. She graduated from Vassar College and now directs the Pittsburgh University Press.

Kim Manley
Kim Manley, the daughter of physicist John Manley, is a geologist in Los Alamos. She turned to science because of the intellectual excitement and teamwork that she sensed at Los Alamos as a child. She grew up "assuming that this was normal" and has been disappointed not to experience that intense cooperation in her own scientific pursuits. "I think it doesn't exist today as it did at that time," she says.

5. The Little Green Schoolhouse

Dorothy Hillhouse

After the war, schoolteacher Dorothy Hillhouse and her husband, George, a butcher, opened a bakery in Los Alamos, which they operated for many years. Their daughter, Barbara Jean Hillhouse Wilson, was away from Los Alamos for some years before returning in about 1977. She has taught school and worked for the Norris Bradbury Science Museum.

Alice Smith

Alice Smith, who taught high school history in wartime Los Alamos, went on to help found and for many years edit the *Bulletin of Atomic Scientists*. She has written extensively about atomic science issues, including the book *The Peril and the Hope*, and edited Robert Oppenheimer's letters. She lives in Cambridge, Massachusetts.

Mary Jeanne Bolan Nilsson

Mary Jeanne Bolan Nilsson came to Los Alamos to teach in the fall of 1945. She has lived there ever since, and still teaches elementary school.

6. Two Views from Bathtub Row

Joan Bainbridge Safford

Joan Bainbridge Safford is the elder daughter of Kenneth Bainbridge, the Harvard physicist who directed the Trinity test. She went to law school at age 37 and is deputy U.S. attorney for the Northern District of Illinois. She recently flew to Santa Barbara for a visit with her Los Alamos childhood friend Martha Bacher Eaton. The reunion included singing together the choruses they had belted out long ago on the banks of the Rio Grande.

7. Fathers and Sons

Severo Gonzales

Severo Gonzales, whose grandparents and great grandparents are among the earliest homesteaders on the mesa, is the son of Bences Gonzales, who was a mainstay of the Los Alamos Ranch School, where he managed the Trading Post and ordered the groceries that had to be shipped in. When the army took over the school, Bences signed up with the Manhattan Project, working in the commissary, until his retirement in 1959. The only one of his brothers and sisters to remain in the area, Severo is retired from a career with the New Mexico state government in Santa Fe. He lives in Espanola.

Bill Jette

Bill Jette is the son of metallurgist Eric Jette and his wife, Eleanor, author of *Inside Box 1663,* which describes the family's wartime experiences at Los Alamos. An architect in Albuquerque, Bill "wound up working for a man I met at Los Alamos when I was a kid." Max Flato was a captain in the Corps of Engineers, when, after the war, the Jettes prevailed upon the army to add on to the Bathtub Row house in which they were living. Flato built the addition, which became Bill's bedroom. When Bill completed architecture school and his stint in the service, he wrote to Flato for a job, and "By golly, he gave me one."

8. Teenagers' Perspectives

Johnnie and Anita Luttrell Martinez

Johnnie Martinez's father brought his family to Los Alamos from Santa Fe when he got a job as a janitor, moving on to a job at the Lab. Anita Luttrell Martinez arrived when her father came to operate the heavy equipment. The couple have remained in Los Alamos, where Johnnie is retired from his job in the weapons division at the Lab, and Anita is retired from her job as a school secretary.

Bill Fox

Bill Fox came to Los Alamos at age 12 when his father got a job there as a fireman. Six years later Bill got a job in the Lab as an apprentice in glass blowing. Over the next 40 plus years he became expert at fabricating the variety of equipment required for the Lab's sophisticated experiments. He is now retired.

Bette Peters Brousseau

Bette Peters Brousseau, whose father, Rex Peters, ran one of the Lab machine shops, has lived on the mesa since 1943, except for two years at Stephens College in Missouri. She has worked at the Lab in various capacities, principally in the travel division and in the supply and property division. She has raised six children and now divides her time between volunteer work for the Los Alamos Historical Society and a docent's job at the Norris Bradbury Science Museum.

Betty Ann Williamson Peterson

In 1945 Betty Ann Williamson Peterson's father left his pharmacist job to sign on as an electrician at Los Alamos. Betty has lived there off and on since—working for the Lab in personnel, in the data base division, and at the Meson Physics Facility.

Neale Byers

Neale Byers, whose father worked as a machinist at the Rock Island arsenal (in Illinois), arrived in Los Alamos in June 1945. After graduating from college with a degree in education, he had planned to study for a master's degree and go into teaching, but he settled instead into a draftsman job at the Lab, where he remained until retiring.

Betty Marchi Schulte

Betty Marchi Schulte, whose father George Marchi, a chef, moved the family to Los Alamos from Santa Fe in 1943 when he took over the dining service at Fuller Lodge, has since lived in Los Alamos, Santa Fe, and, most recently, Albuquerque. She worked at the Lab for some time in the procurement and property division.

9. Nella's Circle

Gaby Peierls Gross

Gaby Peierls Gross is the daughter of Rudolf Peierls, a German-born physicist, and his wife, Genia, a Russian, both of whom had become British citizens. The Peierlses arrived in Los Alamos in 1944 as part of the British delegation of scientists. Gaby returned to England, where she graduated from Oxford University, and later moved to the United States. A lawyer in private practice in the Boston area, she specializes in family law.

Jane Flanders Ziff

Jane Flanders Ziff, whose mathematician father, Donald Flanders, brought the family to Los Alamos in 1943, left the town in 1946 and has not returned even for a visit. She teaches music in Amherst, Massachusetts.

Emma Baca Knowles

Emma Baca Knowles, whose father brought the family to Los Alamos in 1944 when he took a carpentry job there, was married the summer after her high school graduation and followed her Air Force husband to posts around the country. Upon his retirement from the Air Force they moved back to northern New Mexico, where Emma now works as financial specialist for the Emergency Medical Services Bureau of the New Mexico Department of Health in Santa Fe.

10. The Cat Screamed All Night

Paula Schreiber Dransfield
After some years away from Los Alamos, Paula Schreiber Dransfield came home. After her father, physicist Raemer Schreiber, retired as associate director of the Lab, Paula joined the Lab in the personnel division.

11. The War Ends

Frances Smith Weiland
Frances Smith Weiland arrived in Los Alamos in the fall of 1945 when her father, an electrician, brought his family to the place where he had earlier gotten a job. Frances graduated from Los Alamos High School in 1952 and now lives in Alexandria, Virginia. She has taught school and worked in political campaigns and in the personnel field.

13. Arriving after the War—and Again Decades Later

Verne Bell
Verne Bell arrived in Los Alamos in 1946 when his father became chief of a warehouse and soon worked his way up to get a job as engineer with the Atomic Energy Commission. Vern graduated from Los Alamos High School in 1952 and later from the University of Colorado. He did a stint in the service and then worked as a facilities engineer for Martin Marietta for 31 years. Now retired, he lives "in a pueblo style home" in Las Cruces, New Mexico.

Jim Wearin
Jim Wearin, who came to Los Alamos from Iowa in 1948 when his father took a job as a security guard, now lives in California, where he is in the irrigation business.

Vic Heyman
Vic Heyman first set foot in Los Alamos in 1947, when his father took a job as patent lawyer for the Atomic Energy Commission. Vic graduated from high school a year early—in 1951—and six years later had earned a Ph.D. in political science. He taught at Marshall University, then went to work for Defense Secretary Robert S. McNamara. He currently operates a bulk-mail business just outside Washington, D.C.

187

Bob Martin

Bob Martin came to Los Alamos in 1949 when his father took a job as a senior budget analyst for the Atomic Energy Commission. He now lives in Texas, where he is a semi-retired industrial engineer.

Jo Redman

Jo Redman, whose father was a construction worker at Los Alamos, lives in Cyprus, California, and teaches physical education at a state university.

Polly Richardson Boyles

Polly Richardson Boyles moved to Los Alamos in 1948 when her father got a job with the Atomic Energy Commission, then with the University of California, doing the accounting work for the Lab. She attended college in Colorado from 1952 to 1955, when she returned to Los Alamos, later marrying a physicist at the Lab and raising three children in Los Alamos. Following a divorce and remarriage she moved to rural Mexico, where she has lived for the past two decades, fishing and working with search-and-rescue operations for fishing boats.

14. Three Friends

Brant Calkin

Son of mathematician Jack Calkin, Brant Calkin is a biologist/environmental activist. He spent his first several years out of college working for the Lab, was very active in the Sierra Club, and currently works for the Southern Utah Wilderness Alliance.

15. "Atomic Bomb, Atomic Bomb"

Yibi Mark Smith

Yibi Mark Smith lives in Davis, California, where she teaches high school chemistry.

Paul Teller

Paul Teller, son of Edward Teller, majored in mathematics at Stanford University and earned a Ph.D. in the philosophy of science from MIT. After years of teaching the philosophy of science in the Chicago area, he moved to California, where he now teaches at the University of California at Davis.

Henry Bethe

The son of physicist Hans Bethe, Henry Bethe is a former tournament bridge player and a vice president of Chase Manhattan Bank in New York City.

David Bradbury

David Bradbury, son of Norris Bradbury, holds a Ph.D. in biogeography. He taught at the University of Arizona for some years before returning to northern New Mexico, first for a state job in Santa Fe, then to work in environmental restoration at the Lab.

Wendy Teller

Wendy Teller, daughter of Edward Teller, studied mathematics at Radcliffe and at the University of California at Berkeley. A systems engineer in a telecommunications company in Illinois, she specifies designs for telephone companies.

16. The Spy, the H-bomb, and the Hearing

Ron Peierls

Ron Peierls, son of Rudolf Peierls, came to Los Alamos at the age of five, returning to England a year and a half later. He lives in New York State, where he is a physicist at the Brookhaven National Laboratory.

17. A Hat to Remember

Peter Oppenheimer

After high school, Peter Oppenheimer went west to his uncle's sheep farm in Colorado. In the late 1960s he traveled to northern New Mexico to show his wife the countryside he had come to love when the Oppenheimers vacationed there in the late 1940s and early 1950s. He settled in the area, working as a photographer and a carpenter/builder.

Blue Corn

Blue Corn traded in her job as a housekeeper for the Oppenheimers to try her hand at pottery, preferring the more colorful polychrome to the black pottery for which the pueblo is best known.

18. The Lure of the Land

Margaret Montoya Caperton

Margaret Montoya Caperton grew up at the Los Alamos Ranch School, where her father, Adolfo Montoya, was the ranch gardener, coaxing from the desert soil prize-winning flowers and vegetables. A retired educator,

Margaret taught in northern New Mexico for 18 years, then served as a school principal for 21 years.

Peggy Pond Church
Peggy Pond Church spent much of her childhood roaming the mesas and canyons of northern New Mexico—first as a child in the years preceding her father's founding of the Los Alamos Ranch School and later at the school as a faculty wife. She has written extensively about the land and her attachment to it.

Laurie Archer
Laurie Archer arrived in Los Alamos in the summer of 1949 to visit her two sisters who were working on the Hill. She returned a year later to live with her sisters, graduating from Los Alamos High School in 1952. An artist, she now lives in Santa Fe.

Joe Smith
Joe Smith, whose father, an electrician, brought his family to Los Alamos in 1945, graduated from high school there in 1953 and later graduated from the Naval Academy. A lawyer in Upper Marlboro, Maryland, he returns to northern New Mexico for frequent visits.

Lew Agnew
Lew Agnew, a physicist, came to Los Alamos in 1951 to work at the Lab, from which he now is retired.

19. Coming of Age in the 1960s

Graham Mark
Graham Mark, son of mathematician Carson Mark, spent many years away from Los Alamos in graduate and postgraduate study. He is now employed at the Lab doing computer work.

Clayborne Carson
After a year at the University of New Mexico, Clayborne Carson, who moved to Los Alamos in 1948 when his father took a job as a security guard there, set out for Los Angeles in 1964. Active in the civil rights and and peace movements of the 1960s, he is a professor of African-American history at Stanford University and directs the Martin Luther King, Jr., Papers Project.

20. You *Can* Go Home Again, But . . .

Dimas Chavez
Dimas Chavez, whose father was a heavy-machine operator at Los Alamos, lives near Washington, D.C., where he works for the State Department in technical security for embassies. He has given some security talks at Los Alamos, which gave him a particular pride.

Lucia Ortiz y Garcia
Lucia Ortiz y Garcia is the daughter of Walter Garcia, a carpenter with the Army Corps of Engineers. Lucia lives "in the valley" in a town called La Billita. A former nun who has lived around the world and earned two advanced degrees before returning home, she coordinates cooperative education for the University of New Mexico at Los Alamos.

Notes and References

Introduction

1. Lawrence Badash, Joseph O. Hirschfelder, and Herbert P. Broida, eds., *Reminiscences of Los Alamos, 1943–1945* (Dordrecht, Netherlands: D. Reidell Publishing Co., 1980), 43.

Chapter 1

1. Richard Rhodes, *The Making of the Atomic Bomb* (New York: Simon & Schuster, 1986), 425.

2. Edith Truslow, *Manhattan District History: Nonscientific Aspects of Los Alamos Project Y, 1942 through 1946* (Los Alamos, N.M.: Los Alamos Historical Society, 1991), 1.

3. Badash, Hirschfelder, and Broida, eds., *Reminiscences of Los Alamos*, 14.

4. Letter on exhibit at the Los Alamos Historical Museum.

5. Robert Jungk, *Brighter than a Thousand Suns: A Personal History of the Atomic Scientists* (San Diego: Harcourt Brace Jovanovich, 1958), 118.

6. Truslow, *Manhattan District History*, 101.

7. Ibid., 41.

8. Eleanor Jette, *Inside Box 1663* (Los Alamos, N.M.: Los Alamos Historical Society, 1977), 125–26.

9. Jane S. Wilson and Charlotte Serber, *Standing By and Making Do* (Los Alamos, N.M.: Los Alamos Historical Society, 1977), 89.

10. Ibid., 92.

11. Truslow, *Manhattan District History*, 90.

12. Wilson and Serber, *Standing By*, 16.

13. Ibid., 90.

14. Ibid., 91.

15. Truslow, *Manhattan District History*, 67.

16. Ibid., 74.

17. Wilson and Serber, *Standing By*, 2.

18. Los Alamos Scientific Laboratory, *Los Alamos: Beginning of an Era* (Los Alamos, N.M.: Los Alamos Historical Society, 1986), 18.

19. Wilson and Serber, *Standing By*, 46.

20. Ibid., 25.

21. Ibid., 46.

22. Ibid., 10.

Chapter 2

1. Badash, Hirschfelder, and Broida, eds., *Reminiscences of Los Alamos*, 90.

2. Laura Fermi, *Atoms in the Family: My Life with Enrico Fermi* (Chicago: University of Chicago Press, 1954), 200.

3. Ibid., 21.

4. Ibid., 126.

5. Wilson and Serber, *Standing By*, 29–30.

6. Ibid., 30.

7. Ibid., 31.

8. Ibid.

Chapter 3

1. Leslie Groves, *Now It Can Be Told* (New York: Harper & Brothers, 1962), 159.

2. Ibid., 160.

3. Ibid., 161.

4. Ibid.

5. Truslow, *Manhattan District History*, 107.

Chapter 4

1. Wilson and Serber, *Standing By*, 27.

2. Peggy Pond Church, *The House at Otowi Bridge: The Story of Edith Warner and Los Alamos* (Albuquerque: University of New Mexico Press, 1959), 13.

3. Ibid., 124.

4. Ibid.

5. Ibid., 99.

6. Ibid., 96.

7. Ibid., 55.

8. Ibid., 56–57.

Chapter 5

1. Truslow, *Manhattan District History*, 85.

2. Badash, Hirschfelder, and Broida, eds., *Reminiscences of Los Alamos*, 150.

3. Ibid., 149.

4. Interview with Anita Martinez, who worked as a school secretary and was in possession of records of school population.

5. Badash, Hirschfelder, and Broida, eds., *Reminiscences of Los Alamos*, 150.

Chapter 7

1. Jette, *Inside Box 1663*, 11.

2. Ibid., 15.

Chapter 9

1. Rudolph Peierls, *Bird of Passage: Reflections of a Physicist* (Princeton, N.J.: Princeton University Press, 1985), 97.

Chapter 10

1. Fern Lyon and Jacob Evans, *Los Alamos: The First 40 Years* (Los Alamos, N.M.: Los Alamos Historical Society, 1984), 34.

2. Jette, *Inside Box 1663*, 96–97.

3. Los Alamos Scientific Laboratory, *Beginning of an Era*, 32–33.

4. Rhodes, *The Making of the Atomic Bomb*, 571–72.

5. Ibid., 676.

6. Los Alamos Scientific Laboratory, *Beginning of an Era*, 53.

7. Ibid.

8. Ibid., 53–54.

9. Ibid., 53.

10. Ibid., 55.

11. Ibid., 57.

12. Ibid., 54.

13. Jette, *Inside Box 1663*, 107.

14. Ibid.

15. Lyon and Evans, *The First 40 Years*, 38.

16. Franck Report, printed as appendix to Jungk, *Brighter than a Thousand Suns*, 355.

17. Ibid.

18. Ibid., 349.

Chapter 11

1. Lyon and Evans, *The First 40 Years*, 40.

2. Ibid.

3. Eric Chivian, Susanna Chivian, Robert Jay Lifton, and John E. Mack, eds., *Last Aid: The Medical Dimensions of Nuclear War* (New York: W. H. Freeman & Co., 1982), 43–44.

4. Ibid., 44.

5. Ibid.

6. Lansing Lamont, *Day of Trinity* (New York: Atheneum, 1965), 271, and Jungk, *Brighter than a Thousand Suns*, 228–29.

7. Lamont, *Day of Trinity*, 119, and Jungk, *Brighter than a Thousand Suns*, 194.

8. Lamont, *Day of Trinity*, 271.

9. Lamont, *Day of Trinity*, 277–78, and Jungk, *Brighter than a Thousand Suns*, 195–96.

10. Jette, *Inside Box 1663*, 114.

11. On file at the Los Alamos Historical Society.

12. Jette, *Inside Box 1663*, 120.

13. Los Alamos Scientific Laboratory, *Beginning of an Era*, 62.

Chapter 16

1. Norman Moss, *Klaus Fuchs: The Man Who Stole the Atomic Bomb* (London: Grafton Books, 1987), 126.

2. Richard Chadwell Williams, *Klaus Fuchs, Atom Spy* (Cambridge, Mass.: Harvard University Press, 1987), 1.

3. Moss, *The Man Who Stole the Atomic Bomb*, 170.

4. James Gleick, *Genius: The Life and Science of Richard Feynman* (New York: Vintage Books, 1993), 185–86.

5. Williams, *Klaus Fuchs, Atom Spy*, 79.

6. Fuchs's confession to William Skardon, 27 January 1950, in Williams, *Klaus Fuchs, Atom Spy*, 180.

7. Ibid., 182.

8. Groves, *Now It Can Be Told*, 167.

9. Moss, *The Man Who Stole the Atomic Bomb*, 38.

10. Williams, *Klaus Fuchs, Atom Spy*, 132.

11. Moss, *The Man Who Stole the Atomic Bomb*, 170.

12. Ibid., 171.

13. Ibid., 88.

14. John Major, *The Oppenheimer Hearing* (New York: Stein & Day, 1971), 11.

15. Ibid., 245–46.

16. Ibid., 32.

17. Peter Goodchild, *J. Robert Oppenheimer, Shatterer of Worlds* (New York: Fromm International, 1985), 223.

18. Groves, *Now It Can Be Told*, 142.

19. Major, *The Oppenheimer Hearing*, 9.

20. Ibid., 175.

21. Ibid., 176.

22. Goodchild, *Shatterer of Worlds*, 286.

23. Ibid., 272.

Chapter 17

1. Goodchild, *Shatterer of Worlds*, 11.

2. Ibid., 15.

3. Ibid.

4. Ed Regis, *Who's Got Einstein's Office* (Reading, Mass.: Addison-Wesley, 1987), 132.

5. Goodchild, *Shatterer of Worlds*, 22.

Chapter 18

1. Wilson and Serber, *Standing By*, 103.

2. Church, *The House at Otowi Bridge*, 6.

3. Ibid., 2.

4. Ibid., 3.

5. Ibid., 3, 114.

6. Wilson and Serber, *Standing By*, 4.

Epilogue

1. Report of Kennedy visit in Los Alamos Laboratory Archives.

2. Ibid.

3. *New York Times*, 7 September 1991.

4. *Bulletin of Atomic Scientists*, March–April 1995, 5–6.

Bibliography

Badash, Lawrence; Joseph O. Hirschfelder; and Herbert P. Broida, eds. *Reminiscences of Los Alamos, 1943–1945*. Dordrecht, Netherlands: D. Reidell Publishing Co., 1980.

Chivian, Eric; Susanna Chivian; Robert Jay Lifton; and John E. Mack, eds. *Last Aid: The Medical Dimensions of Nuclear War*. New York: W. H. Freeman & Co., 1982.

Church, Peggy Pond. *The House at Otowi Bridge: The Story of Edith Warner and Los Alamos*. Albuquerque: University of New Mexico Press, 1959.

Fermi, Laura. *Atoms in the Family*. Albuquerque: University of New Mexico Press, 1962.

Gleick, James. *Genius: The Life and Science of Richard Feyman*. New York: Vintage Books, 1993.

Goodchild, Peter. *J. Robert Oppenheimer: Shatterer of Worlds*. New York: Fromm International Publishing, 1985.

Groves, Leslie. *Now It Can Be Told*. New York: Harper & Brothers, 1962.

Jette, Eleanor. *Inside Box 1663*. Los Alamos, N.M.: Los Alamos Historical Society, 1977.

Jungk, Robert. *Brighter than a Thousand Suns: A Personal History of the Atomic Scientists*. San Diego: Harcourt Brace Jovanovich, 1958.

Lamont, Lansing. *Day of Trinity*. New York: Atheneum, 1965.

Los Alamos Scientific Laboratory. *Beginning of an Era*. Los Alamos, N.M.: Los Alamos Historical Society, 1977, 1986.

Lyon, Fern, and Jacob Evans. *Los Alamos: The First 40 Years*. Los Alamos, N.M.: Los Alamos Historical Society, 1984.

Manhattan District History. *Nonscientific Aspects of Los Alamos Project Y, 1942 through 1946*. Los Alamos, N.M.: Los Alamos Historical Society, 1991.

Major, John. *The Oppenheimer Hearing*. New York: Stein & Day, 1971.

Moss, Norman. *Klaus Fuchs: The Man Who Stole the Atom Bomb*. London, Glasgow, Toronto, Sydney, Auckland: Grafton Books, 1987.

Peierls, Rudolph. *Bird of Passage: Recollections of a Physicist*. Princeton, N.J.: Princeton University Press, 1985.

Regis, Ed. *Who Got Einstein's Office?* Reading, Mass.: Addison-Wesley Publishing Co., 1987.

Rhodes, Richard. *The Making of the Atomic Bomb*. New York: Simon & Schuster, 1986.

Spivey, Richard L. *Maria*. Santa Fe, N.M.: Northland Publishing, 1979.

Truslow, Edith. *Manhattan District History: Nonscientific Aspects of Los Alamos Project Y 1942 through 1946*. Los Alamos, N.M.: Los Alamos Historical Society, 1991.

Ulam, S. M. *Adventures of a Mathematician*. Berkeley: University of California Press, 1976.

Williams, Richard Chadwell. *Klaus Fuchs, Atom Spy*. Cambridge, Mass.: Harvard University Press, 1987.

Wilson, Jane S., and Charlotte Serber, eds. *Standing By and Making Do: Women of Wartime Los Alamos*. Los Alamos, N.M.: Los Alamos Historical Society, 1988.

Index

The Author

Katrina R. Mason is a journalist who lives in Bethesda, Maryland. She is a graduate of Smith College and received her M.A. in English literature from the University of Pennsylvania.